# Mortgage Lending
## and Race

# Rutgers University
## Center for Urban Policy Research

# Mortgage Lending and Race:

## Conceptual and Analytical Perspectives of the Urban Financing Problem

David Listokin
Stephen Casey

Cover Design by Francis G. Mullen

Published in the United States of America
by the Center for Urban Policy Research
Building 4051—Kilmer Campus
New Brunswick, New Jersey 08903

**Library of Congress Cataloging in Publication Data**

Listokin, David.
  Mortgage lending and race.

  Bibliography:  p.
  Includes index.
  1.  Discrimination in mortgage loans—United States.
I.  Casey, Stephen, 1946-  joint author.  II. Title.
HG2040.5.U5L57       332.7'2       79-12209
ISBN 0-88285-060-1

# Acknowledgments

The preparation of this study would have been impossible without the assistance and cooperation of many individuals. Dr. George Sternlieb inspired the authors to embark on this venture and lent invaluable assistance. Other Rutgers' University faculty, Drs. Susan S. Fainstein, James W. Hughes and Ernest C. Reock, Jr., deserve special thanks for broadening the scope of inquiry and in many ways lending critical guidance. Our colleagues at the Center, Drs. Robert W. Burchell, W. Patrick Beaton and Robert W. Lake also must be thanked for their assistance.

Mrs. Mary Picarella, Mrs. Joan Frantz, Mrs. Lydia Lombardi, Mrs. Anne Hummel, and Mrs. Susan Zondlo, the mainstays of the Center for Urban Policy Research administrative and typing staff, all assisted in preparing the manuscript and performing other necessary tasks.

The authors assume responsibility for any errors or misinterpretations that remain.

D.L.
S.C.

# CONTENTS

# SECTION I
# PROBLEM AND MODEL
# DEFINITION

## CHAPTER 1 THE URBAN FINANCING PROBLEM

## CHAPTER 2 THE ECONOMIC AND
## ECO-RACE MODELS

## CHAPTER 3 THE URBAN FINANCING
## LITERATURE

# SECTION II
# EMPIRICAL INVESTIGATION

## CHAPTER 4 METHODOLOGY

## CHAPTER 5 MACRO DATA ANALYSIS

## CHAPTER 6 MICRO DATA ANALYSIS

# SECTION III
# SUMMARY

## CHAPTER 7 PERSPECTIVE AND
## POLICY IMPLICATIONS

# SECTION IV
# ANNOTATED BIBLIOGRAPHY

# List of Exhibits

**Exhibit**

**Exhibit**

# Introduction

## Research Objectives

Few housing issues have aroused as much controversy in the last few years as the charge leveled by some community groups and politicians that financial institutions are hastening the decline of many American urban neighborhoods by arbitrarily denying them adequate mortgage credit.[1] Lenders vehemently deny this accusation; they claim they merely adhere to sound lending practices and do not unjustifiably discriminate against city locations.[2] Accelerating urban decay, and the perception that a credit shortfall is contributing to this decline, has caused Federal and state governments to enact or consider legislation that ranges from simple requirements that financial institutions disclose where and to whom they grant loans, to more stringent measures such as credit allocation to urban centers.

This monograph examines the urban financing problem—the difficulty faced by residents of some urban neighborhoods in obtaining institutional mortgages or other loans for purchasing, refinancing, or repairing properties. It specifically examines two models of lender behavior which can partially explain some facets of the urban credit shortfall—the *economic and eco-race models*. The economic model perceives lenders as being guided solely by economic considerations; thus the urban financing problem exists because many city neighborhoods, and applicants for loans in these areas, have an objectively unacceptable economic underwriting risk. Guided by neutral lending standards, lenders simply do not approve many urban loans. The eco-race model views lenders as being influenced by both economic *and* racial criteria — underwriting is a composite of both neutral economic standards and racial biases against minority neighborhoods and residents.

The monograph examines whether the economic or eco-race models can more appropriately and adequately explain why certain urban neighborhoods receive inadequate conventional credit.

## Research Strategy And Organization

The influences on urban lending are examined via macro and micro analyses. The macro investigation considers which *neighborhoods* within the City of Chicago are receiving loans. It focuses on the areal (zip code location) distribution of about 24,000 loans granted in Chicago from 1971 to 1973. The micro study examines successful and unsuccessful loan *applications* in six Standard Metropolitan Statistical Areas. It considers the disposition of approximately 12,000 loan requests made in these six areas. Both macro and micro analytic strategy are followed for they offer a more comprehensive opportunity to examine influences on lender behavior. Both the macro and micro analyses test the significance of race, but the former considers *neighborhood* economic and racial data, while the latter focuses on *individual* loan applicant economic and racial characteristics. A finding that lenders consider race, either of a neighborhood or individual nature, would support the eco-race model; a null race outcome would suggest the economic model.

The empirical analysis supports the eco-race model: lenders are guided by both economic and racial influences. Such behavior is exhibited when considering both the macro and micro dynamic. This conclusion has both conceptual and policy implications such as what role should lenders play and what are the most appropriate strategies to encourage reinvestment.

The monograph consists of four sections: (I) Problem and Model Definition; (II) Empirical Investigation; (III) Summary and Conclusions; and (IV) Bibliography. Section I considers the objectives of the analysis; the economic and eco-race models; and the findings of the existing literature. Section II contains the empirical analysis. It first discusses the methodology chosen for the investigation. The section then presents the macro neighborhood and the micro applicant analyses. Section III summarizes findings, interprets their significance, and suggests the linkage of the findings to existing theory. Section IV is an annotated bibliography, citing books, articles, hearings, newspaper reports and other sources on the urban financing problem and proposed solutions.

*Introduction*

## NOTES

1. See, *Hearing on the Home Mortgage Disclosure Act of 1975,* before the Senate Committee on Banking, Housing and Urban Affairs, 94th Congress, 1st Session, (Washington, D.C.: Government Printing Office, 1975), pp. 22-514 (hereinafter cited as *Senate Hearings); Hearings Before Subcommittee on Financial Institutions Supervision, Regulation and Insurance of the House Commission on Banking, Currency and Housing,* 94th Congress, 1st Session (Washington, D.C.: Government Printing Office, 1975), pp. 126-260; (hereinafter cited as *House Hearings*); Michael Agelasto and David Listokin, *The Urban Financing Dilemma: Disinvestment-Redlining* (Monticello, Ill.: Council of Planning Librarians, Exchange Bibliography 890), (October 1975), pp. 21-26 (hereinafter cited as *CPL Bibliography).* See e.g., U.S. League of Savings Associations, Special Management Bulletin, "Guidelines for Management Response to Activist Groups in Crisis in Urban Lending," in *Senate Hearings*, pp. 115-30; D. Crooks, "Redlining Chokes Communities," *People and Taxes,* Vol. 2 (May 1974), p. 6; Michael Tasker, "Battling the Banks," *Shelterforce,* Vol. 1 (November 1975), p. 8: "Chicago Lenders Killing City, Saving Suburbs: MAHA," *Chicago Tribune*, March 25, 1975, p. 9; Tee Taggart, "Redlining — How the Bankers Starve the Cities to Feed the Suburbs," *Planning,* Vol. 40 (December 1974), pp. 14-16; D. Leindorf & D. Etna, *Citibank, Ralph Nader's Study Group Report on First National City Bank* (New York: Grossman Publishers, 1973), p. 155; G. Rafter (editor), *Crisis in Urban Lending: Myth or Reality* (New York: Institute of Financial Education, 1975); "Anti-Redlining Bills Passed," *Practicing Planner,* Vol. 6 (February 1976), p. 44; M. Duncan, E. Hood & J. Neet, "Redlining Practices, Racial Resegregation and Urban Decay: Neighborhood Housing Services as a Viable Alternative," *Urban Lawyer*, Vol. 7 (1975), pp. 510-39; Calvin Bradford & Leonard Rubinowitz, "The Urban-Suburban Investment-Disinvestment Process: Consequences for Older Neighborhoods," *Annals, AAPSS,* Vol. 442 (1975), p. 77.
2. Senate Hearings, pp. 589-940; House Hearings, pp. 19-82; *CPL Bibliography,* pp. 21-26.

Section **I**
*Problem and*
*Model Definition*

# Chapter 1
# The Urban Financing Problem

## Introduction

This chapter introduces the dimensions of the urban financing problem and the possible causes of the credit shortfall. It suggests multidimensional causes of the financing dilemma, encompassing geographic, economic, racial, and other influences, and focuses on the economic and racial factors. These determinants are discussed in terms of two models of lender behavior—economic and eco-race—which can help explain the mortgage crunch. The alternative models set the conceptual base for the analysis.

## The Problem: The Urban Financing Shortfall

The urban financing problem (also shortfall, dilemma, or credit crunch) is defined here as the difficulty faced by residents of some urban neighborhoods in obtaining institutional mortgages or other loans for purchasing, refinancing, or repairing properties.[1] The problem is not new. Four New York City studies, conducted over a 30-year period, illustrate the financing shortfall that has troubled the city. In 1944, Herbert Swan,[2] examining New York real estate activity from the 1920s to the 1940s, reported:[3]

> In every borough there are numerous large areas where (mortgage) terms are so strict as practically eliminating funds for the construction of a new house or the purchase of an existing home. . .the policy of lending institutions to mark out areas within which they will not make loans for new buildings, though designed

3

to safeguard funds of depositors, policyholders, and clients, practically dooms the regeneration of mature areas for new construction.

A study of neighborhoods on the West Side of Manhattan in the 1950s arrived at similar conclusions.[4] According to Chester Rapkin:[5]

> there is little doubt that in the minds of officials of mortgage institutions, the West Side Study Area has become a district in which lending activity is undertaken with extreme caution. In view of the volume of transactions and the value of structures, the amount of new money flowing into the area is extremely small.

Slightly more than a decade later, George Sternlieb examined the New York City housing market as part of a study of the city's rent control law.[6] His findings concerning the financing shortfall paralleled Rapkin's somber conclusions. Based on interviews with both financial institutions and building owners, Sternlieb found that new mortgage money was not only expensive, but was also extremely difficult to obtain.[7] The one seemingly bright note in the analysis was the reported decline in the number of second mortgages.[8] On closer examination, though, even this reflected a weakening in the market, for it indicated that speculators were no longer willing to make these inherently more risky loans.

A 1977 report by the New York State Banking Department found that many New York City neighborhoods were becoming mortgage short and that the credit crunch was exacerbating the city's housing difficulties.[9] Important lenders such as mutual savings bank were granting many of their loans to out-of-state borrowers (mainly in Sunbelt states) or else were abandoning the "whole" mortgage market in favor of more secure mortgage pool investments such as GNMA (Government National Mortgage Association) backed securities.

Other studies conducted in the 1950s and 1960s explored urban financing problems.[10] More recently, a score of monographs have discussed the urban credit shortfall.[11] They report widespread and continued tightening of credit in many urban neighborhoods.[12] The problems encountered by New York City are endemic to urban areas throughout the country.

## Parameters of the Urban Financing Problem and the Adverse Consequences of the Credit Shortfall*

---

*Many studies have examined the neighborhood change and public/private financing interaction dynamic. See Aruthur Solomon *et al.*, *Financial Institutions and Neighborhood Decline. A Review of the Literature* (Cambridge: Harvard MIT Joint Center, 1974); Urban-Suburban Investment Study Group, Center for Urban Studies of the University of Illinois, *Redlining and Disinvestment As a Discriminatory Practice in Residential Mortgage Loans* (Washington, D.C.: Government Printing Office, no date), Calvin Bradford *et al.*, *Maintaining Viable Communities: The Investment-Disinvestment Process* (Chicago: The Center for Urban Studies - University of Illinois at Chicago Circle, 1977); Federal National Mortgage Association, *Redlining: A Special Report by FNMA* (Washington, D.C.: FNMA, 1976).

The urban financing dilemma can take different forms: a reduction in the *volume* of conventional credit and/or a change in the *terms* of such credit. The absence of conventional financing, and/or its lessened desirability, forces borrowers to turn to often less desirable private credit sources.

The urban shortfall affects many urban neighborhoods and residents, but it has often proved especially problematical to minority areas and property owners.

THE URBAN FINANCING PROBLEM: SUPPLY CHANGES

The dominant feature of the credit problem is a reduction in the total number of conventional loan originations or refinancing for certain neighborhoods. Studies in Newark, New York, Los Angeles, Philadelphia, and other urban centers have indicated this downward trend.[13] Such a decline can have a major adverse impact on neighborhood stability and maintenance since owners' maintenance and rehabilitation is at least partially dependent on loan availability. Also, new investors who wish to buy and existing owners who wish to refinance are unable to get mortgages. Refinancing is especially important to both current homeowners and landlords for it is the primary way to recapture equity.

While credit availability includes conventional as well as government monies (either direct loans, as in the Section 236 program, or more commonly, government-insured mortgages, e.g., the 223 (e) program), conventional credit is essential. Since direct public mortgages are often in short or uneven supply, a neighborhood cannot depend on this source of credit. Borrowers who hope to rely on FHA insured loans are confronted with problems. These loans are expensive because they require a mortgage insurance premium; more importantly, because the interest rate on the insured loans is restricted, "points" are paid by buyer and seller. Time delays in obtaining credit approval compound these frustrations.

THE URBAN FINANCING PROBLEM:
TIGHTENING of CREDIT TERMS

This second dimension of the urban financing problem concerns the terms of the loans that are made available. Credit terms encompass a) *loan appraisal,* b) *maturity,* and c) *cost.*

The lower appraisal of urban properties vis-a-vis their suburban competition is another feature of the urban financing dilemma. Lower appraisals force a potential purchaser to make a larger down payment.[14] In addition, the buyer may have to resort to costly secondary mortgage sources such as those offered by private companies or individuals. These factors tend to weaken the urban resale market by limiting the pool of available buyers and/or by forcing residents to sell to speculators. (Speculators can obtain financing because they offer a volume market and are willing to pay high interest rates for their short-term holding.) Alternatively, the existing property owners, unwilling to sell at lower prices, will often let their property deteriorate.

Compared to suburban loans, urban loans must be paid back comparatively faster and at higher interest rates, or they require the payment of additional points at closing.[15] Points raise the initial cost of the house, while higher interest rates increase the total cost of housing. Both phenomena can price out low-income and moderate-income households from purchasing or adequately maintaining their property. For the multifamily investor, the high-cost urban loan may reduce cash flow to a point where, just to break even, maintenance must be kept at a bare minimum.[16] Confronted by a high debt service, the owner of the single or multifamily urban property may decide to free himself of this real estate burden. But sale is impeded by the financing dilemma, forcing the owner to forestall needed maintenance or to sell to a speculator who has his own line of credit. As an extreme resort, the owner simply abandons his parcel.

THE URBAN FINANCING PROBLEM:
THE SHIFT TO PRIVATE CREDIT

The flight from conventional credit usually means the ascendency of private financing. Private mortgages[17] offer certain advantages such as less paperwork and expeditious processing but this type of credit has numerous disadvantages. It is costly for interest rates are higher and terms are shorter. In addition, many private loans have "kited" principals, that is, the amount of the loan is increased to far above the actual value or even initial purchasing price of the property. "Kiting" can be considered as a perverse case of mortgage overappraisal, working to the disadvantage of the purchaser who is forced to pay an artificially inflated loan. In addition to cost factors, private loans sometimes offer little protection to the purchaser in default.[18] With private financing, some default on even one payment will sometimes allow the seller to repossess without standard foreclosure procedures and the buyer will lose all nominally accrued equity.

THE URBAN FINANCING PROBLEM:
MINORITY INCIDENCE

While many urban neighborhoods and residents are affected by the urban credit shortfall, black areas and individuals are the most seriously impacted. Studies by the Center for New Corporate Priorities (Los Angeles), Phoenix Fund (St. Louis), Urban League (six city survey), Richard Mazin (Bronx), Northwest Housing Association (Philadelphia), North Toledo United

Citizens Organization (Toledo, Ohio), Cleveland Coalition of Neighborhoods (Cleveland), New York State Banking Commission (New York) and other groups have graphically shown that the flight of conventional credit has been most pronounced in minority neighborhoods.[19]

The National Housing and Economic Development Project concluded:[20]

> Studies of the impact of redlining amply demonstrate that (it) disproportionately affects minority groups. In light of the overt racially discriminatory policies which created segregated housing patterns, practices which redline also have a certain effect of perpetuating residential segregation.

The Center for National Policy Review summarized:[21]

> Generally speaking, redlining makes it more difficult for minority group members to finance home purchases and repair in those areas where they generally live or seek homes. Moreover, the practice of redlining interracial areas contributes to the destabilization and decline of mixed areas and tend therefore, to enforce or reinforce ghettoized residential patterns.

## Causes Of The Urban Financing Problem: Multidimensional View

There are many reasons why residents of certain urban neighborhoods may encounter problems in obtaining credit. Geographic, economic, racial and other considerations are all possible influences (see Exhibit 1-1).

GEOGRAPHIC CONSIDERATIONS

Lenders may grant few loans to a particular city location because of geographical favoritism. There are inter- and intra-metropolitan as well as neighborhood preferences. Financial institutions often prefer to extend credit to the West and South West— the "Sunbelt" regions—as opposed to the Northeast. While the Northeast has traditionally been a capital exporting area, the flight of capital from this region has accelerated in recent years.

Philip Gabel's study, *The Mortgage Financing of Manhattan Multifamily Income Properties*[22] documents the geographical lending market preferences of New York State lenders and its impact on New York City's financing dilemma. New York savings institutions had always made investments in other regions, but the volume of such out-of-state loans had been restricted by state law. These restrictions were lifted in 1966. Gabel documents how this change resulted in an outflow of capital and was one of the factors responsible for the declining availability of institutional mortgages for multifamily properties in many Manhattan neighborhoods.

EXHIBIT 1-1

## MULTIDIMENSIONAL MODEL OF THE URBAN FINANCING PROBLEM

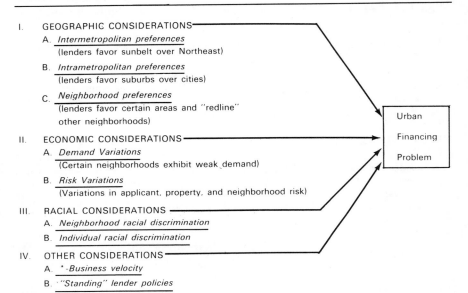

I.  GEOGRAPHIC CONSIDERATIONS
   A. *Intermetropolitan preferences*
     (lenders favor sunbelt over Northeast)
   B. *Intrametropolitan preferences*
     (lenders favor suburbs over cities)
   C. *Neighborhood preferences*
     (lenders favor certain areas and "redline"
     other neighborhoods)

II. ECONOMIC CONSIDERATIONS
   A. *Demand Variations*
     (Certain neighborhoods exhibit weak demand)
   B. *Risk Variations*
     (Variations in applicant, property, and neighborhood risk)

III. RACIAL CONSIDERATIONS
   A. *Neighborhood racial discrimination*
   B. *Individual racial discrimination*

IV. OTHER CONSIDERATIONS
   A. *\*-Business velocity*
   B. *"Standing" lender policies*

Urban Financing Problem

Intrametropolitan variations, specifically the inclination of lenders to give loans in suburban as opposed to urban locations, is another reason for the urban financing dilemma. The Center for New Corporate Priorities, Phoenix Fund, Citizens Housing and Planning Association, Rochester Greenlining Coalition and others have documented the suburban versus urban underwriting preference of financial institutions.[23] This inclination contributes to the problem because it results in an export of capital to suburbs, thereby diminishing the pool of available urban credit.

There are also in-city neighborhood preferences. A lender is often more willing to grant loans in the area(s) surrounding his office(s) for they are more familiar with the underwriting risks of these neighborhoods and may also wish to promote the stability of the locations in which they are doing business.

Certain neighborhoods are sometimes avoided by lenders for allegedly unjustified or near-arbitrary reasons, e.g., age, housing composition, "fear" about the future and other characteristics. This policy has traditionally been called "redlining" and the areas not receiving loans have been termed "redlined neighborhoods."[24] In recent years the usage of the redlining term has sometimes been broadened to encompass racial and even economic factors. Today "redlining" is a muddled term encompassing various conditions of mortgage availability and mortgagee intent. This monograph shall refer to "redlining" as simply unjustified areal differentiation, e.g., the practice of not granting loans to a neighborhood because the area has been subjectively downgraded. The classic definition of redlining focuses on *areal* differentiation and we shall use this term accordingly. In sum then, borrowers in a particular urban neighborhood may receive few loans because lenders prefer to export capital to other regions, prefer suburbs within the metropolitan area, and favor some neighborhoods within the city.

ECONOMIC CONSIDERATIONS

Economic factors may also explain why relatively few conventional loans are granted to some urban neighborhoods and why residents in these areas pay more for the mortgages they do receive. Volume may be lower because of softer urban demand. Many urban neighborhoods have little new housing construction and therefore less need for loans. These areas often contain older and less affluent residents — two groups who move less frequently than younger, more affluent families. Their housing turnover is therefore lower and they demand fewer mortgages.

Urban credit terms may be unfavorable because of undesirable underwriting conditions. There are three basic underwriting criteria: the quality of the loan applicant, quality of the subject property (property being mortgaged), and quality of the surrounding neighborhood.[25] Urban areas may fare poorly on all three standards. Mortgage applicants in urban neighborhoods may have lower incomes and assets in proportion to the acquisition price and hence pose a greater underwriting risk. Since they are less affluent, they will require higher loan-to-value ratio mortgages, thus increasing the lender's exposure. Urban properties tend to be older, have fewer modern amenities, and may be in worse shape than their suburban counterparts. Certain urban neighborhoods may also compare less favorably to suburban locations; they are often older and more crowded, have more deteriorated physical facilities (i.e., schools, parks, etc.), contain inharmonious residential and nonresidential uses, and in other ways are less desirable.

RACIAL CONSIDERATIONS

Racial discrimination may contribute to the urban credit shortfall. Some empirical investigations have documented the paucity of conventional credit extended to many black neighborhoods and have shown that black mortgage applicants are sometime granted loans with unfavorable terms (see Chapter 3).

Two forms of racial bias, neighborhood *and* individual, are cited as possibly contributing to the urban financing problem for both may be factors and it is difficult to dissociate the neighborhood versus individual influence. The black homebuyer will usually purchase, rehabilitate, or refinance a property in a black neighborhood. The financing difficulty encountered, a difficulty which is a distinct feature of the current urban financing dilemma, may result from lender discrimination against himself, or the surrounding neighborhood, or a combination of the two.[26]

## OTHER CONSIDERATIONS

There are other possible influences on the urban financing dilemma. Lenders may favor rapidly developing regions and suburban locations because of their future business potential. This business velocity consideration may be especially important for financial institutions who make their major profit originating loans. (These lenders derive their profit from fees and "points" and repeatedly sell packages of mortgages to long-term investors.) A neighborhood may be given few loans, not entirely because of current geographic, economic or racial reasons, but also because of its limited future business potential.

Lender policies concerning minimum loan size, minimum property width, conformance of the property with current zoning, etc., may also work to the disadvantage of certain urban neighborhoods. A minimum loan amount may restrict conventional financing in low housing cost locations. Property size and type restrictions may steer lenders away from urban areas with narrow row houses and similar housing configurations. And since urban neighborhoods tend to have more nonconforming properties, a strict zoning rule can disqualify many such areas. These supposedly "neutral" policies may therefore unwittingly work to the disadvantage of urban residents.

## The Economic and Eco-Race Models of Lender Behavior and the Urban Financing Dilemma

While there are many possible contributing elements to the urban financing dilemma, a major aspect of the current controversy concerns the influence of economics versus race. Lenders stress the hegemony of economic criteria, while community and civil rights organizations argue that financial institutions are guided by racial as well as economic policies. The clash between these two groups was highlighted at a number of major forums on the credit shortfall, such as the House (1975) and Senate (1975) hearings[27] on the federal mortgage disclosure requirements, and HUD's Philadelphia (1976) "Administrative Meeting on Disinvestment as a Discriminatory Practice in Residential Mortgage Loans."[28] National civil rights organizations, (e.g., the National Committee Against Discrimination in Housing [NCDH] and the Urban League), and scores of local community organizations (see Chapter 3 for examples), emphasized the past and current racial discriminatory roots of the urban financing problem. These charges were answered by lender spokesmen (such as the S&L League and National Association of Mutual Saving Banks), who denied racial bias and emphasized the unswerving influence of economic underwriting criteria.[29]

Two views or models of lender behavior underlie the accusations and rebuttals at the three national forums (and at other hearings concerning the urban financing problem) — the *economic and eco-race models* (see Exhibit 1-2). Both attempt to explain the variation in the *supply* or *volume* of conventional credit to different neighborhoods, a significant element of the urban financing problem. They differ in terms of their perception of the presence and influence of economic and racial factors.

The economic and eco-race models do not attempt to explain all possible causes of the urban financing problem but recognize the multidimensional catalysts which shape the credit shortfall. The two models focus on two major facets of the problem — the influence of economic and racial criteria. The economic model stresses the former's influence; financial institutions are guided by neutral economic forces. Lenders, the strongest proponents of this model, admit there are distinctions in the availability of credit by neighborhood but argue that these differentiations are due to market forces. Urban areas may receive few loans because demand is weak — a function of older resident age, lower income, and other characteristics. Urban applicants, properties and neighborhoods may additionally pose a greater economic risk (see Exhibit 1-2), for such reasons as lower resident affluence, heightened property obsolescence and marginal neighborhood public facilities.

Proponents of the economic model often cite a lender's fiduciary responsibility to depositors as dictating financial prudence that forestalls granting mortgages to urban areas. One lender explained:[30]

> Loans in poverty areas are, by definition, high-risk loans, and there thus is little likelihood they could be collected in the event of such a liquidation. As a result . . . such loans are seldom of bankable quality and are discouraged, not only by the standards of the banking profession, but also by the supervision acting in the name of the very people who criticize banks because they don't do enough for the poor. It is not the social responsibility of bankers to make loans at below market rates of interest, nor to allocate funds in ways which are adverse to the interest of their depositors.

The eco-race model admits that lenders are influenced by economic considerations, but stresses the addition of racial discriminatory policies against minority areas and individuals. Chapters 2 and 3 detail the evidence that advocates of this model bring to substantiate charges of discrimination.

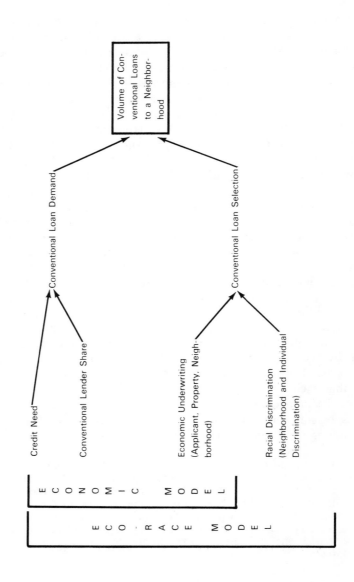

EXHIBIT 1-2

NEIGHBORHOOD MORTGAGE DISTRIBUTION: ECONOMIC AND ECO-RACE MODELS

## Research Objective and Strategy

This monograph evaluates the validity of the economic versus eco-race models. The two imply different policy directions. The former suggests economic supportive strategies (e.g., loan insurance, pool programs, neighborhood preservation strategies) while the latter implies both the economic strategies as well as a vigorous enforcement of anti-discriminatory safeguards. (See Chapter 7 for detailed discussion.)

The economic and eco-race models stand at the core of the proposed analysis. It is therefore important to fully understand their variation. Gaining a better understanding of the two models will also assist the evaluation of the extant literature on the urban financing shortfall. The next two chapters undertake these analyses.

Notes

1. The urban financing problem is commonly referred to as "redlining." The use of the term appears in the Douglas Commission's final report. Discussing the practices of the Federal Housing Administration (FHA) during the postwar decades, the Commission stated:

There was evidence of a tacit agreement among all groups — lending institutions, fire insurance companies, and FHA — to block off certain areas of cities within "red lines," and not to loan or insure within them.

See National Commission on Urban Problems, *Building the American City* (Washington, D.C.: Government Printing Office, 1969). During Congressional consideration of the 1975 Home Mortgage Disclosure Act, confusion over terminology surfaced several times. See, e.g., *Senate Hearings,* p. 874; *House Hearings,* p. 2102.

2. Herbert Swan, *The Housing Market in New York City* (New York: Building Press, 1944).

3. *Ibid.,* p. 213.

4. Chester Rapkin, *The Real Estate Market in An Urban Renewal Area* (New York: New York Building Department, 1958).

5. Rapkin, *The Real Estate Market,* p. 57.

6. George Sternlieb, *The Urban Housing Dilemma* (New York Housing Development Administration, 1971).

7. *Ibid.,* p. 387.

8. *Ibid.,* p. 382.

9. Robert Lindsay, *et al., Mortgage Financing and Housing Markets in New York State: A Preliminary Report* (Albany, New York: New York State Banking Department, 1977).

10. George Sternlieb, *The Tenement Landlord* (New Brunswick, New Jersey: Rutgers University, Center for Urban Policy Research, 1966); Charles Abrams, *The City is the Frontier* (New York: Harper and Row, 1965); Jane Jacobs, *The Death and Life of Great American Cities* (New York: Random House, 1961); Chicago Mayor's Commission on Human Relations, *Selling and Buying Real Estate in a Racially Changing Neighborhood; A Survey* (Chicago: Chicago Commission on Human Relations, 1962), David McEntire, *Residence and Race* (Berkeley: University of California Press, 1960); Charles Abrams, *Forbidden Neighbors: A Study in Prejudice in Housing* (New York: Harper and Row, 1955).

11. George Sternlieb and Robert W. Burchell, *Residential Abandonment: The Tenement Landlord Revisited* (New Brunswick, New Jersey: Rutgers University, Center for Urban Policy Research, 1973). See also Chapter 3 of this monograph.

12. Sternlieb, *The Tenement Landlord,* pp. 108-11; Sternlieb and Burchell, *Residential Abandonment,* p. 244; U.S. Civil Rights Commission, *Hearings on Mortgage Lending and Employment Opportunity in Baltimore Savings and Loan Institutions as they Effect Minorities, Ethnics and Women before the Maryland Advisory Committee to the U.S. Commission on Civil Rights* (Washington, D.C.: Government Printing Office, 1975); National Urban League, *The National Survey of Housing Abandonment* (Washington, D.C.: National Urban League, 1971).

13. Latta Chatterjee, David Harvey and Leonard Kengman, *FHA Policies and the Baltimore City Housing Market* (Baltimore: Johns Hopkins, 1974); Charles Boyer, *Cities Destroyed for Cash,* 1973; Leonard Downie, *Mortgage on America* (New York: Praeger, 1974) See also Chapter 3 of this monograph.

14. Rapkin, *The Real Estate Market,* p. 54. See also Kenneth Holbert "Redlining: A New Direction in Fair Housing Policy," *HUD Challenge,* Vol 7 (April 1976), p. 20; Latta Chatterjee, *et al., FHA Policies,* p. 412; A. Heidkamp and S. Sandy, "Redlining in Milwaukee: Who is Destroying the Westside" (Milwaukee: Citizens Action Group, no date), pp. 4-5.

15. Rapkin, *The Real Estate Market,* p. 53; Sternlieb, *The Tenement Landlord,* p. 113; Sternlieb, *Urban Housing Dilemma,* p. 380. See also Frederick Case, *Inner City Housing and Private Enterprise* (New York: Praeger, 1973). See also Chicago Commission on Human Relations, *Selling and Buying Real Estate in a Racially Changing Neighborhood,* p. 10.

16. George Sternlieb, "Slum Housing: A Functional Analysis," *Law and Contemporary Problems,* Vol. 32, pp. 349-351 (1967): Ad Hoc Subcommittee on Home Financing Practices and Procedures of the House Committee on Banking and Currency, 91st Cong., First Sess., *Financing of Inner-City Housing* (Committee Print 1969), pp. 84-85; George Akahoshi and Edna Gass, *A Study of the Problems of Abandoned Housing and Recommendations for Action by the Federal Government and Localities* (Washington, D.C.: Linton, Mields and Costow, 1971); George Sternlieb, "Abandonment and Rehabilitation: What is to be Done," In U.S. Congress, House of Representatives, Committee On Housing (Washington, D.C.: Government Printing Office, 1971); William Grigsby, Michael Stegman, and J. Taylor, *Housing and Poverty* (New Brunswick, New Jersey: Rutgers University Center for Urban Policy Research and APS Publications, 1976); George Cranker, "Abandoned and Vacant Housing Units: Can They be Used During Housing Crises?," *New York University Review of Law and Social Change* (Spring 1971), pp. 3-66.

17. Michael Stegman, *Housing Investment in the Inner City* (Cambridge, Mass.: M.I.T. Press, 1973); Fredrick Case, ed., *Inner City Housing and Private Enterprise,* Chicago Commission on Human Relations, *Selling and Buying Real Estate; CPL Bibliography.*

18. Chicago Commission on Human Relations, *Selling and Buying Real Estate.* See also Stegman, *Housing Investment in the Inner City.*

19. See Chapter 3 in this monograph.

20. See statements in U.S. Department of Housing and Urban Development, *Administrative Meeting on Redlining and Disinvestment As A Discriminatory Practice in Residential Mortgage Loans,* Vol. 1, July 14-16, 1976. Philadelphia, Pennsylvania (Washington, D.C.: Government Printing Office, 1976).

21. *Ibid.*

22. Philip Gabel, *The Mortgage Financing of Multifamily Income Properties* (Ph.D. dissertation, New York University, 1974).

23. National Urban League, Inc. *The National Survey of Housing Abandonment* (New York: National Urban League, 1971); Center for New Corporate Priorities, *Where the Money Is, Mortgage Lending, Los Angeles County* (Los Angeles: Center for New Corporate Priorities, 1974); District of Columbia, Public Interest Research Group, *et al., Redlining: Mortgage Disinvestment in the District of Columbia* (Washington, D.C.: DC PIRG, 1975); Karren Orren, *Corporate Power and Social Change* (Baltimore: Johns Hopkins, 1974). See also *CPL Bibliography;* Phoenix Fund, "Savings and Loan Lending Activity in the City of St. Louis — A Phoenix Fund Update for 1974" (St. Louis, Missouri: Phoenix Fund, May 5, 1975); Citizens Planning and Housing Association, "1974 in Retrospect: A Review of the Baltimore Housing Market," (Baltimore, Maryland: Citizens Planning and Housing Association, April 1975), p. 3; Rochester Greenlining Coalition, "Memo of Research to Senator William Proxmire " (April 30, 1976), p. 1; See also Chapter 3 in this monograph.

24. See Gale Cincotta and Randy Vereen, *Regulatory Agencies and the Redlining and Disinvestment Process: A Report* (Chicago: mimeographed, 1977); *Senate Hearings; House Hearings;* and *Administrative Meeting on Redlining and Disinvestment.*

25. See Chapter 2 in this monograph.

26. National Urban League, *The National Survey of Housing Abandonment.*

27. See *Senate Hearing; House Hearings;* and *Administrative Meeting on Redlining and Disinvestment.* See also U.S. Commission on Civil Rights Staff Report, "Home Mortgage Financing and Racial and Economic Integration," in *Hearings on the Federal Government's Role in the Achievement of Equal Opportunity in Housing,* before the Civil Rights Oversight Subcommittee of the House Committee on the Judiciary, 91st Congress, 1st and 2nd Sessions (Washington, D.C.: Government Printing Office, 1972); *Hearings Before the Subcommittee on Antitrust and Monopoly of the Senate Committee on Judiciary on Competition in Real Estate and Mortgage Lending,* 92nd Congress, 2nd Session (Washington, D.C.: Government Printing Office, 1971); *Hearings Before Senate Committee on Banking, Housing and Urban Affairs Oversight in Equal Opportunity in Lending Enforcement by the Bank Regulatory Agencies,* 94th Congress, 2nd Session (Washington, D.C.: Government Printing Office, 1976); *Hearings Before Senate Committee on Banking, Housing, and Urban Affairs on Oversight on Home Mortgage Disclosure Act and the Equal Credit Opportunity Act,* 94th Congress, 2nd Session (Washington, D.C.: Government Printing Office, 1976).

28. See footnote 20.

29. See statement of William A. Beasman, Jr. on behalf of National Association of Mutual Savings Banks, *Senate Hearings,* p. 807; Statement of Grover J. Hansen on behalf of National Savings and Loan League, *Senate Hearings,* p. 820; Statement of William B. O'Connell on behalf of U.S. League of Savings Associations, *Senate Hearings,* p. 871; Statement of John H. Perkins on behalf of the American Bankers Association, *Senate Hearings,* p. 884.

30. Herbert Prochnow, *The Changing World of Banking* (New York: Harper and Row, 1974), p. 374.

Chapter 2
# The Economic and Eco-Race Models

---

## Introduction

The economic and eco-race models concern the underwriting practices of institutional lenders — a difficult and multifaceted topic. To better understand the underwriting process and the differing emphases of the economic and eco-race models, this chapter introduces a general mortgage distribution model. This model attempts to show the determinants of the volume of conventional credit to a particular neighborhood. It is general in the sense of showing many possible influences on loan availability. The economic/eco-race models are detailed subsets of the general model.

## Nature of the Mortgage Distribution Model

There are many types of models, ranging from the simple or descriptive to formal and complex mathematical constructions.[1]

The mortgage distribution model is a simple, first-pass approach to help show the different considerations involved in granting a loan and how these different inputs can affect the volume of credit flowing to a specific area. It comes closest to Catanese's perception of a model as a device to help "develop and illustrate meaningful relationships"[2] or Bartos' concept that "models can help express complex ideas."[3]

The model is summarized in Exhibit 2-1. Before its components are discussed, the model's limitations must be realized. It is descriptive rather than analytical, and partial rather than holistic; the model shows components

17

EXHIBIT 2-1

GENERAL MORTGAGE DISTRIBUTION MODEL

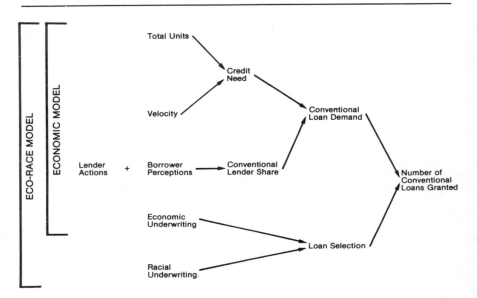

and simple relationships rather than direct and indirect interactions. To illustrate, it considers the influence of housing and neighborhood quality on mortgage supply but does not examine the simultaneous effect of the availability of credit on housing and neighborhood condition. Similarly, in terms of scope, the model is micro rather than macro; it does not attempt to comprehensively explain the urban housing, financing and race dynamic but rather limits itself to considerations of loan demand and selection.

The general model is neutral. It contains some variables emphasized by the economic and others stressed by the eco-race model. It shows the many influences that may explain why there are variations in loan distribution.

## A Theoretical General Mortgage Distribution Model

The amount of conventional credit flowing to a neighborhood is first a function of the *demand* for loans in that area. Lenders then decide which members of the pool of applicants will be granted credit. Thus, volume is a function of first, loan *demand*, and then, lender *selection*.

LOAN DEMAND

The process can be better understood by examining the components influencing conventional loan demand and selection. Conventional demand is influenced by the need for credit in an area and the filtering of part of that need to conventional lenders.

It is difficult to estimate precisely the need for credit in a neighborhood, but the following factors can be expected to play a role.

I. *Number of Units.* All things being equal, the greater the number of parcels (buildings and land) in a neighborhood, the greater the ultimate number of mortgages needed. (Parcels rather than units are employed as an indicator, for by definition, a single mortgage is given on a building regardless of the number of units it contains [ condominiums and co-ops excluded].) The number of parcels sets the parameters of the basic pool of realty that may need credit when ownership transfers or when current owners wish to refinance.

II. *Velocity.** While the number of parcels is certainly an influence, it is equally evident that certain areas may be experiencing more transactions and hence more demand for credit than others of roughly comparable size. This is why the velocity factor, specifically the influence of velocity on an area's existing pool of units, is so important. Velocity is defined as the ownership turnover rate in the housing stock. It is analogous to the velocity or turnover in the money supply. Velocity volume is influenced by such factors as:

1. *Level of new construction.* Neighborhoods experiencing relatively high levels of new construction can be expected to experience a relatively higher number of real estate transactions. In turn these locations will be demanding more credit.

2. *Age of housing stock.* Empirical evidence has shown that greater turnover is common in the younger housing stock.[4] This may be due in part to the resident attracted to these units — typically younger families who tend to be more mobile.

3. *Age of neighborhood residents.* Research by John Kain and John Quigley has revealed that the older the heads of households in an area, the more stable the housing market in terms of turnover.[5] Age influences mobility; older residents are less mobile and therefore remain in their housing longer. Neighborhoods with older residents usually will demand less credit.

4. *Family composition.* Neighborhoods with relatively greater shares of "full family" households, consisting of a husband/wife and children, have lower sales velocity. Studies have found such families to be more "rooted," less mobile, and hence less willing to move from one dwelling to another.[6] Credit demand will be lower in such areas.

Other variables, such as income and race and race-related factors (e.g., blockbusting) are still possible further influences.

---

*The general mortgage distribution model does not consider the feedback or simultaneity issue of the influence of mortgage availability and velocity.

The share of loan requests funnelled to conventional lenders constitutes their market share and is influenced by lender actions in pursuing a strong market position in certain neighborhoods, borrower perceptions concerning the feasibility or desirability of approaching a conventional lender, and other factors such as "tradition," or physical presence (whether the conventional lender has convenient branches in the area).

Borrower perceptions concerning the best sources of credit also will influence the share of conventional institution loan requests (of course, lender actions influence borrower perceptions). For instance, minorities have sometimes displayed a reluctance to approach conventional lenders. This situation was revealed repeatedly in the Frederick Case studies.[7] Case found that blacks often distrusted conventional lenders and had communications problems when dealing with them. In California, Case concluded that blacks often sought private financing because:[8]

> A (conventional) mortgage loan transaction with its archaic documents, implicit comments and fine points is certainly culturally biased . . . Obscure statements and bundles of legal documents are enough to turn many prospective borrowers away.

LOAN SELECTION

The selection of successful loan applicants from a larger pool of home purchasers, sometimes referred to as loan underwriting, is a complex, multifaceted endeavor.

Deferring for a moment questions of emphasis, underwriting may involve both economic and racial considerations.

ECONOMIC UNDERWRITING CRITERIA

Since many of the urban financing studies have focused on single-family loans, the discussion will concentrate on single-family loan underwriting (single-family units comprise approximately two-thirds of the housing stock). For such housing, lenders and lending training texts stress three underwriting factors:[9] (1) *economic characteristics of the borrower;* (2) *economic characteristics of the property that will serve as security for the loan;* and (3) *economic characteristics of the neighborhood in which such property is located.*

While all three carry weight, borrower traits supposedly are very significant in single-family underwriting. The following borrower traits are deemed indicative of an ability and willingness to repay a loan:
1. current and anticipated income and housing expense-to-income ratio;
2. past credit/asset history;
3. equity in property;

4. "personal" characteristics;
5. property characteristics;
6. neighborhood traits.

1. *Income and housing expense-to-income ratio.* Of primary importance is the income of the applicant. What is the annual income? Is this income stable? Does the applicant's occupation suggest that income will be consistent in the future? The length of time a person has been employed as well as his or her type of occupation are considered critical: the longer a person has been working, and the more stable and remunerative the occupation (professionals or managers, for example), the lower the risk.

The composition of income is also examined: part-time and special supplements such as overtime and larger Christmas bonuses are discounted. Previously, a wife's earnings usually were not counted for they were deemed temporary. In line with changing concepts of the woman's role in, and value to, society, the Equal Credit Opportunity Act (ECOA) of 1974 designated that a wife's income be fully counted.

While income itself is important, another crucial consideration is the housing expense-to-income ratio. The most frequently used rule of thumb, popularized by the FHA, is that a borrower's housing expenses should not exceed 25 percent of his income. Another is that the purchase price of the home should not exceed 250 percent of the purchaser's annual income. In considering these ratios, the underwriter not only measures their magnitude, but how they compare to the applicant's prior housing burden; an individual with a 40 percent housing expense-to-income expense ratio might be accepted if this was the burden successfully borne on a prior house.

2. *Past credit/asset history.* Whether or not the applicant has previously used credit, and the past repayment record, is significant. Regular payment, or, conversely, delinquency, are deemed as excellent indicators of future performance.

Underwriters also check an applicant's assets, such as a bank account. Assets are deemed a good proxy of an applicant's ability to manage his financial affairs. They also represent a potential partial security for the lender in the event of foreclosure. (This is particularly true when the mortgagor has signed a note making him personally liable.)

3. *Equity in property.* The mortgagor's monetary interest influences the degree of effort and sacrifice that the mortgagor would normally make to protect the mortgaged property. A major determinant of the borrower's equity is the loan-to-value ratio (LVR).* The higher the LVR, the lower the borrower's equity, and presumably the greater the risk in granting such a loan.

---

\* $\dfrac{\text{Size of Loan}}{\substack{\text{Value or purchase price} \\ \text{of property}}}$ = Loan-to-value ratio (LVR)

4. *Borrower's personal characteristics.* Underwriters maintain that certain traits such as family stability reveal a willingness and ability to repay a loan.

5. *Property characteristics.* In turning from the borrower to property-neighborhood variables, the basic concern is that the commodity (mortgaged property) and environment (neighborhood) will not be adverse or undesirable, an admittedly vague standard. In rating a property these factors may be considered:[10]

Visual appeal of property;
Livability of property;
Natural light and ventilation;
Structural quality;
Resistance to elements and use;
Suitability of mechanical equipment;
Adjustment for nonconformity.

6. *Neighborhood characteristics.* Underwriting manuals discuss a series of neighborhood traits which determine an area's ambience. Some pertain to the physical environment:

proximity to employment centers, shopping, entertainment, schools, etc.;
well defined, preferably natural, boundaries;
homogeneous land uses, proximity to desirable land uses;
availability of public utilities and transportation;
physical attractiveness of structure, subdivision layouts, level of crowding;
natural hazards, e.g., flooding.

Neighborhood social and economic features are deemed very critical. The "quality" of the population which resides in the neighborhood and its stability are two key underwriting considerations.

Closely associated with the stress on stability is the high esteem underwriters often have for single-family areas as opposed to neighborhoods with a mixed (single and multifamily) housing stock. Single-family neighborhoods are considered more desirable in term of owner maintenance, attachment to area, and pride of homeownership, as insurance against decline.

Neighborhood economics are a final key consideration; underwriters consider wealthier areas as "safer," more stable and desirable.

Many of the neighborhood variables are vague, especially as compared to the borrower's economic underwriting considerations. Evaluations of the "physical attractiveness of structures" and the "level of stability" are clearly subjective. Critics further contend that the neighborhood underwriting standards are biased—they explicitly or implicitly lead loan officers to downgrade urban neighborhoods, especially minority areas. These locations are usually relatively old, physically and socially heterogeneous, and more prone to change. Single-family homeownership is less predominant. These neighborhoods are also usually economically weaker—unemployment is higher while average income is lower. All of these traits are adverse or negative ones according to traditional underwriting standards. These rules are currently being challenged as discriminatory to urban and black neighborhoods.

## RACIAL UNDERWRITING CRITERIA

In *addition* to economic considerations, some critics claim that racial criteria influence lenders.[11] These factors include:

1. *Race of loan applicant.* The race of the applicant is viewed as an important determinant of whether or not a mortgage will be granted. Because of racial discrimination, blacks and other minorities are at a disadvantage.

2. *Race of area where secured property is located.* In addition to the race of the applicant, the racial composition of the neighborhood surrounding the would-be mortgaged property allegedly also influences lenders. Loan applications in high minority locations (or transitional areas where whites are leaving) are allegedly denied outright or are scrutinized more closely than in other locations. The black applicant may suffer both because of his color as well as the racial composition of the neighborhood in which he wishes to purchase a home, since individual minority buyers often purchase homes in minority neighborhoods (whether out of choice and/or discriminatory steering practices).

## Influences on Urban Mortgage Lending

The lender behavior models can better be understood if explained in terms of the general mortgage distribution model. If few conventional loans are granted to a neighborhood, then according to the general model, the area would have to exhibit weak loan demand and/or stringent loan selection, i.e., most loan applications are rejected. The advocates of the economic and eco-race models differ in their view of both the loan demand and the economic loan selection procedure in mortgage-short neighborhoods and markedly disagree on the influence of racial loan selection.

## LOAN DEMAND

The eco-race proponents agree that the demand for credit may be less in mortgage-short areas. The mortgage deficient locations will often have less need for credit because of their lower turnover velocity. This occurs for such reasons as less new housing activity, and that residents and the housing stock may be older. Since conventional loan demand is a function of both credit need and conventional lender share, and need in turn is influenced by both total neighborhood units and velocity, if velocity is lower in the mortgage-short areas, then demand will be less in such locations.

But while the eco-race advocates make the above admission—an economic justification of the financing crunch—they argue that demand will not always be lower; not all mortgage-short areas have lower velocity since they are not universally old, or contain only low-income residents. These proponents further charge that it is important to look at the *full* conventional loan demand equation to understand the forces at work. As previously stated, this demand is a product of both need and conventional lender market share. Even if need were greater in some of the credit rationed locations, demand for conventional loans might still be weaker there, not from innocent economic causes, but as a consequence of deliberate lender policy not to pursue a market in certain urban neighborhoods. This policy may either be overt (refusing to accept applications in a particular area) or co.-vert (not advertising).

Eco-race advocates further contend that even if demand were weaker in the mortgage-short locations, the variation would not be an acceptable explanation of the financing crunch since areal differences in demand are far less striking than the extremely sharp contrasts in the number of loans granted to various neighborhoods.

Advocates of the economic model, in turn, argue that one major reason why certain neighborhoods receive few loans is that there is little demand. Need is less for reasons previously discussed. These proponents take issue with the charge that conventional lenders are deliberately reducing their market share. They argue instead that lenders, like good businessmen, want to act in growth markets; few loans are granted, because the market in many urban neighborhoods (in terms of demand) is so limited. Pierre de Vise, a Chicago consultant, for example, attributed the low levels of loans granted in certain Chicago neighborhoods to "supply factors;" namely there were "record new levels of construction of housing, factories and shopping centers in suburbs."[12]

LOAN SELECTION

While the demand question is part of the economic versus eco-race debate, the major controversy concerns loan selection. The general mortgage distribution model states that conventional lender selection can include both economic and racial factors. The eco-race advocates agree that for certain loan applicants, most typically blacks, living in certain areas, usually minority or transition locations, the economic underwriting criteria are evaluated but argue that racial criteria are also unfairly considered. Race may have a subtle, but nonetheless harmful impact, such as when race biases economic underwriting. Blacks might be denied loans in borderline cases where a white applicant would be accepted. To illustrate, underwriting manuals stress that only "stable" incomes should be counted, that is, the regular compensation paid to an individual. The question of how to treat overtime, income from a second job, a spouse's part-time employment, etc., is usually left to the discretion of loan officers. Eco-race advocates claim that such secondary or supplementary income, admittedly hard to classify, would not be counted or would be discounted heavily in the case of blacks, but would be considered for whites. As another example, in considering property characteristics, a loan officer would rate the livability or visual appeal of a row house in an inner city neighborhood as unsatisfactory yet might possibly classify a similar structure in a white, middle-class area as "quaint" and energy efficient.

Proponents of the economic model claim that the above view of the urban lending dynamic is simply not valid today. Economic underwriting criteria are viewed as the guiding considerations in whether a loan is granted or not. Applicant race and neighborhood racial composition are never considered (the same is true with reference to sex and marital status). If black loan applicants are rejected more frequently, it is because their income, credit history, etc. are lower or weaker. If black neighborhoods receive fewer loans, it is because the individual properties and overall neighborhood environments are less favorable.

This discussion of the general mortgage distribution model and economic versus eco-race controversy clarifies this monograph's research objective. The study focuses on the loan selection process; while demand is surely an important consideration, the major controversy of the models has usually centered on the mortgage selection dynamic. There are also pragmatic data constraints: while it would have been desirable to consider demand, no data existed at the time of this analysis to effect such investigation. Instead, this study focuses on the loan selection process and attempts to isolate the influence of the economic versus racial underwriting criteria. It tests whether race, as a variable *separate* from ecomomies, is playing a distinct role in influencing loan selection.

## Notes

1. See Anthony Catanese and Alan Steiss, *Systematic Planning: Theory and Application* (Lexington, Mass.: Lexington, 1970); J. Brian McLaughlin, *Urban and Regional Planning: A Systems Approach* (New York: Preager, 1969); Walter Buckley, *Modern Systems Research for the Behavioral Scientist* (Chicago: Aldine, 1968); Ira Lowry, "A Short Course in Model Design," *Journal of the American Institute of Planners*, Vol. 39 (January 1973), p. 158; Britton Harris, "Quantitative Models of Urban Development: Their Role in Metropolitan Policy Making," and "New Tools for Planning," *Journal of the American Institute of Planners*, Vol. 39 (January 1973), p. 90; Robert Dubin, *Theory Building* (New York: Free Press, 1969); Gordon D. Renyo, *Concepts, Theory and Explanation in the Behavioral Sciences* (New York: Random House, 1967), p. 46.

2. Catanese and Steiss, *Systematic Planning*, p. 167.

3. Otomar Bartos, *Simple Models of Group Behavior* (New York: Columbia University Press, 1967), p. 10.

4. See John F. Tomer, "The Redlining Hypothesis and How to Test It " (Rensselaer Polytechnic Institute, Troy, New York, 1977).

5. John F. Kain and John M. Quigley, *Housing Markets and Racial Discrimination: A Microeconomic Analysis* (New York: National Bureau of Economic Research, 1975), pp. 126-130.

6. *Ibid.*

7. Frederick Case, *Inner City Housing and Private Enterprise* (New York: Praeger, 1972).

8. Frederick Case, Project Director, "Housing the Underhoused: The California Studies " (Los Angeles: UCLA School of Business Administration, 1970), p. 6.

9. American Institute of Banking, *Home Mortgage Lending* (Washington, D.C.: American Institute of Banking, 1972); Robert A. Pease and Lewis O. Kerwood, *Mortgage Banking* (New York: McGraw Hill, 1965), See also U.S. Federal Housing Administration, *Underwriting Training Handbook*, Chapter 5 (Washington, D.C.: Government Printing Office, 1972).

10. *Ibid.*

11. See Appendix 3-A in this monograph.

12. Pierre de Vise, "The Anti-Redliners: How Community Activists Have Forged a Devil Theory of Urban Decay," Working Paper II.24, Chicago Regional Hospital Study (September 1976), p. 1.

Chapter 3
# The Urban Financing Literature

## Introduction

It is important to consider the existing literature on the urban financing dilemma before initiating the empirical analysis. This chapter summarizes and evaluates numerous studies, using the general mortgage distribution model as a conceptual framework. (Appendix 3-A discusses individual analyses at greater length. See also the annotated bibliography.)

## Economic-Eco-Race Studies

At minimum, the eco-race studies indicate that black areas and property owners are receiving fewer loans than they have in the past and/or relative to the current flow in white urban or suburban locations.[1] The economic analyses, more limited both in number and scope, contend that lenders stress economics and discount race and have made limited headway in proving at least isolated cases of economic predominance. Both groups of studies, however, raise sample, conceptual and analytic questions.

SAMPLE SELECTION

The samples (e.g., the neighborhoods examined) in the urban financing studies can sometimes be faulted for being small and perhaps biased. Many analyses examine only one or a handful of neighborhoods. Other things being equal, if the sample is small (a characteristic of many loan analyses), then the idiosyncracies or non-universal characteristics of the individual members selected as part of the sample, which are more likely to be offset or balanced in a larger sample, will likely remain and increase the chance of error in making generalizations.

While small sample size is a deficiency of many economic and eco-race studies, the drawback must be kept in perspective. First, some analyses have considered city-wide rather than individual neighborhood lending patterns. Second, while individually many investigations do have a limited geographical purview, in aggregate the sum of areas considered by the urban financing studies is quite large.

A more significant question than sample size is possible sample bias. Bias is not the same as small sample size. With a small sample, average error is higher because generalizations are drawn from fewer cases; increased sample size means increased reliability. Bias is a different problem in that the selection procedure is not neutral — a large biased sample would be flawed because it offers just a larger collection of atypical cases.

The neighborhoods examined by many of the lending studies are biased; they are atypical from the universe of urban neighborhoods for they are in far worse condition, often terminal in nature. Examples are neighborhoods in New York's South Bronx and North Philadelphia. These areas are clearly not typical urban neighborhoods. Given their uniqueness, one cannot generalize that race is a prevalent consideration in all types of urban lending, but only that race is a consideration in the highly impacted neighborhoods. Racial discrimination could therefore be present only in the more atypical situation of the terminal neighborhoods — a much more limited finding than some of the eco-race analyses purport to show.

CONCEPTUAL ISSUES

Investigations of the economic versus eco-race models would ideally consider both the demand and selection stage of underwriting and the finer points of the selection process. At minimum, since the controversy focuses on the loan selection dynamic, the specific underwriting considerations would be minutely examined.

In reality, many of the financing studies fail to consider either the full process (demand plus selection) or even the selection phase alone. Demand is almost never examined. This discussion is not meant to imply that the failure to adequately consider demand is a fatal flaw. It is unlikely that all mortgage-short areas always have a lesser demand. And demand is a secondary issue in the economic versus eco-race controversy as compared to the debate over selection. Although not fatal, avoiding the demand question raises some doubts. As expressed by **Senator Jake Garn:**[2]

> Specifically, what good does it do to come to a conclusion that because there are so many loans made in a particular area, that area was discriminated against without knowing what the demand factor was? How many people applied for loans? I happen to know of a situation where redlining is charged where only three loans were made but 3 out of 5 or 60 percent were approved. Now the raw statistics may or may not be worth a darn. We should know all the facts.

There are also questions concerning the analysis of the loan selection process. This stage may involve both economic and racial factors. Since race and economics are intertwined, at minimum the studies should attempt to consider the interaction of racial and economic criteria and disentangle which influence remains. Many of the reports do not do this, however. They (in this instance referring to the eco-race studies) attempt to prove non-justifiable lender activity by implication, by looking at the end product, the actual loan patterns, and drawing from that suspect lender motives and actions. This kind of second hand analysis does not control for the intertwining economic and racial influences; it confirms the sharp differences in the number of loans granted in particular areas, but begs the question of why this happens.

The suspect patterns deemed to confirm racial discrimination or other unjustified practices include:

1. Few loans granted in minority versus nonminority areas.
2. Few loans granted in cities versus suburbs.
3. Few loans granted relative to the volume of deposits (Loan-to-deposit [LDR] ratios are low).
4. Few conventional loans granted relative to FHA/VA volume.

From pattern 1, the eco-race analyses surmise racial discrimination as follows:

A. Certain areas are not granted mortgages.
B. These areas are often minority locations.
C. The reason for the paucity of loans in minority locations is therefore racial discrimination.

In a similar fashion, the analyses surmise from pattern 2 that lenders subjectively favor suburban as opposed to urban locations (an indirect form of racial discrimination, since blacks are concentrated in cities). From pattern 3 they conclude that financial institutions are ignoring the needs of certain neighborhoods for they are not giving loans to locations where deposits do exist. Pattern 4 is said to clearly show that lenders are unjustifiably ingoring a potential loan market, that of the FHA/VA buyer.

These arguments are questionable; they unjustifiably impugn intent (an intent that is illegal) using evidence that depicts only loan patterns, not lender policy. It does not necessarily follow that because many black areas receive few loans (pattern 1), racial discrimination is therefore at play rather than objective underwriting based on consideration of loan demand or loan security. The following exchange illustrates the issue:[3]

*Lawson* - I think that the lending institutions work actively with builders and with real estate brokers to create a market which Negro buyers cannot enter. [The Northwest Section of Washington, D.C.]* . . . the fact that we see here a picture of the bulk of the loan money going to an area where the fewest number of Negroes live seems to me to make a definite statement.

*Griswold* - Could I interrupt here? I must confess I don't find the information you have gathered that the bulk of the money goes to the Northwest very indicative of anything except that that's where there are opportunities for loans. Do your figures or any other information you have indicate in any way that Negroes in general or as a class, have difficulty in getting mortgage loans . . .

*Lawson* - I think these things don't just happen. I think that they come about as a result of policy, and I think the fact that Negroes don't live in these forbidden neighborhoods means they couldn't get there because they couldn't get loans to move there.

*Griswold* - I think you are entitled to think that, but I don't think your figures prove it.

The conclusions drawn from the other three patterns are equally suspect. Urban locations may be receiving fewer loans because of softer demand and higher risk than suburban areas. The urban loan deposit ratio argument is especially problematical. The bibliographic essay discusses some of the premises for arguing that there should be parity between loans and deposits. Deposits made in a particular bank are not a very good proxy of local economic health, for they may not be made by local depositors or by local businesses; financial institutions in downtown areas bordering on slum residential neighborhoods may very well have large deposits, but these may be derived from commercial-industrial firms, not local residents.[4] While lenders are obliged to provide credit to their "local service area," this does not necessarily mandate the granting of local mortgages in complete parity with local deposits.

The conclusion drawn from the fourth pattern (FHA/VA versus conventional loans)—that lenders are ignoring a viable market—is also questionable. Clearly, there is less risk when the Federal government provides security for loans, whether they are FHA-insured or VA-guaranteed. Thus, a high ratio of conventional-to-FHA/VA loans may very well be a product of an objective evaluation of a lending environment and an economically justifiable conclusion that is suitable only for insured mortgages.

ANALYTIC ISSUES

It is important to mention the spirit in which this evaluation is made. The analyses that have gone beyond the descriptive, that is those which do not merely show unequal patterns of loans but try to analyze why it occurs, were made after painstaking efforts in collecting basic data. To illustrate, before

*Note added.

the 1975 Home Mortgage Disclosure Act, the only way to tell how many mortgages were being made in a neighborhood was to search out *every* transaction in that area, usually via the county title record or some commercial real estate directory (i.e., LUSKs, REDI, etc.) and then hand tabulate those institutions providing the financing for each transaction—a truly laborious task. (This difficulty, in part, explains why analyses often were limited to one neighborhood.) That these studies were even conducted under such conditions is a tribute to their authors' persistence.

Certain analytic questions, however, cannot be ignored. Some are minor and/or unavoidable. One problem concerns loan standardization. Holding aside the issue of demand, there is the question of how loan volume should be expressed. Some approaches, such as number of mortgages per number of housing structures, are appropriate, but others are questionable. Comparing the gross number of loans in different zip code locations or Census tracts without standardizing them (i.e., number of loans per 1,000 mortgagible parcels per zip code) is misleading, for zip codes as well as Census tracts can contain substantially different numbers of parcels and population. Other measures are also questionable. The number of loans per capita (LPC), a measuring device found in some studies, has little significance; to say that area X has .001 LPC while area Y has .01 LPC means very little if X has a higher density of multifamily rental structures than Y.

Other inadequacies are more serious. One of them is the limited information on the condition of housing in a neighborhood—one economic underwriting variable. The Census is very deficient in this regard; early Census measures, such as substandard or deteriorating units, were deemed unreliable. Current more objective standards (i.e., percentage units lacking plumbing) are often inadequate, especially in an urban context.[5] Another problem is a time gap—analyzing the current loan distribution with Census data which may reflect conditions of a decade earlier.

The most serious analytic issue involves the detailed consideration of the loan selection process. In considering the selection dynamic, one should examine racial and economic components, e.g., applicant income, credit, equity, personal characteristics, property and neighborhood traits, the race of the loan applicant and the racial composition of the area surrounding the mortgaged property.

This comprehensive analysis was rarely undertaken by the early economic and eco-race studies and is only sometimes followed by more recent investigations (see Appendix 3-A). Additionally, certain data, used as proxies for critical economic and social and racial values, are suspect.

Some of the data considered are perfectly acceptable. In terms of the racial composition of the neighborhood it is legitimate to use Census data on percentage minority residents per zip code or Census tract. Similarly, the spectrum of Census variables (median rent and median values of homes, for example) used by the financing studies are reasonably acceptable as showing neighborhood condition, albeit the neighborhood quality underwriting standards are themselves vague and there is scant Census information on housing-neighborhood quality.[6]

But these are the exceptions. Most of the other economic-racial underwriting criteria, especially those concerning individual applicant characteristics, are examined with questionable data. To illustrate, one item of utmost importance is the income of mortgage applicants. The financing studies use average income in the neighborhood as a proxy for mortgagor income. While average income is a valid indicator for neighborhood wealth, it may under or overstate the income of specific applicants applying for mortgages. In a transition area, neighborhood income will overstate applicant income if there is a high-to-low socio economic status change and will tend to understate applicant wealth in situations where middle-income families are replacing the poor.

Certain loan selection criteria are usually not examined at all. These include the credit history of the mortgage applicant, applicant's downpayment, and personal characteristics—all important background information. This shortcoming is especially serious, for in single-family underwriting the personal characteristics are considered to be especially important.

To play devil's advocate, a lender could explain that black neighborhoods and property owners receive fewer loans (a major finding of the eco-race studies) because blacks fail the personal underwriting criteria; they have less income and less steady means of support; they may not have much of a past credit record, and they desire riskier high loan-to-value ratio mortgages.

This statement cannot be easily refuted or confirmed. The issue of economics versus eco-race requires continued study.

## Appendix 3-A
## A Bibliographic Essay on the
## Urban Financing Literature

---

## Introduction

This bibliographic essay examines a number of studies considering the presence and causes of the urban financing problem. These can be grouped into three categories:

1. Political-economic;
2. Minority housing opportunity;
3. Empirical economic and eco-race.

The first group of analyses considers the mortgage crunch as a manifestation of deficiencies in the overall political-economic system; the second views it as one facet of the larger discriminatory network encountered by minorities; and the third attributes the credit shortfall to the economic or eco-race models of lender behavior.

The first two groups share certain common traits. They discuss the financing dilemma as a secondary issue, often to illustrate their major thesis. They also do not examine the mortgage crunch via empirical data, but rather assume that it exists and is due to various reasons. Similar themes are found in the economic and eco-race studies, but they focus on the financing problem and usually employ empirical information to attempt to prove or disprove the existence of the mortgage crunch and to explain its origins. Many of the economic and eco-race studies also go beyond just considering economic and racial influences and evaluate such issues as the presence of geographic redlining and the impact of FHA financing. They also discuss meliorative strategies to the urban financing problem.

This appendix focuses on early or pioneer studies, mostly conducted prior to the mid-1970s. These investigations proved very influential not only in molding subsequent research efforts but in shaping the very tenor of the economic versus eco-race debate. More current analyses, completed in the past few years, are briefly summarized.

## Political-Economic Studies

This group of analyses examines the political-economic forces that have influenced the nature, form and spatial distribution of the "built environment." Many are influenced by Marxist thought and interpret the formation of cities, suburban outmigration and urban problems according to the Marxian view of capital, labor and class exploitation. Some examples include David Harvey's *Social Justice of the City* and James O'Connor's *The Fiscal Crisis of the State.*[7]

These studies view most urban difficulties as the inevitable undesirable products of a capitalist system. To illustrate, Francois Lamarche sees urban renewal displacement and "insalubrious" housing conditions as resulting from the priorities of market capital and exploitation by those possessing capital.[8] Suburban growth and prosperity, as compared to urban misfortunes, is viewed by James O'Connor as suburban economic exploitation of the city.[9] Michael Stone similarly views urban decay as a product of profit motivated activity:[10]

> The crucial decisions in the housing sector — as in most major areas of the society are not made primarily on the basis of human needs. Instead the important decisions revolve around the flow of investment capital into housing and these decisions of course are made on the basis of the opportunities for profit ... American families will continue to live in substandard homes and neighborhoods and continue to pay exorbitant sums for housing needs unless there are radical changes in the American political economy.

The urban financing problem is mentioned by some of the political-economic studies as an additional undesirable urban fault attributable to capitalist exploitation. David Harvey's writings give the fullest attention to this issue. He accepts the mortgage crunch as a prevalent urban ill:[11]

> The obvious "red-line" in mortgage finance is an excellent example of how something very firmly etched into the geographical landscape of the city can arise by the complex of interactions and expectations in the housing market.

Harvey views the urban credit shortfall as economically rational behavior. In his words, "nobody in particular is at fault but the red-line nevertheless exists."[12] Harvey elaborates on the "rational" reasons for redlining in *Social Justice and the City.* He sees the capitalist acceptance of the practice as one illustration of this system's undesirability:[13]

The banks naturally have good rational business reasons for not financing mortgages in inner city areas . . . In fact, it is a general characteristic of ghetto housing that if we accept the mores of normal, ethical entrepreneurial behavior, there is no way in which we can blame anyone for the objective social conditions which all are willing to characterize as appalling and wasteful of potential housing resources . . . Consequently, it seems impossible to find a policy within the existing economic and institutional framework which is capable of rectifying these conditions . . .

This group of studies gives a systems framework for viewing the urban financing crunch. It views the credit shortfall as quite prevalent in cities and attributes this phenomenon to profit-motivated lender behavior. The analyses thus give an economic interpretation to the urban financing dilemma;[14] they do not accept it as a desirable economic practice, but rather view the mortgage shortage as a failing of the capitalist system.

## Minority Housing Opportunity Studies

This literature has focused on three key issues:
1. Does discrimination cause minorities to pay more for housing than whites?
2. Does discrimination contribute to the relatively low rate of minority homeownership?
3. Does discrimination force minorities to live in cities (and in ghettoes within cities), thereby forestalling their access to job and educational opportunities?

The studies attempt to show that discrimination *is* an important factor in all three areas. Originally the analyses were conducted by sociologists, planners and political scientists. Economists dominate this literature today.[15] The discussion below highlights some of the more significant minority housing cost, choice, and location monographs.

Charles Abrams (1955) discussed the difficulties blacks faced in obtaining access and credit to purchase houses in New York City and other communities.[16] David McEntire (1956) analyzed Census data to show that blacks had a lower rate of homeownership and paid more for their rental housing than white tenants.[17] The U.S. Civil Rights Commission (1961) concluded, that while progress had been made, minorities still were confronted with restricted housing opportunity in terms of location and mortgage financing.[18] Roger Pitts (1964), summarized that realtors, builders and lenders discriminated against blacks.[19] George and Eunice Grier (1966) investigated and criticized the racial housing and lending practices of the Federal Housing Administration (FHA).[20] Rose Helper (1969) discovered widespread evidence that blacks experienced difficulties in obtaining housing and mortgages in Chicago, while Luigi Laurenti (1969) showed that minorities in San Francisco paid a premium for the housing and financing they secured.[21]

In recent years economists have dominated the minority housing opportunity literature. Two analyses by John F. Kain and John M. Quigley spearheaded the current economic approach. The first was an article, "Housing Market Discrimination, Homeownership and Savings Behavior,"[22] the second, a monograph, *Housing Markets and Racial Discrimination.*[23] Kain and Quigley used St. Louis and cross-city macro data to show that blacks have a lower incidence of homeownership and that they pay more for housing. They utilized statistical analyses to reject the hypothesis that these differentiations were due to neutral economic forces and suggested instead that discriminatory "supply restrictions" were the cause. Supply restrictions include actions by realtors and local officials.[24] Limited and/or costly mortgage financing was another hurdle that minorities faced:[25]

> Blacks who buy homes in the ghetto either are forced to pay more for theft and fire insurance than would be the case in suburban communities or are unable to obtain coverage at all. Mortgage financing is more difficult to obtain and often can be had only on less favorable terms than in the suburbs. These premiums are in addition to the discrimination markups and home ownership considerations discussed previously.

Kain and Quigley also considered the economic effects of suburban housing restrictions on blacks. This exclusion denied access to blacks, thereby limiting their income and housing potential.

Other studies examining some of these issues first considered by Kain and Quigley have been conducted by Raymond J. Struyk, Charles Daniels, Elizabeth Roistacher and John L. Goodman, Jr., and others.[26] While many of these confirm the Kain and Quigley findings, others have questioned the extent of discrimination, especially among blacks who have recently purchased homes. One author summarized:[27]

> The absence of a significant race differential among movers suggests a reduction in the barriers to home ownerhip for blacks in terms of segregation and mortgage market discrimination, but not necessarily an elimination of these problems.

The minority housing opportunity literature focuses on examining the overall presence and consequences of racial discrimination. Except for the early analyses (McEntire, Helper and Grier, for example), few studies specifically examine mortgage financing problems.

## Economic and Eco-Race Studies: Overview

These studies were prompted by the growing interest in the urban financing problem. Unlike monographs cited previously that only tangentially considered the credit shortfall, these analyses usually focus on that problem. They are the ones most relevant to this monograph for they attempt to empirically document the credit shortfall and isolate its causes.

ECO-RACE STUDIES

*Urban League Abandonment Study.* In 1971, the National Urban League examined housing decay and abandonment in seven American cities:[28] St. Louis, Cleveland, Chicago, Hoboken, New York, Detroit and Atlanta. It employed a case study methodology. Local planners, community leaders, public officials, bankers, and real estate brokers were interviewed in the sample cities and asked to explain the reasons for housing abandonment in their communities.

The League interpreted the urban mortgage crunch as being one of the last steps in neighborhood decline. The first stage was change in neighborhood socio economic status. The second step was racial-ethnic change with whites leaving and blacks entering. Then followed a third stage characterized by property speculation and exploitation. The fourth step was a continued deterioration of market conditions with an emergence of "crisis ghetto" conditions. This in turn was followed by rapid disinvestment by both institutional lenders as well as property owners who stopped maintaining their parcels. Abandonment was the culmination of all these pathologies.

While the League recognized the urban financing problem as having certain economic origins, race, both that of the neighborhood and mortgage applicants, was deemed a major influence on lending. To illustrate, the St. Louis case study showed:[29]

> The flow of conventional mortgage funds to most areas . . . has been shut-off. With the exception of the far South Side of the City (which is an exclusively white community) no savings and loan association will consider either a conventional home-repair or home-purchase loan. Not unexpectedly, the segments of the suburban market into which a few blacks are making inroads have also been deemed a "high-risk" investment by the same institutions.

*The National Survey of Housing Abandonment* proved to be quite influential. It sparked not only a flurry of further abandonment research, but also highlighted the urban financing problem.

*Public-Community Group Studies.* The early to-mid-1970s saw a multitude of reports issued by community organizations, public research interest groups and similar bodies. The Center for New Corporate Priorities (CNCP) analysis is a typical example.[30] The CNCP examined the distribution of loans by area in Los Angeles during 1974. (Data were derived from the monthly loan register kept by the California Savings and Loan Commissioner.) "Redlined" areas with over a million population — one-seventh of the total for Los Angeles County — received less than 1 percent of the County's loans.[31] There were many neighborhood contrasts. Beverly Hills and Palos Verdes were receiving up to 100 times the mortgages granted to comparably sized areas.

The CNCP examined basic 1970 Census data (total population, minority population, median income, median value, etc.) for the locations receiving or not receiving loans. In addition to loan volumes, they viewed areal, population, and racial and housing characteristics. Juxtaposing the loan volume and Census data, the Center attempted to show that high minority, lower-income neighborhoods fared poorest with respect to loan allocation.

1. The all-white areas of the city received about double the loans (on a per capita basis) of integrated neighborhoods.
2. Areas with a median family income of over $25,000 had four times the per capita loan dollars of the next highest income category, and 900 times the loan dollars of the lowest income areas.
3. Areas with the highest home values (above $50,000) received $256 per capita in single-family loans, compared to 75 cents for areas with the lowest home values.

A final iniquity alleged by the Center concerned the relationship of local loans granted by financial institutions to the deposits made in these institutions (presumably by local residents.). Other studies concern themselves with this matter, so this Appendix will briefly discuss the loan-deposit relationship. Deposit volume is viewed as a proxy of neighborhood economic health; the larger the size of deposits, the "healthier" the area. Deposits also are seen as setting a level of obligation by the lender to grant a commensurate number of loans. If the annual deposits of a financial institution located in a particular area equals $1,000,000 (the $1,000,000 is presumed to come from the surrounding neighborhood), then this lender should grant roughly $1,000,000 in loans. If the loan-to-deposit ratio or LDR* is substantially less than 1, lenders are deemed to be insensitive to the needs of supposedly economically healthy neighborhoods and/or are not fulfilling their "fair share" obligation to the neighborhood.

CNCP found the LDR to be very low in inner-city, minority locations. It therefore concluded that a large part of Los Angeles was being discriminated against in terms of receiving loans despite "a sizeable amount of money on deposit in or adjacent to lower-income communities."[32]

The Center's study, with a focus on areal distribution of loans, simple

---

$$*LDR = \frac{\text{Loans granted to a neighborhood}}{\text{Deposits flowing from that neighborhood}}$$

manipulation of Census data, and attention to the LDR, is similar to many other analyses. One example is, *Redlining: Mortgage Disinvestment in the District of Columbia*,[33] conducted by the District of Columbia's Public Interest Research Group (DCPIRG). The group examined a Real Estate Directory which listed detailed information for all real estate transactions, including the name of the buyer, date of transaction, selling price, mortgage amount, name of the lender, etc. The financing information was summarized for each zip code within the city and Census data (total population, minority population, median income, percentage owner-occupied units, percentage one-unit structures, etc.) for the different zip codes also were collected. Finally, deposit data were estimated in order to compute the loan-to-deposit ratios.

After examining the simple distribution of loans by area and the geographic-social identity of the different locations, DCPIRG concluded that center-city, high-minority neighborhoods in the nation's capital were receiving fewer loans than white locations, and in general, the city fared poorly as compared to suburban locations. Specifically:[34]

1. Only 11.6 percent of the total real estate loans made by D.C. savings and loan associations were made on property located in Washington, D.C.

2. Only 36 percent of the total D.C. loan volume went to eleven zip codes with high black populations (80 percent or greater) and containing 69 percent of the city's total population. Nearly one-half of the loans to these eleven zip code areas went to Capitol Hill neighborhoods with rapidly increasing white populations.

*Karen Orren Analysis.* Numerous early investigations went beyond the simple reporting of the case study approach and the simple areal loan volume and Census data juxtaposition common to the community group investigations. One example is Karen Orren's, *Corporate Power and Social Change*.[35] The author examined the social role and activities of the life insurance industry. In the course of her analysis, she considered the industry's mortgage investments, specifically where loans were granted.

To better examine the existing allocation of credit, Orren constructed a mortgage density measure.* In the Chicago area, density was much higher in suburbs as opposed to the city proper, and in white neighborhoods as opposed to black areas. (These loan distinctions were statistically significant.) Was this bifurcation due to economic causes? Orren believed not. She first

---

*Equals the number of mortgages granted by life insurance companies per tract with the lots per tract standardized at 500. The densities were ordered on a scale of one through five with one indicating that no loan was made in the tract and five indicating a density of 25 percent; that is,125 loans were granted (500 × 25 percent = 125).

isolated (via chi-square testing) the economic variables that correlated with mortgage .density. These included median family income, median home value, etc. She then asked whether or not the urban-suburban and white-black loan density gradations were due to economics (i.e., blacks having lower incomes, suburban homes having higher values) or race (white-black) of neighborhood and, controlling for neighborhood economic variables, Orren found the racial and area loan gradations could not be explained on economic grounds. Rather, cities, and particularly black areas within cities, received fewer loans for arbitrary and discriminatory reasons.[36]

Orren's study was one of the first to statistically analyze the racial versus economic causes of the urban mortgage crunch. Others have followed.

*Richard Devine Study.* This analysis examined the changes in and patterns of mortgage lending in the Bronx, New York.[37] It showed that financial institutions within the Bronx shifted a major share of their lending activity out of the Bronx over the 1960-to-1970 period. Devine also considered the factors influencing the intra-Bronx mortgage distribution in 1960 and 1970. Were variations in the number of loans received by each Community Planning District (CPD) due to racial (percentage minority per CPD) or economic factors (percentage 1-4 family housing units per CPD, weighted median family income, weighted median rent, etc.)?

Devine employed the technique of multiple regression analysis to answer this question. He used a regression equation with the number/value of mortgages per 1,000 occupied housing units as the dependent variables and both race (proportion blacks and Puerto Ricans in each CPD) and economic factors (percentage 1-4 family homes per CPD, total rent, etc.) as independent variables. The analysis showed that race did not play a role in the distribution (both number and value) of Bronx mortgages in 1960; the economic variables could sufficiently explain loan variations across CPDs. In 1970, however, race was a statistically significant factor influencing the number of loans made to a neighborhood. (Race was not significant in explaining distinctions in mortgage value, however.)

*Other Eco-Race Studies.* The analyses examined here (Urban League, CNCP, DCPIRG, Orren, and Devine) represent a sampling of some early eco-race studies that have been conducted. The Urban Legue analysis, a case study, is comparable to investigations of the Chicago Commission on Human Rights, and the Illinois Legislative Investigating Committee, among others.[38] The simple loan and basic Census data juxtaposition conducted by the CNCP and DCPIRG typify the approach common to many investigations, especially those conducted by community organizations. Others of a similar nature include reports by the Coalition of Cincinnati Neighborhoods (1975), National Training Information Center (1975), Baltimore Department of Community Development (1974), Phoenix Fund

(1975), Disinvestment Committee of Milwaukee Alliance of Concerned Citizens (1973), the Rochester Greenlining Coalition (1974), and Erie County Citizens Organization (1975).[39]

Up until the mid-1970s, there were few studies comparable to the Orren and Devine statistical efforts. An exception was a series of analyses conducted by the Northwestern University Center for Urban Affairs (1974).[40] The Center briefly considered mortgage loan data made available by the Chicago Federal Home Loan Bank Board (the same data analyzed in Chapter Five) and concluded that race was a statistically significant influence. It also conducted an investigation of regulatory agencies and how their policies affected urban neighborhoods.

More recent statistical investigations are discussed later.

ECONOMIC STUDIES

This section first examines a number of early reports purporting to show that economics is the only significant mortgage influence and then briefly summarizes selected analyses conducted in recent years.

*Lender Survey.* Knowledge of lender attitudes is important for furthering the understanding of the urban financing dilemma and also for pinpointing which strategies would be accepted most readily by the financial community.

In 1974, Rutgers University Center for Urban Policy Research conducted a large-scale interview of financial institution views of the restraints to urban lending and the potential of selected strategies to alleviate the urban mortgage shortfall.[41] Two hundred and fifty lenders in the New York-New Jersey metropolitan area were contacted and asked whether or not they wished to participate in a survey of urban lending practices. The 250 represented a broad sample of both large and small lenders of different institutional types (i.e., savings and loan, savings associations, mortgage bankers, etc.) throughout the region. Sixty agreed to participate. They were asked for the name of their most knowledgeable lending officer experienced in granting urban loans. This person was then contacted and an in-depth, in person interview was conducted with both the lending officer and another staff person (usually a vice-president in charge of operations) present.

The interview instrument consisted of a 25-question form. It listed a wide range of alleged restraints to urban lending (including economic and social considerations) and possible strategies to alleviate the financing crunch (including economic supports and anti-discrimination measures). The lenders were asked to evaluate (on a 1-4 scale with 1 representing "the greatest degree of difficulty" and 4 representing "no problem experienced") the actual problems posed by the alleged restraints as well as the real potential of each of the suggested reform policies (again, a 1-4 rating scale was used with 1 denoting the "greatest potential" and 4 representing "will have no impact").

The answers to the questionnaire are summarized in Exhibit 3-A-1. Lenders emphasize economic factors, both in terms of the restraints to lending in urban areas as well as the potential of ameliorative strategies. While the response is not surprising, the degree of difference in terms of the economic versus social restraints and policies is illuminating; lenders gave the economic restraints a 1-to-2 rating, meaning they view economics as being a very important if not the most important obstacle. Problems involving loan disposition and security were emphasized compared to loan processing and administrative difficulties. Social restraints, in contrast, were given a rating of 3 to 4, in other words having little or no significance. Within the social restraints, race was downplayed to a level indicating practically no bearing on the urban financing dilemma. This pattern was repeated when discussing policies for the future: economics were emphasized as opposed to social strategies, and anti-discrimination measures were seen as having little or no import.

The survey also showed practically no intra-group variations* in lender views. Different types of lenders (i.e., S & Ls versus commercial banks) in different locations (urban versus suburban) similarly emphasized economics.

*Andrew Brimmer Study. Risk vs. Discrimination in Expansion of Urban Mortgage Lending*[42] was published by Brimmer and Co., economic and financial consultants in Washington, D.C. The analysis was commissioned by the United States League of Savings Associations.

Brimmer did not empirically examine loan distribution in a particular area, but rather cited other analyses that he felt at least indirectly supported risk rather than discrimination as the major lender influence. Some examples:

1. Black applicants and black neighborhoods are receiving fewer loans because they have lower incomes.
2. Studies on loan delinquency-foreclosure show risk is inversely related to mortgage equity and positively associated with property age. These factors may explain the reduction in loans to urban neighborhoods. (Brimmer assumes that properties in such locations are older and applicants can make only smaller down payments.)

---

* There are at least theoretical grounds why distinctions might exist. One differentiation might concern bank location. Do banks located in cities suffering severe deterioration have a different view of urban lending compared to financial institutions located in less impacted areas? Another possible distinction lies between different categories of financial institutions, including savings and loan associations (S&Ls), mutual savings, and commercial banks. There may also be differences between large and small banks (in terms of assets) with the latter having the more negative view since they have thinner reserves with which to take any risks.

## EXHIBIT 3-A-1

## LENDER EVALUATION OF THE ECONOMIC AND SOCIAL INFLUENCES ON URBAN MORTGAGE FINANCING

### Economic Variables

| Current Economic Restraints to Lending | Lender Evaluation (1-4 Rating)* |
|---|---|
| a. Mixed land uses in urban areas | 3.7 |
| b. Title problems in urban areas | 3.0 |
| c. Difficulty in obtaining fire/theft insurance | 1.5 |
| d. Property vandalism | 1.3 |
| e. Mortage collection-servicing problems | 1.0 |
| f. High administrative costs | 1.2 |
| g. High foreclosure rate | 1.2 |
| h. Minimal appreciation of urban property values | 2.0 |

| Future Economic Policies to Increase Lending | Lender Evaluation (1-4 Rating)** |
|---|---|
| a. Demolition of abandoned properties | 1.0 |
| b. Faster-cheaper mortgage foreclosure | 1.7 |
| c. Property tax abatement-deferment for housing rehabilitation | 1.8 |
| d. Encouragement of resident property owners | 1.3 |
| e. Homeowners and management counseling | 2.0 |
| f. Additional public mortgage insurance | 2.0 |
| g. Supervision-regulation of speculators | 2.1 |
| h. Private lender mortgage pools | 2.5 |
| i. Removal of usury ceilings | 3.0 |

### Social Variables

| Current Social Restraints to Lending | Lender Evaluation (1-4 Rating)* |
|---|---|
| a. Urban families not familiar with credit procedures | 3.5 |
| b. Difficulty/uncertainty in underwriting urban loans (dual income, etc.) | 3.4 |
| c. Lending officers inexperienced in evaluating special problems of urban families and neighborhoods | 3.0 |
| d. Lender discrimination against minority areas | 3.8 |
| e. Lender discrimination against minority loan applicants | 3.9 |

| Future Social Policies to Increase Lending | Lender Evaluation (1-4 Rating)** |
|---|---|
| a. Enforce existing anti-discrimination regulations | 3.5 |
| b. Enact new prohibitions against racial redlining | 3.9 |
| c. Offer special training and consultation services for urban lending office | 3.0 |
| d. Make branching contingent upon urban mortgage activity | 3.7 |
| e. Emphasize government deposits of reserves in institutions increasing their present levels of urban financing | 2.8 |

*One represents "the greatest restraint" while four is the "weakest restraint"

**One represents "the greatest potential" while four has "the least potential"

*Source:* Survey conducted by the Center for Urban Policy Research for the New Jersey Department of Community Affairs, 1974.

3. Minority-owned associations, doing a larger share of their business in cities, have assumed a relatively cautious lending posture (they rely more heavily on FHA/VA guarantees and keep a fairly high liquidity ratio). Since these associations cannot readily be accused of discrimination, the evidence of their conservative lending posture confirms the higher risk of urban lending.

4. Mortgage foreclosure is an expensive and time-consuming process. There are therefore significant elements which cannot be overlooked in an assessment of the added risks of inner-city home financing.

*Ahlbrandt-Hutchinson, et al. Analyses.* These two studies were early statistical investigations which employed regression analysis and concluded that economics and not race were important loan determinants.[43]

Ahlbrandt examined the distribution of loans in Pittsburgh's Census tracts. Loan volume (number and value) was the dependent variable and a number of independent variables, both economic (i.e., income, percentage owner occupied units, vacancy rate, etc.) and racial (i.e., 1960-1970 racial change), were entered into the regression equation. Ahlbrandt found that income and neighborhood economic risk factors were significant, while race was not—mortgage lending in Pittsburgh occurs in response to fundamental economic circumstances.[44]

Peter Hutchinson, *et al.*, followed a similar approach in examining the loan pattern of four large savings and loan associations in the Toledo (Ohio) SMSA. The study utilized more detailed data (i.e., a breakout of loans by conventional versus public [FHA/VA] categories and mortgages versus home improvement loans), but its findings were similar to Ahlbrandt's. The racial composition of a neighborhood was not significant in affecting the number of mortgages granted, although it did influence the share of government loans (higher in black areas), and seemed to have some impact on the number of home improvement loans that were made (lower in black neighborhoods).


RECENT STUDIES

This appendix has focused on a selection of early studies, mostly conducted prior to the mid-1970s. In recent years many additional analyses have been undertaken. Some of these more current investigations are considered chronologically below.[45]

In 1976 the New York State Banking Department commissioned a study of lending practices in the state.[46] The principle authors of the analysis were Robert Lindsay, Emmanuel Tobier and Richard Schafer. The study utilized data made available by the New York State Mortgage Disclosure Regulations—Supervisory Procedure G107 (promulgated April 1976) and also implemented in-depth case studies in Brooklyn and Rochester.

This pioneering investigation yielded a detailed look into mortgage trends and investment in New York State. It documented growing exports of capital to other states and a declining volume of lending especially for multifamily buildings. The Brooklyn case study showed specific patterns of lending change in different racial and social class neighborhoods. The Rochester case study contested the charge that inner-city Rochester neighborhoods were redlined.*

The California Department of Savings and Loan has been very active in examining credit access. In 1977 it published *Fair Lending Report No. 1.*[47] This analysis considered Mortgage Deficient Areas (MDA)—an index derived by considering loan dollars per capita. The report concluded that black areas were frequently characterized by a relatively high share of loan denials. It considered the possible confounding influence of income (e.g., blacks were being denied because of their lower income) and concluded that race was still an independent influence.[48]

> Summarizing the material presented on loan denials by ethnic groups, which has been controlled by income classes, we may conclude that blacks were being denied loans more frequently than any other ethnic group. Although in some counties certain Black income groups fare better than in other counties, there are instances in every country where Blacks are denied loans at a higher ratio than other ethnic groups.

Numerous other analyses have been considered utilizing data made available by state and federal mortgage disclosure requirements. In 1977, Dennis Dengemans *et al.,* examined loan patterns and influences in Sacramento.[49] The authors of *Redlining and the Geography of Residential Loans in Sacramento* concluded that economic and racial factors are correlated with census tract variations in loan availability as shown below:

*Data from the New York State Banking Department Study were used in other analyses. See George Leyland, *Determining Priorities of Need for Guaranteed Mortgage Funds* (New York: Bernard Baruch Legislative Institute, 1978).

STEPWISE MULTIPLE REGRESSION MODEL: PREDICTING THE NUMBER OF HOME MORTGAGE LOANS ISSUED PER 1000 UNITS OF 1-4 UNIT DWELLINGS

| | R Square | RSQ Change | Simple R |
|---|---|---|---|
| Household Income | 0.42760 | 0.42760 | 0.65392 |
| Average Household Size | 0.47727 | 0.4967 | 0.11824 |
| Distance from Tract to CBD | 0.55105 | 0.07378 | 0.11824 |
| Percent White Population | 0.57647 | 0.02542 | 0.42402 |
| Age of Housing Stock | 0.58470 | 0.00822 | −0.24073 |
| Income Change, 1070-75 | 0.59252 | 0.00782 | 0.46183 |
| Household Mobility, 1968-70 | 0.49762 | 0.00510 | −0.10179 |
| Percent of Homes Owner-occupied | 0.60102 | 0.00340 | 0.24972 |
| Upper White Collar Employment | 0.60157 | 0.00055 | 0.64398 |

*Data from the New York State Banking Department Study were used in other analyses. See George Leyland, *Determining Priorities of Need for Guaranteed Mortgage Funds* (New York: Bernard Baruch Legislative Institute, 1978).

Dengemans identified a modest race effect. Percent white population alone explained about 18 percent of the variation in mortgage loans granted; however, after household income and two other variables were controlled, the racial variable (percent white) added little to the explanatory power of the regression equation.

A race effect was contested in three 1978 studies by George Benston *et al.*, Philip Hauser, and the California Department of Savings and Loan but supported in a third major analysis by Robert Schafer.

George Benston *et al.*, considered lending practices in Rochester, New York.[50] They delineated two areas; one in inner-city Rochester and the second, a suburban control. The study concluded that economic considerations rather than arbitrary "redlining" appear to explain lender behavior.[51]

> The empirical study of mortgage lending practices conducted in Rochester, N.Y. yields findings that are inconsistent with hypothesized redlining practices. If anything, the lenders may not be taking sufficient account of the risks of writing mortgages on the central city residential property. Of course, the behavior studied may not be typical of other areas. However, it should be noted that Rochester, N.Y. is an older, northeast city with a metropolitan area of about 700,000 people, and probably is more typical of U.S. cities than is New York or Chicago.

A 1978 study conducted by the California Department of Savings and Loan, *Fair Lending Report No. 2*,[52] considered the variables associated with the disposition of about 600 mortgage applications in "high" and "low" loan volume neighborhoods in Los Angeles. The analysis considered both racial and economic variables. After applying multiple regression analysis, it concluded that race was not a statistically significant influence.

Philip Hauser and Hekmat Elkhanialy examined loan volume variables in different Chicago Census tracts.[53] They employed multiple regression analysis and considered a range of economic and racial Census tract characteristics. The authors concluded that race was not an important consideration, especially as compared to economic variables such as median value of home, percent owner occupied, median income, and single-family dwelling.

The most extensive recent analysis has been conducted by Robert Schafer of the Harvard—MIT Joint Center for Urban Studies.[54] The Schafer study employed the most detailed economic and racial data base assembled to date. It evaluated economic, geographic and racial influences in lending in New York State and concluded that:[56]

> - Most of the mortgage lending in New York State is based on objective factors such as the income and net wealth of the applicant and the value of the property
> - The results are consistent with allegations that at least some savings banks discriminate against minority applicants in four out of five of the metropolitan areas.

- The results contradict allegations that a particular neighborhood is redlined in 22 of 30 cases; are consistent with redlining allegations in two neighborhoods; and are equivocal in six neighborhoods.
- The results regarding the allegation that older neighborhoods are redlined are equivocal in all five metropolitan areas.

Numerous other recent analyses have been conducted, many following a similiar analytical strategy as those described in this appendix. Examples include:[56] the Leland and Michigan Governor's Task Force on Redlining investigations of the relationships of loan volume and neighborhood racial profile; studies by Crunkel and Ingrams and Naparstek and Cincotta on the association of lending availability and neighborhood income; evaluations by Rosser *et al,* Tee Taggart, and the New York Public Interest Group on the disparity of neighborhood deposits and loan volume; and in-depth case analyses by Feins and Lyons on the distribution and consequences of FHA financing. In addition to the burgeoning and empirical studies, conceptual analyses, most notably by Guttentag and Wachter, have broken new ground in formulating the problem of urban lending and stating the issues.[57]

In sum, from an issue of sometimes secondary concern, the question of the availability and determinants of credit in urban areas has assumed major importance and is the topic of a growing literature. This study is one of numerous attempts to examine the influences on urban lending, but it is important to realize that this analysis has a limited purview. It is not examining such questions as whether certain neighborhoods are "redlined" or what is the impact of increasing FHA versus conventional financing. Many of the studies cited in this appendix, in addition to considering the economics and racial influences on lending, have tackled these broader issues. This monograph concentrates on the more limited goal of evaluating the presence, if any, of racial discrimination in lending.

## Notes

1. See Richard Devine, *Institutional Mortgage Investment in An Area of Bronx County, 1960-1972*, Ph.D. dissertation, New York University (1974); George Jay Mazin, *The Impact of Credit Availability on Housing Abandonment: The Case of the Mid-Bronx*, Master's Thesis, Cornell University (June 1974); Northwest Community Housing Association, "Mortgage Disinvestment in Northwest Philadelphia " (Philadelphia: Northwest Community Housing Association, 1973); Cincinnati Coalition of Neighborhoods, "Housing Analysis in Oakley, Bond Hill and Evanston " (Cincinnati: Cincinnati Coalition of Neighborhoods, June 1974); National Training and Information Center, "Lender Policies Exposed: Prime Factor in Neighborhood Decay" (Chicago: National Training and Information Center, 1976) Center for New Corporate Priorities, *Where the Money Is, Mortgage Lending, Los Angeles County* (Los Angeles: Center for New Corporate Priorities, 1974); Karen Orren, *Corporate Power and Social Change* (Baltimore: Johns Hopkins, 1974).
2. See Hearings before the Committee on Banking, Housing and Urban Affairs, United States Senate, 94th Congress, 2nd Session, *Home Mortgage Disclosure and Equal Credit Opportunity* (Washington, D.C.: Government Printing Office, 1976), p. 37.
3. U.S. Commission on Civil Rights, *Hearings on Housing in Washington* (Washington, D.C.: Government Printing Office, 1962).
4. Pierre de Vise, "The Anti-Redliners: How Community Activists have Forged a Devil Theory of Urban Decay," Working Paper II.24 Chicago Regional Hospital Study, (September 1976), p. 1.
5. Stephen C. Casey, "The Effect of Race on Opinions of Structural and Neighborhood Quality," Report prepared for U.S. Department of Housing and Urban Development, 1978.
6. *Ibid.*
7. David Harvey, *Social Justice and the City* (Baltimore: Johns Hopkins Press, 1973); James O'Connor, The *Fiscal Crisis of the State* (New York: St. Martins Press, 1973); C.G. Pickvance, ed., *Urban Sociology: Critical Essays* (New York: St. Martins Press, 1976); Michael E. Stone, *"The Politics of Housing:* Mortgage Bankers,"*Society*, Vol. 9 No. 9 (July/August 1972), pp. 31-37.
8. Francois Lamarche, "Property Development and the Economic Foundations of the Urban Questions," in Pickvance, ed., *Urban Sociology: Critical Essays,* pp. 85-118.
9. O'Connor, *The Fiscal Crisis of the State*, p. 125.
10. Stone, "The Politics of Housing."
11. David Harvey, "The Political Economy of Urbanization in Advanced Capitalist Societies: The Case of the United States," in Gary Gappert and Harold Rose, *The Social Economy of Cities, Urban Affairs Annual Review* Vol. 9 (1975), p. 149.
12. *Ibid.*, p. 151
13. David Harvey, *Social Justice and the City,* p. 140.
14. For a discussion of economic and racial influences see Dwight M. Jaffee, "Credit for Financing Housing Investment: Risk Factors and Capital Markets," unpublished paper for the HUD National Housing Policy Task Force (1973); Paul Noah Courant, *Economic Aspects of Racial Prejudice in Urban Housing Markets,* Ph.D. Dissertation, Princeton University (1973).
15. See John F. Kain and John M. Quigley, *Housing Markets and Racial Discrimination: A Microeconomic Analysis* (New York: National Bureau of Economic Research, 1975), pp. 377-385.

16. Charles Abrams, *Forbidden Neighbors* (New York: Harper Books, 1955).
17. David McEntire, "Housing Problems of Minority Groups in the United States," Interim Research Report to the Commission on Race and Housing (February 1956).
18. U.S. Commisiion on Civil Rights, *Housing - 1961 Commission on Civil Rights Report* (Washington, D.C.: Government Printing Office, 1961).
19. Robert Pitts, "Mortgage Financing and Race," in John H. Denton, ed., *Race and Property* (Berkeley: Diablo Press, 1964), p. 100.
20. George and Eunice Grier, *Equality and Beyond* (Chicago: Quandrangle Books, 1966).
21. Rose Helper, *Racial Policies and Practices of Real Estate Brokers* (Minnesota: University of Minnesota Press, 1969); Luigi Laurenti, *Property Value and Race* (Berkeley: University of California Press, 1969), pp. 213-231.
22. John F. Kain and John M. Quigley, "Housing Market Discrimination, Homeownership, and Savings Behavior," *American Economic Review,* Vol. 62 (June 1972), pp. 263-277.
23. John F. Kain and John M. Quigley, *Housing Markets and Racial Discrimination, A Microeconomic Analysis* (New York: National Bureau of Economic Research, 1975).
24. Kain and Quigley, *"Housing Market Discrimination,"* p. 220.
25. Kain and Quigley, *Housing Markets and Racial Discrimination,* p. 298.
26. Raymond J. Struyk, "Determinants of the Rate of Home Ownership of Black Relative to White Households," *Journal of Urban Economics,* Vol. 2 (1975), pp. 291-346; Elizabeth Roistacher and John L. Goodman, Jr., "Race and Home Ownership: Is Discrimination Disappearing?", *Economic Inquiry,* Vol. 14 (March 1976), pp. 59-70; Charles Daniels, "The Influence of Racial Segregation on Housing Prices," *Journal of Urban Economics,* Vol. 2 (1975), pp. 105-122.
27. Roistacher and Goodman, "Race and Home Ownership," p. 69.
28. National Urban League, Inc., *The National Survey of Housing Abandonment* (New York: National Urban League, 1971).
29. *Ibid.,* p. 190.
30. Center for New Corporate Priorities, *Where the Money Is, Mortgage Lending.*
31. *Ibid.*
32. *Ibid.*
33. District of Columbia, Public Interest Research Group, et al., *Redlining: Mortgage Disinvestment in the District of Columbia.*
34. *Ibid.,* pp. 4-6.
35. Karen Orren, *Corporate Power and Social Change.*
36. *Ibid.*
37. Devine, *Institutional Mortgage Investment in An Area of Bronx County.*
38. See footnote 1, and Illinois Legislative Investigating Commission, *Redlining-Discrimination in Residential Mortgage Loans* (Chicago: Legislative Investigating Commission, 1975).
39. See footnote 1 and *CPL Bibliography.*
40. Center for Urban Affairs, Northwestern University, *The Role of Mortgage Lending Practices in Older Urban Neighborhoods* (Evanston, Ill.: Center for Urban Affairs, 1974).
41. Lender survey conducted by the Center for Urban Policy Research for the New Jersey Department of Community Affairs (1974). Reprinted in *The Urban Financing Dilemma* (New Brunswick, N.J.: Rutgers University Center for Urban Policy Research, 1974, mimeographed).

50                                                    Mortgage Lending and Race

42. Brimmer and Co., *Risk vs. Discrimination in the Expansion of Urban Mortgage Lending* (Washington, D.C.: Brimmer and Co., 1977). Prepared for the United States League of Savings Associations.
43. Roger S. Ahlbrandt,Jr.,"Explanatory Research on the Redlining Phenomenon," *Journal of the American Real Estate and Urban Economics Association,* Vol. 5, No. 4 (Winter, 1977), p. 473  Peter Hutchinson *et al,* "A Survey and Comparison of Redlining Influences in Urban Mortgage Lending Markets," *Journal of the American Real Estate and Urban Economics Association,* Vol. 5, No. 4 (Winter, 1977), p. 463.
44. Ahlbrandt, "Redlining: An Economic Phenomenon."
45. See also the annotated appendix in this monograph.
46. Robert Lindsay et. al., *Mortgage Financing and Housing Markets in New York State: A Preliminary Report* (Albany, New York: New York State Banking Department, 1977).
47. California Department of Savings and Loan Fair Lending Report No. 1 Vol. 1 and 2 (Sacramento, California: California Department of Savings and Loan, 1977).
48. *Ibid.,* p. 18.
49. Dennis Dengemans et al., *Redlining and the Geography of Residential Mortgage Loans in Sacramento* (Davis, California: University of California at Davis, 1977).
50. George Benston, Dan Horsky and H. Martin Weingarter, *An Empirical Study of Mortgage Redlining* (New York: Salomon Brothers Center for the Study of Financial Institutions, 1978).
51. See also George Benston, "The Urban Financing Dilemma Reconsidered'.' Paper prepared for the Fourth Annual Conference, Federal Home Loan Bank of San Francisco, December 7, 1978.
52. California Department of Savings and Loan, *Fair Lending Report, No. 2.* (Sacramento, California: California Department of Savings and Loan, 1978).
53. Philip Hauser and Hekmat Elkhanialy, *The Hauser Report on Lending Practices, of Savings and Loan Associations in Chicago — 1977.* (Chicago: Study Prepared for Federal Savings and Loan Council of Illinois, 1978).
54. Robert Schafer, *Mortgage Lending Decisions: Criteria and Constraints* (Executive Summary). (Cambridge: Harvard-MIT Joint Center, 1978).
55. *Ibid.,* p. III-IV.
56. George P. Leyland, *Determining Priorities of Need for Guaranteed Mortgage Funds* (New York: New York State Legislative Institute, no date): Governor's Task Force On Redlining, *An Analysis of Mortgage Lending Activity in Flint, Michigan* (Lansing: 1976); Jon R. Crunkleton and Franklin J. Ingram, "Path Analysis and the Need for An Alternative Approach to the Investigation of Redlining," unpublished paper 1978; Lawrence B. Rosser, Calvin Bradford and Barbara Beck, "Bank Structure and the Public Interest in Urban Centers: An Advance Summary of Research and Recommendations," Woodstock Project and the Chicago Illinois Center for Urban Studies (June 1976); Harriet T. Taggart,"Home Mortgage Lending Patterns in Metropolitan Boston" (December 1977); New York Public Interest Research, *Take the Money and Run! Redlined in Brooklyn* (New York: NYPIRG, 1976); Arthur Lyons, *Conventional Redlining in Chicago* (Chicago: 1975); Judith D. Feins, *Urban Housing Disinventment and Neighborhood Decline: A Study of Public Policy Outcomes,* Ph.D. dissertation, University of Chicago, 1976.
57. Jack M. Guttentag and Susan M. Wachter, "Redlining and Public Policy, "unpublished paper (1978).

Section **II**
*Empirical*
*Investigation*

## Introduction

Section II turns from a discussion of the financing problem and the economic versus eco-race models to an analysis of which model is more valid. Chapter Four describes the methodology that is followed in pursuing the research question, Chapter Five evaluates macro (neighborhood) data to examine the possible impact of race on underwriting, and Chapter Six considers micro (individual applicant profile made available by the Comptroller of the Currency) data to similarly test for a racial influence. The empirical examination reaches the following conclusions:

1. Neighborhood race and the race of the individual mortgage applicant are both statistically significant. In the Chicago analysis, neighborhood race is associated with neighborhood loan volume, after neighborhood economic variables have been controlled. In the Comptroller analysis an individual mortgage applicant's race is associated with the disposition of the loan request, after individual economic variables have been controlled.

2. Going beyond statistical significance, how "strong" is the race effect? It is important to realize the difficulty of segregating the separate effect of an individual variable such as race from those of economic distinctions such as income and asset. While keeping in mind these difficulties, the macro analysis indicates that neighborhood race explains about half of the variation in neighborhood loan volume not accounted for by economic

characteristics. The micro study reveals that race of an individual is a small but measurable effect.

3. Similar findings are reached after applying various statistical techniques. The outcome does not appear to be merely a function of a specific type of analysis.

To facilitate reference to the empirical investigation section, the following list defines the economic and racial variables that are considered in Chapters Five and Six.

| SYMBOL | EXPLANATION |
| --- | --- |
| AGEHOUS | Median age of all year-round housing units in zip code area |
| AGE 55 | Percentage persons 55 years or older in zip code area |
| AMT | Amount of mortgage applied for |
| ASSET | Amount of assets, including savings and other forms |
| BLACK FHH | Percentage of families with income below poverty level (Social Security Administration's poverty index) in zip code area |
| BLACK 55 | Percentage of blacks 55 years or older in zip code area |
| BLACKUE | Percentage of black labor force 16 years or over that is unemployed in zip code area |
| BURDEN | The required annual mortgage payment compared to annual income |
| CROWD | Percentage units with 1.01 or more persons per room in zip code area |
| DEBT | Outstanding debt of loan applicant |
| DBPY | Debt payments of loan applicant |
| DISP | Loan application disposition |
| ETH | Ethnicity; nonwhite (NW) and white (W) |
| EXDB | Relationship of existing debt payments to existing income |
| FEMALE HH | Percentage female-headed households in zip code area |
| INCO | Income of loan applicant |
| INCOME | Family median income in zip code area |
| INST | Financial institution |
| IPPR | The relationship of annual income to the total purchase price |
| LDR | Loans-to-deposit ratio |
| LPC | Loans per capita |
| LVR | The size of the loan compared to the purchase price |
| MAR | Marital status of loan applicant |

| | |
|---|---|
| MGTDR | The size of the mortgage compared to the size of the existing debt. |
| MPDP | The size of the mortgage payments compared to the existing debt payments |
| MS7172 | Number of mortgages granted per 1000 structures in a specified zip code area in 1971-1972 |
| MS7273 | Number of mortgages granted per 1000 structures in a specified zip code area in 1972-1973 |
| MU7172 | Number of mortgages granted per 1000 units in a specified zip code area in 1971-1972 |
| MU7273 | Number of mortgages granted per 1000 units in a specified zip code area in 1972-1973 |
| NEGROCRW | Percentage black-occupied overcrowded units in zip code area |
| OO | Owner-occupied dwelling |
| OWN | Percentage owner-occupied units in zip code area |
| PERSONU | Median persons per unit in zip code area |
| POVERTY | Percentage employed population that is professionally employed in zip code area |
| PROF | Percent professionally employed |
| PURPR | Purchase price of home for which a mortgage applicant is seeking a loan |
| RCR | Relationship of assets to the home purchase price |
| RENT | Median gross monthly rent of renter-occupied units in zip code area |
| SAME 65 | Percentage of population residing in same house in 1965 in zip code area |
| SERVICE | Percentage of labor force employed at service occupations in zip code area |
| SEX | Sex of loan applicant |
| SPANISH | Percentage of Spanish residents in zip code area |
| UNEMPL | Percentage of labor force 16 years or over that is unemployed in zip code area |
| VACANT | Percentage of year round units for rent that are vacant (60 days or more) |
| VALUE | Median value of owner-occupied units (in $000s) in zip code area |
| WHITE 55 | Percentage whites 55 years or older in zip code area |
| WHITE | Percentage white residents in zip code area |
| YEA | Years loan applicant has been employed |
| YES | Years the spouse of a loan applicant has been employed |

Chapter **4**
# Methodology

## Introduction

Chapter Four considers the research methodology used to evaluate the possible significance of racial underwriting criteria. It discusses two data sources, one macro and one micro, selected for analysis. The conceptual and analytic advantages and disadvantages of these two sets of data are described. The chapter concludes by discussing the methodological approach for analyzing the selected lending information.

## Macro and Micro Data Sets

This monograph selects two data sources: (1) the Federal Home Loan Bank Board Chicago Survey (macro data) and (2) the Comptroller of the Currency's Fair Housing Lending Practice Survey (micro data).

### FHLBB CHICAGO SURVEY (1973)

In 1972, CAP (Citizen's Action Program) leaders appoached the Chicago FHLBB office and requested that a survey be conducted to ascertain whether racial discrimination was being practiced by lenders in the city.[1] They asked that each financial institution supervised by the Chicago FHLBB reveal where it was granting loans. In a compromise move, the FHLBB said that pooled data for all institutions would be made available. Accordingly, 189 lenders were contacted and asked to fill out a complex form showing their lending activity in Chicago. The specific data requested included:

1. The zip codes where all loans on 1-4 family dwellings were made by the associations from June 30, 1971 to June 30, 1973.
2. Terms of the granted mortgage, including LVR and interest rate.
3. The zip codes for all home improvement and construction loans made in the same period.

Approximately 80 percent (144 out of 189) of the contacted lenders responded. Information on about 24,000 mortages and 16,000 loans was collected. There have been conflicting interpretations of the data. The FHLBB claims that its survey revealed that loans were being made in supposed "redlined areas," while community groups charged that the data confirmed that black areas and property owners were being discriminated against. Preliminary analysis by the Center for Urban Affairs at Northwestern University appeared to support the discrimination charge.[2]

## FAIR HOUSING LENDING PRACTICES PILOT PROJECT

The first national disclosure effort came about as a result of a suit by the Center for National Policy Review. In 1971, the Center was retained by the National Urban League, NAACP and 11 other organizations to seek enforcement of non-discrimination lending statutes. The Center brought suit against the four major financial regulatory bodies—Federal Reserve, Federal Home Loan Bank Board, Federal Deposit Insurance Corporation and the Comptroller of the Currency—to assure compliance of non-discrimination by the institutions they monitored. One objective of the suit was to improve loan data collection. The need for better data was discussed by William Taylor, director of the Center:[3]

> . . . almost every federal agency with statutory duties to protect civil rights has understood the necessity of collecting racial data as an aid to enforcement. While statistical disparities in the benefits accorded to particular racial groups do not constitute conclusive proof of discrimination, the courts in various contexts have held that they can create a presumption that the law has been violated, shifting the burden to defendants to establish that their practices are free from the taint of illegality. In areas such as lending where discrimination often takes subtle forms and where the victim himself may not be aware that he has been discriminated against, such data is indispensable.

In 1974, the agencies responded with a pilot disclosure project.[4] Lenders in eighteen SMSAs were required to make public certain data on loans and loan applications made between June and November of 1974. Information on approximately 105,000 mortgage applications was collected.

Three survey forms were used, known as the survey A, B, and C approaches. All three showed that minority mortgage applicants were rejected far more frequently than white applicants, in many cases twice as often. To illustrate, whereas 7 percent of the white loan applicants in Chicago were unsuccessful in seeking credit, 18 percent of the blacks were denied.

While all three indicated similar black-white disparities, they differ in their value as data bases for examining the economic versus eco-race question. Survey B is not very informative. While it does indicate the number of white versus black applicants in various zip codes and the disposition of these applications, this survey yields *no* information on either the personal economic characteristics of those seeking credit or on the properties for which they wish to acquire a mortgage. Neighborhood economic and racial characteristics, though, can be obtained from the Census fifth count data (zip code information).

Survey A is more fertile. It indicates the race of loan applicants and the outcome for those seeking credit. The survey reveals certain personal social traits, namely the marital status, sex and age of those seeking credit—information that can be useful for examining sex, marital status and age discrimination in lending. Another plus is its reporting by Census tract, rather than zip codes; the former are more homogeneous and Census data are richer and more readily accessible than zip code information. (See Chapter Five.)* But while offering more than Survey B, Survey A has many of the former's shortcomings. Personal economic data are not revealed, for example.

Survey C is the richest data base. It shows the disposition of loan applicants and the race of those seeking credit. This information is collected on a zip code-Census tract basis so that the neighborhood profile can be obtained. (In practice areal information was not made available to researchers.) The applicant's sex and marital status is also shown. Most important is the wealth of data on the personal, social and economic characteristics of successful and unsuccessful applicants. These include: (1) income, (2) spouse's income, (3) number of years employed, (4) number of years spouse has been employed, (5) assets, (6) total debt, and (7) debt payments. There is also relatively considerable data on the property to be mortgaged, namely purchase price and whether it will be owner occupied; the former is surely a good proxy for the "worth," "desirability," and "amenity" level of the home—three variables mentioned by underwriters. Finally, the size of the requested loan is also available, allowing the calculation of LVR ratios. This profile, available for almost 13,000 loan applications, makes Survey C a large, fertile loan data base.

---

*See Chapter Seven for a brief discussion of the advantages and disadvantages of zip code versus Census tract information.

## Characteristics of the Selected Data

The Chicago financing information, indicating the areas receiving and not receiving credit but not the profile of successful and unsuccessful bidders for credit, constitutes the *macro data base,* while the Comptroller of the Currency Survey, with its detailing of economic and social characteristics of loan applicants, serves as the *micro data set.*

Before describing why these particular information sets were chosen, it is important to realize the difference between them. The Chicago survey focuses on the distribution of loans by area, while the Comptroller of Currency survey concentrates on the acceptance/rejection rates for different groups of loan applicants. The former shows that predominantly black areas receive fewer mortgages than predominantly white areas, while the latter indicates that black mortgage applicants are rejected more frequently than white applicants. If the racial variation (area or applicant) is significant and cannot be explained by the economic position of black areas and families, the eco-race model would be supported. If economic underwriting criteria can explain the racial mortgage differences, the economic model would be supported.

### ADVANTAGES OF THE MACRO AND MICRO DATA SETS

*Sample Advantages and Disadvantages* The selected data have certain disadvantages. The surveys do not include the loan activity of such important urban loan originators as mortgage bankers. They are somewhat dated although admittedly most more current data are not more revealing. Additionally, the very fact of ''dating'' means that the surveys are more current with the 1970 Census — the basic housing and socioeconomic source used by this and other urban mortgage lending studies. There are significant drawbacks in utilizing more current mortgage data sources, e.g., Home Mortgage Disclosure Act loan volume for 1977, 1978, etc., and then drawing on the 1970 Census. The Comptroller information also suffers from response editing problems — a common occurrence in mortgage surveys.

At the same time the data sets offer numerous advantages. The macro and micro data are large samples; unlike many other studies which have focused on one neighborhood or portion of a city, the data sets selected are comprehensive. The Chicago survey shows the loan distribution for the nation's second largest city, specifically the allocation of 24,000 mortgages over a two-year period; Survey C yields loan acceptance/rejection rates for 12,000 applicants across six SMSAs.

The two also minimize the danger of a biased sample because they include areas with a wide range of geographical, social and economic characteristics. Lending is being examined in communities throughout the country: the Northeast (Bridgeport and Cleveland); the South (Memphis and Montgomery), and the North Central and Western regions (Chicago, Topeka and Tucson). These areas range in population from over 3,000,000 in Chicago to slightly over 100,000 in Montgomery and Topeka. The areas also differ in type—encompassing large, older central cities (Chicago and Cleveland), a smaller central city (Bridgeport) and "Sunbelt" and "Deep South" communities (Tucson, Memphis and Montgomery).

The locations have wide ranging social, economic and housing profiles. Cleveland, Montgomery and Memphis have large black communities (over 30 percent), while the remainder are closer to the national incidence of between 10 and 30 percent. In terms of housing, Chicago and Cleveland (the two large central cities) have a relatively small number of single-family units (20 to 50 percent) while the others have much larger shares (about 75 percent of all housing units) of single-family units. Clearly, both the macro and micro samples cannot be accused of containing areas so unique and limited that generalizations cannot be made from the data.

*Conceptual and Analytic Advantages and Disadvantages.* The conceptual issues discussed in Chapter Three included the considerations of loan demand and selection. This study does not examine demand although this factor is considered briefly in Appendix 5-A. It is important to consider how the two data sets differ in this regard, however. When examining loan volume by area, loan demand clearly affects such volume. In conducting the analysis of the macro data, it is important to remember that the loan demand is not directly considered. This problem does not arise with the micro data for here acceptance/rejection rates are examined—a ratio not affected by loan demand, for it shows the experience of those who applied for credit.

Both data sets allow the examination of the loan selection dynamic, thus avoiding one of the drawbacks characteristic of some past studies. Both contain social and racial data needed to scrutinize the justification of why certain groups/areas are not receiving loans. In this respect, the micro data, with a more detailed breakdown of applicant and property characteristics, are far superior.

From an analysis point of view, the micro and macro data sets are also attractive. Chapter 3 noted three prevalent analytical issues: 1) mortgage loan-Census time gap; 2) questionable loan standardization; and 3) inadequate detailed consideration of the loan selection process. The two information sets, especially the macro data, offer numerous advantages. While the macro data do have a loan-Census time gap, this break is less lengthy than, for example, 1976 or late loan patterns (as with federal disclosure data) with 1970 Census characteristics. The micro loan data are current with social economic traits, the Comptroller survey displays 1974 loan disposition and 1974 economic and property data of the mortgage applicants.

Loan volume standardization is also no problem. The Chicago data can be standardized* by looking at loans per 1,000 structures, 1,000 units or other measures. (These considerations are fully discussed in Chapter Five.) The micro data do not present a standardization problem, for they can be expressed on a standardized measure of observation—the percentage of white versus black loan applicants who are successful.

The data also allow the detailed examination of the loan selection process. Again the micro set is superior in this respect for it contains racial data plus an entire series of property and personal economic information such as the purchase price of the mortgaged parcel and the applicant's income, assets, credit and work history, etc.

The above discussion indicates that the micro data set is richer than its macro partner. In fact, the latter has data limitations similar to those discussed in Chapter Three. Why then include macro information and analysis? This monograph opts for a combined (macro and micro) approach for the following reasons:

1. While the macro base source does have data limitations, it contains macro loan data and other racial/social information, albeit of a limited nature, for a large area—Chicago. Previous macro data bases have usually had a much more limited scope.
2. The macro data base contains time series information—data for Chicago are available for two years. By contrast, the micro set examines mortgage patterns for a six-month period only.**
3. The macro data, focusing on loan volume by area, allow the examination of areal loan distribution by areal economic and racial characteristics. This dimension is not considered by the micro data. The latter is suited for examining the individual loan distinctions, namely the issue of whether black applicants are rejected at a disproportionate rate.

---

*The loan standardization problem is one that usually arises from the way the data is handled rather than being endemic to certain types of information.
**See Chapter Seven for discussion of the limitations of using the Chicago data to consider time effects.

## Analysis Strategy

In the macro (Chicago) case, race (percentage white) and economic indices are used to predict* the volume of loans granted and, if this is done successfully, to measure the relationship of loan volume with race after economics** has been controlled. The statistical technique of regression is utilized since all the variables are interval scales, and regression analysis is an appropriate technique with which to measure the strength of prediction and/or association for such data.[5] The overall adequacy of the model is measured by $R^2$, the F-statistic, and residual plots. The association of race and loan volume when economics is controlled is analyzed via t-tests, partial correlations and regression coefficients.

In the micro (Comptroller of the Currency) case, the objective is to measure the relationship between disposition of a loan request and the race of the applicant when economic factors are controlled. Since disposition and race are dichotomous and the economic variables are polytomous with three or four levels each, a method of contingency table analysis is needed. Although several techniques are available for data of this type (including discriminant analysis and weighted least squares), log-linear analysis and several peripheral techniques are utilized because this approach lends itself to testing the two most relevant hypotheses: (1) the independence of race and disposition given economics, and, (2) the interaction between economics and race.

---

*The use of the terms "predict," "influence" or "explain" in this study do not imply a casual relationship but just association.

**In this monograph the term "economics" is used in a singular sense to refer to all non-racial influences.

## Notes

1. Illinois Legislative Investigating Commission, *Redlining—Discrimination in Residential Mortgage Loans* (Chicago: Illinois Legislative Investigating Commission, 1975), p. 11.

2. Center for Urban Affairs, Northwestern University, *The Role of Mortgage Lending Practices in Older Urban Neighborhoods* (Evanston, Ill.: Center for Urban Affairs, 1975).

3. Testimony of William Taylor, Director, Center for National Policy Review, in *Equal Opportunity in Lending* (Washington, D.C.: Government Printing Office, 1976), p. 194.

4. See Exhibit B submitted by James H. Blair, Assistant Secretary for Fair Housing and Equal Opportunity, Department of Housing and Urban Development, in U.S. Senate, 94th Congress, *Equal Opportunity in Lending* (Washington, D.C.: Government Printing Office, 1975), pp. 130-149.

5. See Morris Hamburg, *Statistical Analysis for Decision Making* (New York: Harcourt, Brace and World, 1970), pp. 304-308; John H. Mueller and Karl F. Schuessler, *Statistical Reasoning in Sociology* (Boston: Houghton Mifflin Co., 1961), pp. 388-391; Hubert M. Blalock, Jr., *Social Statistics* (New York: McGraw Hill, 1960), pp. 119-130; Sidney Siegel, *Nonparametric Statistics for the Behaviorial Sciences* (New York: McGraw Hill, 1956), Chapter 2.

Chapter 5
# Macro Data Analysis

---

## Introduction

This chapter analyzes macro data to test for the possible influence of race on underwriting. It utilizes information available from a 1972 survey conducted by the Federal Home Loan Bank Board in Chicago. The chapter first considers this survey and then evaluates economic and racial loan factors. The discussion evaluates whether neighborhood race is a statistically significant variable after controlling for neighborhood economic characteristics. The chapter concludes that race is a significant independent influence.

## Data Base

The Chicago macro data consist of two items:
1. Loan information by zip code area derived from the Federal Home Loan Bank Board Survey;
2. Census information available by zip code area from the fifth count of the 1970 Census.

The background to the FHLBB survey was described in the previous chapter. In September 1973, the Chicago CAP (Community Action Program Board) requested the Chicago FHLBB office to investigate and take action against alleged redlining. The Board responded by requesting the 189 savings and loan associations in Cook County to:[1]

reveal certain data as to the geographical distribution, by zip code, of the
volume of savings and loan real estate lending in these various zip code areas
during the last two years and certain other data.

It further commented:[2]

> The reason for this survey is the increasing concern of many residents . . . that
> conventional mortgage loans for purchase or rehabilitation of homes either can-
> not be obtained or are very difficult to obtain by people who would otherwise
> qualify for loans under proper underwriting standards . . .

The Board assured each lender that only total data would be released,
not the data on the performance of individual associations. (The Chicago
CAP had requested individual institutional disclosure.)

The following information was requested for the years 1971-1972 (June
30, 1971 - June 30, 1972) and 1972-1973 (June 30, 1972 - June 30, 1973).
Lenders were asked to show how they allocated different categories of credit
for all the zip code areas within the city, including:

*Conventional Loans*
  1. Number of loans
  2. Total loan amount
  3. Average down payments (in percent of purchase price)
  4. Average interest rates of the loans granted.
*FHA/VA Loans*
  1-4. Same information as for conventional loans.
*Construction Loans*
  1. Number of loans
  2. Total loan amount
*Home Improvement Loans*
  1. Number of loans
  2. Total loan amount
  3. Average interest rates of the construction loans granted.
*Savings*
  1. Total deposits by zip code area.

One hundred and forty-four savings and loan associations (S&Ls) gave
the requested information (a response rate of 76 percent). The respondents
had assets of almost $8 billion and included some of the largest S&Ls in
Chicago.

The FHLBB made this data public on February 21, 1974. Exhibits 5-1
and 5-2 indicate the gross loan totals for 1971-1972 and 1972-1973. In a
press release, the Board claimed that a significant amount of loans had been
made in alleged credit-short neighborhoods.[3] It cited that 933 conventional
loans aggregating $22,467,677 were granted in the Austin neighborhood (zip
code 60644) and 894 loans with a total value of $15,956,700 were made in

## EXHIBIT 5-1
## FHLBB CHICAGO SURVEY: GROSS LOAN DATA

| Year | CONVENTIONAL MORTGAGES | | | | FHA/VA MORTGAGES | | | |
|---|---|---|---|---|---|---|---|---|
| | Total Loans | Total Loan Amount | Average Down-payment | Average Interest Rate | Total Loans | Total Loan Amount | Average Down-payment | Average Interest Rate |
| 1971-1972 | 10,991 | $262,844,834 | 28.2% | 7.25% | 656 | $13,025,625 | 5.4% | 7.02% |
| 1972-1973 | 12,556 | $305,950,711 | 27.4% | 7.21% | 102 | $ 2,222,600 | 4.0% | 6.99% |
| TOTAL | 23,547 | $568,795,545 | 27.8%[1] | 7.23%[1] | 758 | $15,248,225 | 4.7%[1] | 7.01% |

EXHIBIT 5-2

FHLBB CHICAGO SURVEY: CONSTRUCTION AND HOME IMPROVEMENT LOAN DATA

| Year | CONSTRUCTION LOANS | | HOME IMPROVEMENT LOANS | | |
| | Total Loans | Total Loan Amount | Total Loans | Total Loan Amount | Average Interest Rate |
|---|---|---|---|---|---|
| 1971-1972 | 429 | $26,095,595 | 1753 | $26,095,595 | 8.5% |
| 1972-1973 | 375 | $23,675,420 | 1011 | $ 2,818,190 | 7.0% |
| TOTAL | 804 | $ 49,771,015 | 2764 | $28,913,785 | 7.8%[1] |

[1]*Note*: Average rate is shown in total.

*Source*: Loan data from Federal Home Loan Bank Board of Chicago Survey (1973). See text.

the Rogers Park area (zip codes 60626 and 60660) — two predominately black and allegedly "redlined" locations.

The Chicago CAP (specifically its Anti-Deterioration Coalition) reached an entirely different conclusion. It claimed that the FHLBB's own data "proves that Chicago's oldest neighborhoods have been victimized by the S&Ls with the connivance of the FHLBB."[4] The CAP also cited the prevalent "redlining" of black neighborhoods such as South Chicago and Roseland.[5]

## FHLBB Loan Information Selected for Analysis

The FHLBB and CAP studies were preliminary investigations that merely summarized gross flows of credit and the availability of credit as compared to savings flows. Clearly more substantial analysis is required.

In examining the loan data released by the Chicago FHLBB, this monograph concentrates on the number of conventional loans made in the different zip code areas for the following reasons:

- ° A principal aspect of the urban financing dilemma is the dearth of conventional credit in certain neighborhoods (See Chapter One).
- ° It would be extremely hard to examine some data, such as construction and home improvement loans, because little is known about the specific underwriting criteria influencing these categories of credit.
- ° Sample size is largest for the conventional loans. To illustrate, the FHLBB survey contains data for almost 11,000 conventional loans made in 1971-1972 as compared to about 650 FHA/VA loans.
- ° It might be invalid to examine FHA/VA, home improvement, and construction patterns from the FHLBB survey, for these types of credit are not predominately granted by savings and loan associations, the group responding to the FHLBB survey. In contrast, S&Ls are the main sources for conventional mortgages.
- ° While all of the respondents to the FHLBB survey disclosed the volume of conventional loans made per zip code area, many did not reveal other requested information such as interest rates and down payments. To illustrate, while 48 lenders reported the number of conventional loans they approved for zip code 60644 (for 1972-1973), only 15 disclosed the interest rate of these loans and only 9 stated the downpayments they required.

## Standardizing the Mortgage Data

The basic loan data from the Chicago Board survey are mortgages by zip code area. Since zip code locations are not uniform in size (population, number of structures, number of housing units, etc.), it is important to standardize the loan information. Chapter Three examined some common methods of standardization such as expressing the number of loans per given number of structures or units. Two standardized measures are utilized here:

1. Number of mortgages per 1000 structures (coded MS)
2. Number of mortgages per 1000 units (coded MU)

MS and MU each offer certain advantages. MS is the more sensible measure because mortgages are given on a per structure basis, i.e., a 10-unit multifamily building will be granted one mortgage. However, zip code Census data do not give an exact count of the number of structures per zip code area. The number of structures can be estimated indirectly because the zip code Census data show the number of units in structures of different sizes (i.e., number of units in structures with one unit, number of units in structures with 2-4 units, etc.). From this latter measure, it is only possible to approximate the number of structures. In contrast, the MU measure is exact, albeit it is more sensible only in predominately single-family areas (where it does make sense to examine mortgages granted per unit). MS and MU are both used, for the former is the more logical measure, while the latter in certain areas is more exact.

Since the Chicago survey contained data for two years (1971-1972 and 1972-1973), four sets of data are examined:

1. MS for 1971-1972 (coded MS7172)
2. MS for 1972-1973 (coded MS7273)
3. MU for 1971-1972 (coded MU7172)
4. MU for 1972-1973 (coded MU7273)

## ZIP CODE SYSTEM

The Chicago loan data were reported by zip code area. Zip code is a five digit geographic code that "identifies areas within the United States and its possessions for purposes of simplifying distribution of mail by the U.S. Postal Service."[6] The zip code system of regions is "territorially exhaustive"[7] (all areas have a code) and is based on "functional relationships"—it is roughly sensitive to population density.[8] When population is sparse, code areas are large and conversely, when population is dense, the areas are small.[9]

Zip codes identify different areas. The first digit identifies a major region,[10] such as the Southeast. The first two digits taken together identify states. The first three digits together designate a sectional center (a key post office in each area that receives and transmits mail both between and into or out of post offices within the area) or a metropolitan city. If the first three digits designate a sectional center, the last two refer to specific satellite post offices within the region. If the first three numbers refer to a metropolitan city, then the last two designate zones within that city.

Zip code areas have begun to be accepted as appropriate separate "regions."[11] They are used for marketing and statistical purposes. Periodicals, for example, have special "geodemic" editions which are sent only to specific zip code areas (often affluent locations) and for which advertisers pay a premium.

Fifth Count summary tapes from the 1970 Census of Population and Housing are available both for 3-digit zip code areas for the entire country (File A) and 5-digit zip code areas that fall within SMSAs (File B).[12] This study utilizes the latter file for the Chicago SMSA.

SELECTING AND STANDARDIZING THE ZIP-CENSUS DATA

Initially, 22 population, social and housing variables were selected as appropriate indicators of neighborhood economic and racial profile. These variables are shown in Exhibits 5-3 (variable numbers 5 through 26) and 5-4. They include the share of white residents (coded WHITE), professional workers (coded PROF), resident income (coded INCOME), and median value of housing (coded VALUE). Clearly, there is a considerable intercorrelation between these measures (e.g., between INCOME, PROF and VALUE). Later in the analysis variables that are highly associated with one another are deleted. The goal at this juncture is merely to select an appropriate group of characteristics.

All of the variables shown in Exhibit 5-3 are standardized in percentage or dollar terms. WHITE and PROF, for example, refer to the percentage white and professional residents, respectively; INCOME and VALUE are the dollar earnings of residents and dollar value of neighborhood housing units. See below for a full listing.

### EXHIBIT 5-3

### POPULATION-SOCIAL-HOUSING VARIABLE LIST

*MORTGAGE DATA VARIABLES (entered into regression equation as dependent variables):*

| CODE | GEOGRAPHIC UNIT | VARIABLE |
|------|----------------|----------|
| 1 MS7172 | zip code area | Number of mortgages granted per 1000 structures in 1971-1972 |
| 2 MS7273 | zip code area | Number of mortgages granted per 1000 structures in 1972-1973 |
| 3 MU7172 | zip code area | Number of mortgages granted per 1000 units in 1971-1972 |
| 4 MU7273 | zip code area | Number of mortgages granted per 1000 units in 1972-1973 |

## EXHIBIT 5-3 (cont'd)

## POPULATION-SOCIAL-HOUSING VARIABLE LIST

**POPULATION-SOCIAL VARIABLES *(entered into regression equation as independent variables)*:**

| CODE | GEOGRAPHIC UNIT | VARIABLE |
|---|---|---|
| 5 WHITE | zip code area | % white residents |
| 6 CROWD | zip code area | % units with 1.01 persons per room |
| 7 AGE 55 | zip code area | % persons 55 years or older |
| 8 PROF | zip code area | % employed population that is professionally employed |
| 9 VALUE | zip code area | Median value of owner-occupied units (in $000s) |
| 10 AGE HOUS | zip code area | Median age of all year-round housing units |
| 11 INCOME | zip code area | Family median income |
| 12 PERSONU | zip code area | Median persons per unit |
| 13 UNEMPL | zip code area | % labor force 16 years or over that is unemployed |
| 14 RENT | zip code area | Median gross monthly rent of renter-occupied units |
| 15 OWN | zip code area | % owner-occupied units |
| 16 VACANT | zip code area | % of year-round units for rent that are vacant (60 days or more) |
| 17 SAME 65 | zip code area | % of population residing in same house in 1965 |

**POPULATION-SOCIAL VARIABLES *(not entered into regression equation)***

| CODE | GEOGRAPHIC UNIT | VARIABLE |
|---|---|---|
| 18 POVERTY | zip code area | % of families with income below poverty level (Social Security Administration's poverty index) |
| 19 FEMALE HH | zip code area | % female-headed households |
| 20 NEGROCRW | zip code area | % of black-occupied overcrowded units |
| 21 BLACKUE | zip code area | % of black labor force 16 years or over that is unemployed |
| 22 BLACK 55 | zip code area | % blacks 55 years or older |
| 23 WHITE 55 | zip code area | % whites 55 years or older |
| 24 BLACK FHH | zip code area | % black female-headed households |
| 25 SERVICE | zip code area | % labor force employed at service occupations |
| 26 SPANISH | zip code area | % Spanish residents |

*Source:* See text.

EXHIBIT 5-4

INDEPENDENT RACIAL AND ECONOMIC VARIABLES: EXPLANATION AND EXPECTED AND ACTUAL RELATIONSHIPS

| Variable[1] | Indicating Following Condition | Expected Relationship with Mortgage Volume Dependent Variable | Actual Relationships | | | |
|---|---|---|---|---|---|---|
| | | | Reduced Equation | Full Equation | Reduced-Log Equation | Reduced-Log Cluster Equation |
| **Race** | | | | | | |
| WHITE | Neighborhood Racial Composition | None under economic model | (Positive for MS7172 MS7273, MU7172 and MU7273) | (Positive[2] for MS7172 MS7273, MU7172 and MU7273) | (Positive for MS7172 MS7273, MU7172 and MU7173) | (Positive for MS7172, MS7273 MU7172, and MU7273) |
| **Economic** | | | | | | |
| OWN | Level of resident ownership | Positive | (Positive for MU7172 and MU7273) | (Positive for MU7172 and MU7273) | (Positive for MU7172and MU7273) | (Positive for MU7172 MU7273) |
| PERSONU | Level of crowding | Negative | Not considered | Negative | Not considered | Not considered |
| VACANT | Market strength | Negative | Negative | Negative | Negative | Negative |
| AGEHOUS | Housing condition | Negative | Not considered | Positive | Not considered | Not considered |
| VALUE | Market strength housing condition | Positive | Not considered | Positive | Not considered | Not considered |
| CROWD | Housing condition | Negative | Not considered | Negative | Not considered | Not considered |
| RENT | Market strength housing condition | Positive | Not considered | Negative | Not considered | Not considered |
| INCOME | Affluence of residents | Positive | (Positive for MS7172 and MS7273) | (Positive[2] for MS7273) | (Positive for MS7172 MS7273 and MU7273) | (Positive for MS7172 and MS7273) |
| PROF | Affluence of residents | Positive | Not considered | Positive for MS7273 | Not considered | Not considered |

(continued)

EXHIBIT 5-4 (cont'd)

INDEPENDENT RACIAL AND ECONOMIC VARIABLES: EXPLANATION AND EXPECTED AND ACTUAL RELATIONSHIPS

| | Economic condition | | | | |
|---|---|---|---|---|---|
| UNEMPL | Negative | Not considered | Positive | Not considered | Not considered |
| **Other (Turnover)** | | | | | |
| SAME 65 | Proxy for stability or turnover (the higher SAME 65, the greater the stability) | Positive (though weak) | Not considered | Positive | Not considered | Not considered |
| AGE 55 | Proxy for turnover (the higher AGE 55, the lower the turnover) | Negative (though weak) | Not considered | Negative | Not considered | Not considered |

¹See Exhibit 5-3 for definition.

²Values in parentheses indicate a significant relationship. Models shown in this Exhibit are explained later in chapter

*Source:* Loan data from Federal Home Loan Bank Board of Chicago Survey (1973). U.S. Department of Commerce. Census Fifth Count for Zip Codes. See text.

## Data Analysis Strategy

The influence of race on loan underwriting is tested via multiple regression equations with loan volume (MS7172, MS7273, MU7172 and MU7273) as the dependent variable and economic and racial indicators (INCOME, VALUE, PROF, WHITE, etc.; see Exhibit 5-3) as the independent variables. If race (WHITE) is significant in explaining variations in loan volume, after controlling for economic influences (INCOME, VALUE, PROF, etc.; see variables 6-17 in Exhibit 5-3), then the null hypothesis that race has no influence on urban underwriting is rejected. Conversely, if race is not significant in explaining mortgage frequency after controlling for economics, then the null hypothesis is not rejected.

There are 22 possible independent variables shown in Exhibit 5-3. It would be redundant to enter all of these into a regression equation for there are strong intercorrelations among the independent variables (INCOME and PROF, for example). To pinpoint the collinear relationships among the independent variables and to examine the simple correlations between the independent and dependent variables, an intercorrelation matrix is formulated.

CONSTRUCT AN INTERCORRELATION MATRIX AND
FORMULATE THE FULL REGRESSION EQUATION

Originally a 26 x 26 matrix was devised. (See Exhibit 5-3 for the twenty-six variables.) It showed a high collinearity ($r = .8$ or above) among many of the variables. There was a .91 negative correlation between PROF and SERVICE, and a .83 positive correlation between BLACK FHH and UNEMPL, for example. The matrix also showed certain variables, such as WHITE 55 and BLACK 55, to be only weakly associated with the variations in loan volume.

Nine* economic variables were then deleted in order to construct a more manageable and sensible regression equation. Variables were eliminated if they were judged to be not very significant from an underwriting perspective (e.g., AGE 55), or if they were highly correlated ($r = .80$ or more) with other characteristics deemed more important. While this selection process is somewhat arbitrary, the retention of one economic variable versus another should not bias the analysis of the significance of race because of the high intercorrelation of the economic variables.

---

*POVERTY, FEMALE HH, NEGROCRW, BLACKUE, BLACK 55, WHITE 55, BLACK FHH, SERVICE, SPANISH. See Exhibit 5-3 for definitions.

EXHIBIT 5-5

INTERCORRELATION MATRIX: CHICAGO CENSUS AND MORTGAGE DATA

VARIABLES

| Variables | WHITE | CROWD | AGE55 | PROF | VALUE | AGEHOUS | INCO | PERSONU | UNEMPL |
|---|---|---|---|---|---|---|---|---|---|
| WHITE | 1.00 | -0.68 | 0.65 | 0.22 | 0.30 | -0.18 | 0.63 | -0.12 | -0.75 |
| CROWD | -0.68 | 1.00 | -0.79 | -0.56 | -0.52 | 0.13 | -0.70 | 0.36 | 0.78 |
| AGE55 | 0.65 | -0.79 | 1.00 | 0.50 | 0.33 | 0.17 | 0.50 | 0.56 | -0.53 |
| PROF | 0.22 | -0.56 | 0.50 | 1.00 | 0.61 | -0.27 | 0.55 | -0.42 | -0.37 |
| VALUE | 0.30 | -0.52 | 0.33 | 0.61 | 1.00 | -0.61 | 0.84 | -0.12 | -0.61 |
| AGEHOUS | -0.18 | 0.13 | 0.17 | -0.27 | -0.61 | 1.00 | -0.59 | -0.32 | 0.46 |
| INCOME | 0.63 | -0.70 | 0.50 | 0.55 | 0.84 | -0.59 | 1.00 | -0.03 | -0.83 |
| PERSONU | -0.12 | 0.36 | 0.56 | -0.42 | -0.12 | -0.32 | -0.03 | 1.00 | -0.01 |
| UNEMPL | -0.75 | 0.78 | -0.53 | -0.37 | -0.61 | 0.46 | -0.83 | -0.01 | 1.00 |
| RENT | 0.36 | -0.63 | 0.43 | 0.69 | 0.68 | -0.44 | 0.65 | -0.37 | -0.54 |
| OWN | 0.45 | -0.32 | -0.01 | -0.13 | 0.31 | -0.58 | 0.54 | 0.54 | -0.64 |
| VACANT | -0.34 | 0.40 | -0.30 | -0.07 | -0.30 | 0.08 | -0.34 | -0.08 | 0.36 |
| SAME65 | 0.33 | -0.08 | -0.07 | -0.35 | -0.02 | -0.34 | 0.20 | 0.43 | -0.36 |
| POVERTY | -0.75 | 0.71 | -0.51 | -0.30 | -0.57 | 0.39 | -0.81 | -0.08 | 0.91 |
| FEMALE HH | -0.82 | 0.50 | -0.39 | -0.22 | -0.57 | 0.52 | -0.82 | -0.21 | 0.89 |
| MS7172 | 0.68 | -0.55 | 0.47 | 0.20 | 0.20 | -0.17 | 0.47 | -0.13 | -0.60 |
| MS 7273 | 0.61 | -0.48 | 0.44 | 0.29 | 0.29 | -0.14 | 0.38 | -0.24 | -0.51 |
| MU 7172 | 0.65 | -0.42 | 0.18 | 0.06 | 0.33 | -0.43 | 0.51 | 0.18 | -0.58 |
| MU 7273 | 0.53 | -0.39 | 0.18 | 0.09 | 0.34 | -0.40 | 0.49 | 0.16 | -0.56 |

(continued)

EXHIBIT 5-5 (cont'd)

INTERCORRELATION MATRIX: CHICAGO CENSUS AND MORTGAGE DATA

| VARIABLES | RENT | OWN | VACANT | SAME65 | POVERTY | FEMALE | MS7172 | MS7273 | MU7172 | MU7273 |
|---|---|---|---|---|---|---|---|---|---|---|
| WHITE | 0.36 | 0.45 | -0.34 | 0.33 | -0.75 | -0.82 | 0.68 | 0.61 | 0.55 | 0.53 |
| CROWD | -0.63 | -0.32 | 0.40 | -0.08 | 0.71 | 0.50 | -0.55 | -0.48 | -0.42 | -0.39 |
| AGE55 | 0.43 | -0.01 | -0.30 | -0.07 | -0.51 | -0.39 | 0.47 | 0.44 | 0.18 | 0.18 |
| PROF | 0.69 | -0.13 | -0.07 | -0.35 | -0.30 | -0.22 | 0.20 | 0.29 | 0.06 | 0.09 |
| VALUE | 0.68 | 0.31 | -0.30 | -0.02 | -0.57 | -0.57 | 0.20 | 0.29 | 0.33 | 0.34 |
| AGEHOUS | -0.44 | -0.58 | 0.08 | -0.34 | 0.39 | 0.52 | -0.17 | -0.14 | -0.43 | -0.40 |
| INCOME | 0.65 | 0.54 | -0.34 | 0.20 | -0.81 | -0.82 | 0.47 | 0.38 | 0.51 | 0.49 |
| PERSONU | -0.37 | 0.54 | -0.08 | 0.43 | -0.08 | -0.21 | -0.13 | -0.24 | 0.18 | 0.16 |
| UNEMPL | -0.54 | -0.64 | 0.36 | -0.36 | 0.91 | 0.89 | -0.60 | -0.51 | -0.58 | -0.56 |
| RENT | 1.00 | 0.21 | -0.21 | 0.06 | -0.43 | -0.41 | 0.31 | 0.40 | 0.32 | 0.32 |
| OWN | 0.21 | 1.00 | -0.41 | 0.78 | -0.68 | -0.73 | 0.39 | 0.27 | 0.70 | 0.68 |
| VACANT | -0.21 | -0.41 | 1.00 | -0.32 | 0.43 | 0.41 | -0.39 | -0.31 | -0.44 | -0.45 |
| SAME65 | 0.06 | 0.78 | -0.32 | 1.00 | -0.32 | -0.34 | 0.29 | 0.22 | 0.55 | 0.53 |
| POVERTY | -0.43 | -0.68 | 0.43 | -0.32 | 1.00 | 0.94 | -0.56 | -0.44 | -0.54 | -0.50 |
| FEMALE HH | -0.41 | -0.73 | 0.41 | -0.34 | 0.94 | 1.00 | -0.61 | -0.48 | -0.61 | -0.56 |
| MS 7172 | 0.31 | 0.39 | -0.39 | 0.29 | -0.56 | -0.61 | 1.00 | 0.90 | 0.85 | 0.82 |
| MS 7373 | 0.40 | 0.27 | -0.31 | 0.22 | -0.44 | -0.48 | 0.90 | 1.00 | 0.75 | 0.79 |
| MU 7172 | 0.32 | 0.70 | -0.44 | 0.55 | -0.54 | -0.61 | 0.85 | 0.75 | 1.00 | 0.97 |
| MU 7273 | 0.32 | 0.68 | -0.45 | 0.53 | -0.50 | -0.56 | 0.82 | 0.79 | 0.97 | 1.00 |

*Source:* Loan data from Federal Home Loan Bank Board of Chicago Survey (1973). See text.

Exhibit 5-5 shows the simple intercorrelations of the four dependent variables and 13 independent variables remaining after the selection process discussed in the previous paragraph. It also shows the inter-relationships of two deleted characteristics—POVERTY and FEMALE HH—illustrating the high collinearity of the group of characteristics that were removed with the group preserved. There is a .91 positive correlation between POVERTY and UNEMPL and a .89 correlation between FEMALE HH and UNEMPL, for example.

Exhibit 5-6 shows the simple correlations between the dependent variables. Loan patterns are fairly consistent over time; high correlations are found between MS7172, MS7273, MU7172 and MU7273 (correlations of .75 to .97). The best way to predict the relative neighborhood loan frequency in one year is its frequency in the prior year. As a result of this the findings for MS7172-MS7273 and MU7172-MU7273 will be very similar.

It is important to realize that the consistency discussed here is over a short period of time—in this case two years. Over a longer period, dynamic change in neighborhood economic conditions, neighborhood racial com-position and lender activity can be expected.

What variables are associated with the variations in loan volume by area? The FHLBB survey showed certain zip areas obtaining 40 and 50 times the number of loans of other neighborhoods. Race is clearly related to loan distribution; there is a .68 correlation between WHITE and MS7172, for example. Economic influences are also associated with loan patterns. There is a positive correlation of .68 between OWN and MU7273, a negative correlation of .58 between UNEMPL and MU7172, and a positive correlation of .47 between INCOME and MS7172. Racial and economic characteristics are interrelated, however; there are correlations of .63 between WHITE and INCOME, −.75 between WHITE and UNEMPL, and −.68 between WHITE and CROWD. The basic question is whether or not race still influences loan distribution after disentangling the race and economic collinearity. This question is addressed via multiple regression analysis.

The multiple regression equation can show the influence of race versus economics by controlling the influence of one set of variables while allowing

EXHIBIT 5-6

INTERCORRELATION MATRIX OF 1972-1973 LOAN FREQUENCY MEASURES

|         | MS7172 | MS7273 | MU7172 | MU7273 |
|---------|--------|--------|--------|--------|
| MS7172  | 1.00   | .90    | .85    | .82    |
| MS7273  | .90    | 1.00   | .75    | .79    |
| MU7172  | .85    | .75    | 1.00   | .97    |
| MU7273  | .82    | .79    | .97    | 1.00   |

Source: Loan data from Federal Home Loan Bank Board of Chicago Survey (1973). U.S. Department of Commerce, Census Fifth Count for Zip Codes. See text.

the other to independently explain the variation in the dependent variable. The first regression equation is termed the reduced* equation because it enters a representative set of a large group of economic independent variables to explain the variation in the dependent or loan volume variables.

## REDUCED REGRESSION EQUATION

This regression equation enters a reduced number of the strongest economic independent variables (in terms of their correlation with Y or the dependent [loan volume] variable). Exhibit 5-5 shows that INCOME has one of the highest simple correlations with the MU and MS variables (correlations of .4 to .5). Additionally, it is a standard measure used in underwriting. Two other strong economic characteristics that show a reasonable influence on Y, but are not overly intercorrelated with each other are VACANT (correlations of −.30 to −.45 with Y) and OWN (correlations of .3 to .7). WHITE, of course, should be included to examine race's influence. Tentatively the reduced regression equation includes: INCOME, VACANT, OWN, and WHITE**.

A caveat about the content and form of this regression model should be mentioned: the independent variables include racial and economic characteristics. The interpretation of the variables and their expected relationship with the dependent variable are shown in Exhibit 5-4. WHITE indicates the neighborhood racial composition (specifically, percentage white). Under the null hypothesis that race is not an influence, no significant relationship between WHITE and the dependent variable is expected. INCOME and OWN are examples of economic indicators. If economics is indeed the sole guiding force in underwriting, then INCOME, OWN and similar variables should be associated positively with the dependent variable and WHITE should not be significant.

Exhibits 5-7 and 5-8 show the results of the equations, for dependent variables MS7172 and MU7172 respectively, when the economic variables are entered first followed by WHITE. (Results for MS7273 and MU7273 are similar.) Both the MS7172 and MU7172 regressions are significant at the .001 level (via the F-test) and explain roughly half of the variance (50 percent for MS7172, 58 percent for MU7172).

The influence of the individual independent variables also are shown in Exhibits 5-7 and 5-8. The regression coefficients indicate the change in Y as-

---

*"reduced" refers to the number of variables included in the equation. More detailed equations will be used later.

**A similar regression equation with UNEMPL, VACANT, OWN and WHITE was also considered (UNEMPL was used instead of INCOME) and yielded similar results.

sociated with a given change in one of the independent variables with the other independents held fixed or "constant." It is difficult to gauge the strength of the regression coefficients themselves because they have different standard errors. Partial correlations and individual F-tests can be used, however, to measure and test the significance of the relationship between an individual independent variable with the dependent variable when the remaining independent variables are controlled.

Exhibits 5-7 and 5-8 (step 4) show the importance of the *race* (or WHITE) independent variable. It has the highest partial correlation with MS and second highest with MU. The partial correlation analysis indicates the WHITE can explain 8.4 percent of MU's variation and 29.2 percent of MS's variation in loan volume after economics is controlled.*

While partials are revealing, significance measures are also regarded with great interest in an exploratory analysis such as this. Race (WHITE) *is significantly associated with loan volume.* The results from the reduced equation would force the rejection of the null hypothesis that race is not playing a role in urban underwriting, for they show that race is significant, at the .05 level for MU and .001 level for MS (see Exhibits 5-7 and 5-8, step 4).

The effects of economics and race are interestingly shown by the display of results for the different stepwise regression entries. (There are four such entries — one for each of the four independent variables.**) In the MU7172 equation, for example, INCOME is significant as the first variable entered, and this one independent variable explains 26 percent of MU7172's variation. When VACANT is added (2nd step), the equation is significant and explains 35 percent of the variation in MU7172. When OWN is added (at the 3rd step), 54 percent of MU7172's variation is explained. At this point, however, only OWN is significant. INCOME and VACANT are relatively weak; they are reflecting OWN's influence (INCOME is higher and VACANT is lower in high OWN neighborhoods). Therefore, INCOME and VACANT become insignificant at the 3rd step when OWN is entered. When race (WHITE) is entered, the regression is significant and the explanatory power of the regression model is increased to 58 percent of MU7172's variation. Most important, race (WHITE) is significant (at the .05 level), and OWN also remains significant. For MS7172, INCOME remains significant through the third step in which 29 percent of MS7172's variation is explained. When race is entered, the explanatory power is increased to 50 percent and only race is significant.

---

*29.2 percent in MS's case is computed by squaring WHITE's partial correlation: .54 x .54 = .292. A similar procedure is followed for MU. These partial correlations are from the complete equation (Step 4 in the exhibits).

**The economic variables were forced first into the stepwise regression to measure their interrelationships.

## EXHIBIT 5-7

## MS7172 REDUCED REGRESSION EQUATION RESULTS

**Dependent Variable:** MS7172, Mean = 16.51, S. = 13.18 (arithmetic measure)
**Independent Variables:** Reduced (4 Variables) regression: INCOME, VACANT, OWN AND WHITE.

**Sample:** Chicago
**Sample Size:** 54 (zip code areas)

**STEP 1: INCOME**    $R^2$ = .22   $S_{yx}$ = 11.83   F = 14.42   Significance = .001[1]

| | b | Correlation | F | Significance[5] |
|---|---|---|---|---|
| INCOME | 2.24 | .47 | 14.42 | .001 |

**STEP 2: INCOME, VACANT**    $R^2$ = .28   $S_{yx}$ = 11.44   F = 9.98   Significance = .001[2]

| | b | Partial Correlation | F | Significance[6] |
|---|---|---|---|---|
| INCOME | 1.79 | .38 | 8.66 | .01 |
| VACANT | -0.41 | -.29 | 4.56 | .05 |

**STEP 3: INCOME, VACANT, OWN**    $R^2$ = .29   $S_{yx}$ = 11.50   F = 6.68   Significance = .001[3]

| | b | Partial Correlation | F | Significance[7] |
|---|---|---|---|---|
| INCOME | 1.55 | .30 | 4.97 | .05 |
| VACANT | -0.37 | -.25 | 3.31 | — |
| OWN | -0.06 | -.10 | 0.54 | — |

**STEP 4: INCOME, VACANT, OWN, WHITE**    $R^2$ = .50   $S_{yx}$ = 9.74   F = 12.25   Significance = .001[4]

| | b | Partial Correlation | F | Significance[8] |
|---|---|---|---|---|
| INCOME | 0.01 | .00 | .00 | — |
| VACANT | -0.27 | -.22 | 2.39 | — |
| OWN | 0.02 | .04 | 0.08 | — |
| WHITE | 0.25 | .54 | 20.66 | .001 |

1. Degrees of freedom equal 1 and 52.
2. Degrees of freedom equal 2 and 51.
3. Degrees of freedom equal 3 and 50.
4. Degrees of freedom equal 4 and 49.
5. Degrees of freedom equal 1 and 52.
6. Degrees of freedom equal 1 and 51.
7. Degrees of freedom equal 1 and 50.
8. Degrees of freedom equal 1 and 49.

*Source:* Loan data from Federal Home Loan Bank Board of Chicago Survey (1973).

## EXHIBIT 5-8

## MU7172 REDUCED REGRESSION EQUATION RESULTS

**Dependent Variable:** MU7172. Mean = 9.02, S. = 10.13 (arithmetic measure)
**Independent Variables:** Reduced (4 variable) regression. INCOME, VACANT, OWN AND WHITE.

**Sample:** Chicago
**Sample Size:** 54 (zip code areas)

### STEP 1: INCOME

| | b | Correlation | F | |
|---|---|---|---|---|
| | | | | $R^2 = .26$   $Syx = 8.79$   $F = 18.61$   Significance = .001[1] |
| | | | | Significance[5] |
| INCOME | 1.89 | .51 | 18.61 | .001 |

### STEP 2: INCOME, VACANT

| | b | Partial Correlation | F | |
|---|---|---|---|---|
| | | | | $R^2 = .35$   $Syx = 8.36$   $F = 13.49$   Significance = .001[2] |
| | | | | Significance[6] |
| INCOME | 1.50 | .43 | 11.40 | .01 |
| VACANT | −0.36 | −.33 | 6.42 | .05 |

### STEP 3: INCOME, VACANT, OWN

| | b | Partial Correlation | F | |
|---|---|---|---|---|
| | | | | $R^2 = .54$   $Syx = 7.10$   $F = 19.43$   Significance = .001[3] |
| | | | | Significance[7] |
| INCOME | 0.57 | .19 | 1.78 | — |
| VACANT | −0.19 | −.21 | 2.32 | — |
| OWN | 0.21 | .54 | 20.84 | .001 |

### STEP 4: INCOME, VACANT, OWN, WHITE

| | b | Partial Correlation | F | |
|---|---|---|---|---|
| | | | | $R^2 = .58$   $Syx = 6.87$   $F = 16.64$   Significance = .001[4] |
| | | | | Significance[8] |
| INCOME | 0.07 | .02 | 0.02 | — |
| VACANT | −0.15 | −.18 | 1.67 | — |
| OWN | 0.20 | .53 | 19.48 | .001 |
| WHITE | 0.08 | .29 | 4.36 | .05 |

1. Degrees of freedom equal 1 and 52.
2. Degrees of freedom equal 2 and 51.
3. Degrees of freedom equal 3 and 50.
4. Degrees of freedom equal 4 and 49.

5. Degrees of freedom equal 1 and 52.
6. Degrees of freedom equal 1 and 51.
7. Degrees of freedom equal 1 and 50.
8. Degrees of freedom equal 1 and 49.

Source: data from Federal Home Loan Bank Board of Chicago Survey (1973). See text

The first reduced equation is designed to examine the importance of race in a fairly simple manner. Is the analytical strategy biasing the finding? Perhaps the significance of race is due to a lack of sufficient economic controls. A full regression equation, including all thirteen economic variables (see Exhibit 5-9), is therefore tested (full regression model).

*Evaluating the Full Regression Equation.* Exhibit 5-9 shows the results of the full equation with MS7172 and MS7273 as dependent variables. Exhibit 5-10 displays the output for MU7172 and MU7273. In each case, the equation is significant at the .001 level. The equations explain about 60 percent of the variation in the dependent variable (multiple coefficients of determination or R-squared range from .55 to .62).

Is the race variable significant? The analysis indicates that WHITE is important as measured by its partial correlation and F-tests. For the MU measures, race explains about 10 percent (9 percent for MU7172, 12 percent for MU7273) of the variation in loans after economics has been controlled. Race also explains approximately 20 percent in the MS measures when economics is entered into the equation (17 percent for MS7172 and 24 percent for MS7273). Most important is the finding that race is significant in all cases, at the .05 level for MU and the .01 level for MS.

The weak economic effects in the full equations are due to their multicollinearity. None of the individual economic variables are very strong although together they are strong predictors of loans. (This point is discussed later.)

It is interesting to note that the full equation, with twelve economic variables, explains only slightly more of the loan volume variation than the reduced equation. (Compare Exhibits 5-7 and 5-8 with 5-9 and 5-10.) Thus, little was gained by adding the additional economic controls to the equations.

TESTING SCEDASTICITY OF DATA AND
CORRECTING FOR HETEROGENEITY

The analysis thus far indicates that race is a significant underwriting variable. The regression equations, though, appear to be only mediocre in explaining the variation in loans across the areas in Chicago. One possible reason for this is heterogeneity in the variances of the errors in our models. The commonly made assumption of homoscedasticity (i.e., homogeneity of the variances) has been assumed to be correct in the regressions.*

There are no generally accepted significance tests for homogeneity vs. heterogeneity of the variances in regression. Instead, graphical procedures,

---

*The assumption is commonly made, since regression is affected only slightly by small to moderate departures from homoscedasticity.

## EXHIBIT 5-9

## MS7172 AND MS7273 FULL REGRESSION EQUATION RESULTS

| Dependent Variable: | | Dependent Variable: | |
|---|---|---|---|
| Independent Variables: | Full Regression Equation | Independent Variables: | Full Regression Equation |
| Sample: | Chicago | Sample: | Chicago |
| Sample Size: | 54 (zip code areas) | Sample Size: | 54 (zip code areas) |
| | MS7172, Mean = 16.51, S = 13.18 | | MS7273, Mean = 19.09, S = 14.87 |

| Regression Equation | $R^2$ | Syx | F | Significance[1] | Regression Equation | $R^2$ | Syx | F | Significance[1] |
|---|---|---|---|---|---|---|---|---|---|
| | .55 | 10.17 | 3.76 | .001 | | .55 | 11.48 | 3.77 | .001 |

| Independent Variables | b | Partial Correlation | F | Significance[2] | Independent Variables | b | Partial Correlation | F | Significance[2] |
|---|---|---|---|---|---|---|---|---|---|
| 1. UNEMPL | −1.41 | −.11 | 0.52 | — | 1. UNEMPL | −1.58 | −.10 | 0.44 | — |
| 2. VACANT | −0.20 | −.15 | 0.98 | — | 2. VACANT | −0.13 | −.08 | 0.27 | — |
| 3. PERSONU | −5.50 | −.18 | 1.40 | — | 3. PERSONU | −9.89 | −.28 | 3.40 | — |
| 4. VALUE | 1.24 | .15 | 0.94 | — | 4. VALUE | 2.26 | .24 | 2.55 | — |
| 5. SAME 65 | 0.11 | .07 | 0.19 | — | 5. SAME 65 | 0.07 | .04 | 0.05 | — |
| 6. RENT | −0.05 | −.13 | 0.73 | — | 6. RENT | −0.001 | .00 | 0.00 | — |
| 7. AGE 55 | −0.53 | −.08 | 0.25 | — | 7. AGE 55 | −0.86 | −.11 | 0.48 | — |
| 8. AGE HOUS | 0.05 | .03 | 0.03 | — | 8. AGE HOUS | 0.32 | .16 | 1.03 | — |
| 9. OWN | 0.10 | .08 | 0.24 | — | 9. OWN | 0.29 | .22 | 1.97 | — |
| 10. INCOME | 2.13 | .19 | 1.44 | — | 10. INCOME | −4.47 | −.34 | 5.13 | .05 |
| 11. PROF | 0.35 | .12 | .058 | — | 11. PROF | 0.99 | .30 | 4.01 | — |
| 12. CROWD | −0.08 | −.01 | 0.01 | — | 12. CROWD | 0.79 | .14 | 0.80 | — |
| 13. WHITE | 16.39 | .41 | 7.72 | .01 | 13. WHITE | 0.36 | .49 | 12.39 | .01 |

1. Degrees of freedom equal 13 and 40.
2. Degrees of freedom equal 1 and 40.

*Source:* Loan data from Federal Home Loan Bank Board of Chicago Survey (1973). See text.

## EXHIBIT 5-10

## MU7172 AND MU7273 FULL REGRESSION EQUATION RESULTS

| Dependent Variable: | MU7172, Mean = 9.02, S = 10.13 | | | | Dependent Variable: | MU7273, Mean = 9.98, S = 11.14 | | | |
|---|---|---|---|---|---|---|---|---|---|
| Independent Variables:<br>Sample:<br>Sample Size: | Full Regression Equation<br>Chicago<br>54 (zip code areas) | | | | Independent Variables:<br>Sample:<br>Sample Size: | Full Regression Equation<br>Chicago<br>54 (zip code areas) | | | |
| *Regression Equation* | $R^2$ | *Syx* | *F* | *Significance[1]* | *Regression Equation* | $R^2$ | *Syx* | *F* | *Significance[1]* |
| | .62 | 7.21 | 4.97 | .001 | | .62 | 7.92 | 4.99 | .001 |
| *Independent Variables* | *b* | *Partial Correlation* | *F* | *Significance[2]* | *Independent Variables* | *b* | *Partial Correlation* | *F* | *Significance[2]* |
| 1. UNEMPL | −0.45 | −.05 | 0.01 | — | 1. UNEMPL | −0.78 | −.07 | 0.22 | — |
| 2. VACANT | −0.15 | −.15 | 0.97 | — | 2. VACANT | −0.15 | −.14 | 0.82 | — |
| 3. PERSONU | −4.42 | −.20 | 1.72 | — | 3. PERSONU | −6.11 | .25 | 2.72 | — |
| 4. VALUE | 0.55 | .10 | 0.39 | — | 4. VALUE | 1.15 | .18 | 1.38 | — |
| 5. SAME 65 | 0.03 | .02 | 0.02 | — | 5. SAME 65 | 0.05 | .04 | 0.06 | — |
| 6. RENT | −0.01 | −.03 | 0.04 | — | 6. RENT | −0.02 | −.07 | 0.22 | — |
| 7. AGE 55 | −0.73 | −.15 | 0.87 | — | 7. AGE 55 | −0.82 | −.15 | 0.90 | — |
| 8. AGE HOUS | 0.02 | .02 | 0.01 | — | 8. AGE HOUS | 0.17 | .12 | 0.59 | — |
| 9. OWN | 0.28 | .32 | 4.66 | .05 | 9. OWN | 0.39 | .40 | 7.42 | .01 |
| 10. INCOME | −0.89 | −.11 | 0.51 | — | 10. INCOME | −1.50 | −.17 | 1.22 | — |
| 11. PROF | 0.26 | .13 | 0.69 | — | 11. PROF | 0.59 | .26 | 2.98 | — |
| 12. CROWD | −0.03 | −.00 | 0.00 | — | 12. CROWD | 0.30 | .08 | 0.24 | — |
| 13. WHITE | 0.13 | .30 | 4.10 | .05 | 13. WHITE | 0.17 | .35 | 5.71 | .05 |

1. Degrees of freedom equal 13 and 40.
2. Degrees of freedom equal 1 and 40.

*Source:* Loan data from Federal Home Loan Bank Board of Chicago Survey (1973). See text.

usually a plot of fitted (i.e., predicted) values vs. residuals, is generally used. A flat pattern of type (a) below shows homogeneity while the envelope pattern of type (b) shows increasing variance with fitted values, thereby suggesting heterogeneity of the variances. In the latter case, logs are generally used in an initial attempt to correct the problem.

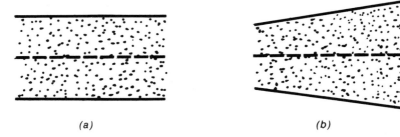

(a)                                                              (b)

Exhibit 5-11 shows the plot of residuals by fitted Ys for MS7172. The data form an almost classical heteroscedastic pattern of the triangular or envelope type. As the fitted Ys increase, so does the spread of the residuals—thereby violating the assumption of equal variances or homoscedascity. The other data of the MS7273, MU7172, MU7273 equations show a similar heteroscedastic pattern.

One possible cause of heterogeneity is an incorrect model for the relationship between the independent and dependent variables. When using the arithmetic form of the dependent variable, or Y, the implication is that, all other things being equal, a change of one unit in an independent variable, or X, corresponds to an expected change of $\beta$ units in Y for some number $\beta$. When using a log form, a one unit change in X should result in a $\beta$ units change in log (Y) which corresponds to an $(e^{\beta} - 1)$ x 100 percent change in Y.* In addition to possibly correcting for heterogeneity of variances, the log transformation also changes the model from analyzing arithmetic differences in the dependent variable to analyzing percentage changes — a possibly more appropriate approach.

For example, assume X is WHITE, Y is MU7273 and we want to compare the expected value of MU7273 for two areas which are identical for all independent variables in the model except that the first area is one unit higher on the WHITE scale. If we use the model: MU7273 = $\beta_0 + \beta_1$ WHITE + other variables and $\beta_1$ is .25, the first area should be about .25 units higher on MU7273 than the second area. If the log model is used so that log (MU7273) = $\beta_0 + \beta_1$ WHITE + other variables and $\beta_1$ = .25, then the first area should be about 28 percent higher ($e^{.25} = 1.28$) on the MU7273 scale than the first location.

---

*e is the base of natural logarithms. Its value is approximately 2.72.

EXHIBIT 5-11

## MS7172 REGRESSION EQUATION PLOT OF RESIDUALS WITH Y MEASURED IN ARITHMETIC FORM

PLOT: RESIDUAL (DOWN)—FITTED VALUE (ACROSS)

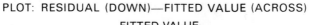

FITTED VALUE

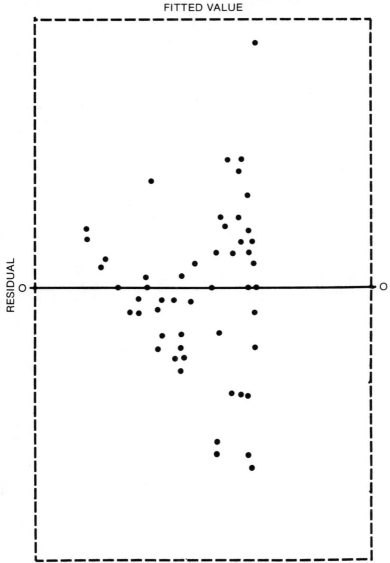

---

*Source:* Loan data from Federal Home Loan Bank Board of Chicago Survey (1973). See text.

EXHIBIT 5-12

MS7172 REGRESSION EQUATION PLOT OF RESIDUALS WITH Y
MEASURED IN LOG FORM

PLOT: RESIDUAL (DOWN)—FITTED VALUE (ACROSS)

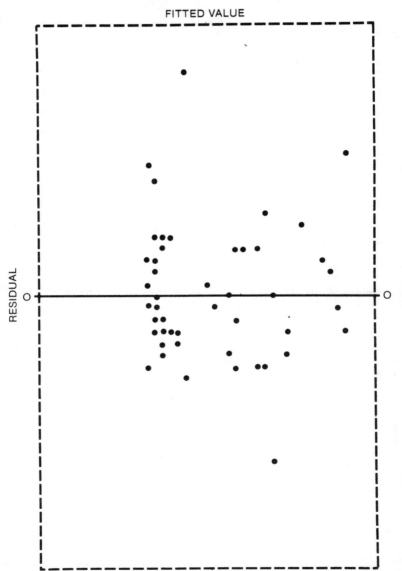

What is the distribution of the data after conversion to log form? Exhibit 5-12 shows the residuals (vertical axis) against the predicted MS7172 Ys (horizontal axis). The pattern is roughly similar to form (a) on page 86 , thereby indicating a homoscedastic condition. The new distribution stands in clear contrast to MS7172's previous heteroscedastic pattern when Y was expressed on an arithmetic scale. (Compare Exhibits 5-11 and 5-12.) There are similar corrections for the other dependent variables (MS7273, MU7172 and MU7273). The log transformation, by converting the heteroscedastic data to homoscedastic observations, satisfies the regression data distribution requirement.

## REDUCED-LOG REGRESSION EQUATION

This equation incorporates the strategies of utilizing four independent variables and expressing the dependent variable in a log form.

### EXHIBIT 5-13
### MU7172 AND MS7172 REDUCED-LOG EQUATION RESULTS

| Dependent Variable: | Log MS7172, Mean = 2.29, S = 1.26 | | | |
|---|---|---|---|---|
| Independent Variables: | Reduced Regression Equation | | | |
| Sample: | Chicago | | | |
| Sample Size: | 54 (Zip Code Areas) | | | |
| *Regression Equation* | $R^2$ | *Syx* | *F* | *Significance*[1] |
| | .70 | .72 | 28.70 | .001 |
| | | *Partial* | | |
| *Independent Variable* | *b* | *Correlation* | *F* | *Significance*[2] |
| INCOME | .026 | .07 | 0.27 | — |
| VACANT | −.012 | −.14 | 0.95 | — |
| OWN | .000 | .01 | 0.01 | — |
| WHITE | .030 | .73 | 54.61 | .001 |
| Dependent Variable: | Log MU7172, Mean = 1.36, S = 1.61 | | | |
| Independent Variables: | Reduced Regression Equation | | | |
| Sample: | Chicago | | | |
| Sample Size: | 54 (Zip Code Areas) | | | |
| *Regression Equation* | $R^2$ | *Syx* | *F* | *Significance*[1] |
| | .80 | .74 | 50.44 | .001 |
| | | *Partial* | | |
| *Independent Variable* | *b* | *Correlation* | *F* | *Significance*[2] |
| INCOME | −.065 | −.18 | 1.60 | — |
| VACANT | −.015 | −.16 | 1.29 | — |
| OWN | .030 | .66 | 37.76 | .001 |
| WHITE | .030 | .72 | 52.10 | .001 |

1. Degrees of Freedom equal 4 and 49.
2. Degrees of Freedom equal 1 and 49.

*Source:* Loan data from Federal Home Loan Bank Board of Chicago Survey (1973). See text.

Exhibit 5-13 shows the reduced-log equation results for MS7172 and MU7172. (The stepwise results are deleted.) Both the equations are significant at the .001 level. The squared multiple correlations, .70 for log MS7172 and .80 for log MU7172, are much higher than even those obtained with the full regression equation (.55 to .62 squared multiple correlations) when nine more independent variables were allowed to explain the variation in loans granted. (Similar results are obtained for the log MS7273 and MU7273 equations.)

*Race or WHITE is significant* in both equations at the .001 level. The partial correlations for WHITE are high: .73 for MS7172 and .72 for MU7172; race explains about 50 percent of the variation in loans after economics has been controlled. As in the two previous equations (full regression and reduced form), the reduced-log equation compels the rejection of the null hypothesis that race is not playing a role in urban lending.

The model with all twelve economic variables and logged dependent variable is considered in Appendix 5-A. Similar results are found.

## Summary of Findings

This chapter considered whether race is an underwriting criterion in Chicago. *The analysis shows that race, in this case racial composition of the neighborhood, is significantly associated with loans granted.* A racial impact is found even after controlling for economic influences. All of the regression results (full, reduced and reduced-log) show the significance of race (see Exhibit 5-4). When the arithmetic form of loans granted is used, WHITE is significant at the .05 level or better. Race is significant at the conservative .001 level when the log form (offering a better "fit" for the regression analysis) is used.

The analysis in this chapter is tested and refined in Appendix 5-A which checks the distribution and appropriateness of the sample data. It also examines the influence of Chapter Five's model and data handling to check whether the results derived are unduly influenced by the decisions made in formulating the analysis. The appendix considers other statistical approaches and different models, including deletion of suspect points and several transformations of the economic variables, but these yield the same finding — race is significant.

MEASURING STRENGTH OF ECONOMICS AND RACE

How strong is the race-underwriting relationship? Tests of significance merely state that non-zero relationships exist (with a specified confidence). In interpreting the individual and relative effects of race and economics, it is helpful to know more than just an effect is present; a measure of absolute size is needed.

The strength of an independent variable* can be measured by its total effect and/or its unique effect. The former is the proportion of variation in the dependent variable explained by the specific independent variable, i.e.,its $R^2$ when it is the only independent variable in the model. The unique influence considered in this section is the proportion of the original variation in MU or MS that is explained by the variable after the other relevant variables are controlled. In considering the strength of race, the unique effect is the $R^2$ for the full model (including race and economics) minus the total effect of economics. The unique effect for economics is similarly defined.

Partial correlations are another measure of a singular influence. The partial correlations for WHITE, given economics, were considered in Chapter Five (see also Appendix 5-A). These partial correlations are relatively high; race explains a reasonable proportion of the variation in loan volume after economics has been entered.

This finding still begs the question. If economics alone explains most of the variation, little residual variation is left for race or any other variables to explain so that, even if race does explain much of this residual variation, it still may not be substantively important. Another question concerns the selection of variables used to define the economic influence.** If too few variables are retained, then the economics effect is not adequately described. If too many are retained, the redundant variables relate to random noise in the data, rather than displaying a substantive link between economics and loan volume.

To obtain a better sense of the "true" economic influence, three models were employed:

1) *Reduced model:* This strategy is based on the reduced regression model which uses INCOME, VACANT and OWN as its economic variables. This model was formulated for substantive and statistical factors (see page 79 ) and acts as a reasonable lower bound for the economics effect.

2) *Principal Components:* This strategy uses the first three principal components of the economic variables as the economic indices. (See Appendix 5-A for discussion of principal components.)

3) *Maximum Adjusted R²:* This strategy determines the appropriate variables via a modified stepwise procedure. Variables are added un-

---

*In this section economics is considered as one variable although it is actually composed of several component variables.

**Previous analyses in the chapter and appendix considering race and economics were based on various models containing three to twelve economic variables. Since tests of significance for race showed strong resistance to the amount of economics controls, a precise definition of economics was not needed. For absolute and relative measures of strength such a definition is potentially important.

til the maximum adjusted $R^2$ is reached. (This procedure retains more variables than standard stepwise analysis.) Maximum adjusted $R^2$ gives a reasonable upper bound to the number of economic variables that need to be included.*

Log MU7273 and Log MS7273 were used as dependent variables in all three models. (The benefit of using logs and the similarity of results for the 7172 measures to the 7273 measures have been discussed previously.) The three economic models give slightly different results for these dependent variables.

The full results for all the models are shown in Exhibit 5-14. For the sake of brevity, this section discusses the findings of the principal components model. The economics and race effects are similar in strength for log MU7273, although the former is slightly stronger. Race explains 61 percent of the variation in log MU7273, while the three economic indices explain 66 percent. More interesting are the unique effects. Since the total $R^2$ is .77, race explains an additional 11 percent of the variation in loans after economics has explained its 66 percent. Similarly, economics explains an additional 16 percent of the variation after race. Both variables predict loan volume fairly well and, although most of this explanatory power is in common, each explains more than 10 percent of the original variation that the other does not.

Further, in the principal components model, WHITE is somewhat stronger than economics when considering LOG MS7273. The $R^2$ for the full model is .66, lower than that for log MU7273. This decrease in $R^2$ is primarily due to a relative weakness in the economic indices. Economics alone explains 46 percent of the variation and just 1 percent of the variation after race. In contrast, race alone explains 65 percent of the variation which includes 20 percent after economics.

The findings for the reduced and maximum adjusted $R^2$ models are similar. Exhibit 5-14 indicates that for the MS measure, race is always stronger than economics; for the MU measure, economics is generally stronger. There are also variations depending on which model is used. The reduced model, retaining the most narrow selection of economic variables, shows the weakest economic association; the maximum adjusted $R^2$ model, with its stepwise addition of economic variables, shows a higher absolute economic effect. Race's unique effect is approximately 10 to 20 percent of the variation for Log MU and about 20 percent for Log MS.

This finding must be kept in perspective, however. The analysis here focuses on neighborhood characteristics, rather than the full universe of underwriting criteria. It is also important to bear in mind that the chapter has

*For the MU measures OWN, INCOME, UNEMPL, VACANT, PROF, CROWD, PERSONU and AGEHOUS were retained. For the MS measures INCOME, UNEMPL, VACANT, PROF, CROWD, PERSONU, AGE55 and SAME65 were retained.

demarcated neighborhoods on a zip code basis. It is difficult to definitively delineate homogeneous areas (as viewed by lending officers and others); the selection of a zip code definition of neighborhood has been dictated by the data. There is a further question concerning the stability of the statistics in considering the absolute and relative strength of race. The same analysis applied to different area or time data will likely show that race is statistically significant, but may indicate a weaker absolute and relative effect. In this respect, race appears to be playing a reasonably strong role. The findings of this chapter, especially the discussion of the strength of variables, must be viewed in light of these caveats.

EXHIBIT 5-14

TOTAL AND UNIQUE VARIATION DUE TO RACE AND ECONOMICS

A) Dependent Variable = LOG **MU7273**

|  | Reduced Model | Principal Components Model | Maximum Adjusted $R^2$ Model |
|---|---|---|---|
| Total $R^2$ | .80 | .77 | .85 |
| Race Total Effect | .61 | .61 | .61 |
| Economics Total Effect | .57 | .66 | .74 |
| Race Unique Effect | .23 | .11 | .11 |
| Economics Unique Effect | .19 | .16 | .24 |

B) Dependent Variable = LOG **MS7273**

|  | Reduced Model | Principal Components Model | Maximum Adjusted $R^2$ Model |
|---|---|---|---|
| Total $R^2$ | .66 | .66 | .75 |
| Race Total Effect | .65 | .65 | .65 |
| Economics Total Effect | .30 | .46 | .57 |
| Race Unique Effect | .36 | .20 | .18 |
| Economics Unique Effect | .01 | .01 | .10 |

*Source:* Loan data from Federal Home Loan Bank Board of Chicago Survey (1973). See text.

## Appendix 5-A: Additional Data and Analysis

This Appendix refines Chapter Five's regression analysis. It consists of four parts:

Part 1. Checking the distribution and appropriateness of the sample data.

Part 2. Applying regression on principal components.

Part 3. Considering Log-Log models.

Part 4. Evaluating the influence of demand.

CHECKING THE DISTRIBUTION AND APPROPRIATENESS OF THE SAMPLE DATA

The regression model utilized in Chapter Five assumes normality of the loan measures. If this condition is not satisfied, then an inappropriate model has been employed.

Nonnormality generally consists of some extreme values scattered within otherwise acceptable data. If these "extreme" points do not truly belong in the sample, then they should be removed; retaining them can significantly skew results by showing a stronger or weaker relationship than actually exists.

Two scattergrams are used to check the normality assumption. The first is a normal probability plot of the observed residuals and the second is the scattergram of fitted values vs. residuals. (Exhibit 5-12 is the latter scattergram for log MS7172.)

EXHIBIT 5-A-1

MU7172 REDUCED LOG-CLUSTER RESULTS

---

Dependent Variable:    Log MU7172     Mean = 1.47     S = 1.47
Independent Variables: Reduced Regression Equation

Sample     Chicago
Sample Size: 51 (Zip Code Areas)

| Regression Equation | $R^2$ | $Syx$ | $F$ | Significance[1] |
|---|---|---|---|---|
| | .80 | .68 | 46.41 | .001 |
| | | *Partial* | | |
| Independent Variable | b | Correlation | $F$ | Significance[2] |
| INCOME | .033 | .06 | 0.15 | — |
| VACANT | −.019 | −.17 | 1.37 | — |
| OWN | .022 | .45 | 11.80 | .01 |
| WHITE | .025 | .66 | 36.10 | .001 |

[1]Degrees of freedom equal 4 and 46.
[2]Degrees of freedom equal 1 and 46

*Source:* Loan data from Federal Home Loan Bank Board of Chicago Survey (1973). See text.

The scattergrams indicate three potentially troublesome points: zip code areas 60611, 60627 and 60633. Zip code 60611 is a high-rise residential area\*, and 60627 and 60633 are largely industrial locations.

As a final step, a regression equation was considered which incorporated the following modifications: reducing the number of independent variables to four;\*\* expressing the dependent variable in log form; and including data for only the appropriate zip codes. Will the deletion of the three zip codes affect the analysis?

This question was tackled by considering another regression termed the reduced-log-cluster equation. It is similar to the reduced-log form, but examines relationships of a smaller and slightly different sample (three zip code areas removed).

The results of the reduced-log-cluster equation are almost identical to those of the reduced-log form. Exhibit 5-A-1 shows the output for the MU7172 reduced-log-cluster equation, and is almost identical to Exhibit 5-13 (MU7172 reduced-log equation). Both explain 80 percent of MU's variation, and show a mixed behavior pattern—economics as well as race are related to loan volume. Similar relationships exist for the full and reduced (three zip codes out) samples. The results for the other three dependent variables are similar.

---

\*The underwriting criteria employed in Chapter Five make the most sense in lower density neighborhoods.

\*\*The results with four variables are essentially identical to the results with twelve variables because of the collinearity of the economic variables.

REGRESSION ON PRINCIPAL COMPONENTS

Another approach to the problem of multicollinearity (or redundancy) among the economic independent variables is a slightly modified version of the method of regression on principal components. (It is modified in the sense that principal components is applied to the economic independent variables, but not the racial independent variable, whereas principal components is generally applied to all the independent variables.) This method addresses the problem in a purely mathematical, hence "unbiased," way.

EXHIBIT 5-A-2

DERIVATION OF THE PRINCIPAL COMPONENTS

I. Correlations between the factors (indices) and the variables and variance explained by each factor.

|  | Factor 1 | Factor 2 | Factor 3 |
|---|---|---|---|
| CROWD | −.84 | .24 | .34 |
| AGE55 | .62 | −.51 | −.49 |
| PROF | .65 | −.54 | .33 |
| VALUE | .84 | −.05 | .38 |
| AGEHOUS | −.55 | −.49 | −.59 |
| INCOME | .93 | .09 | .12 |
| PERSONU | −.17 | .84 | .14 |
| UNEMPL | −.88 | −.19 | .16 |
| RENT | .79 | −.23 | .22 |
| OWN | .53 | .80 | −.14 |
| VACANT | −.46 | −.23 | .50 |
| SAME65 | .24 | .78 | −.32 |
| Amount of Variance Explained | 5.33 | 2.96 | 1.44 |
| % of Variance explained | 44.4 | 24.6 | 12.0 |

II. Percentage of variance of each variable explained by the three factors together

|  | Variance Explained |
|---|---|
| CROWD | .89 |
| AGE55 | .89 |
| PROF | .82 |
| VALUE | .82 |
| AGEHOUS | .89 |
| INCOME | .89 |
| PERSONU | .75 |
| UNEMPL | .82 |
| RENT | .72 |
| OWN | .93 |
| VACANT | .51 |
| SAME65 | .77 |

Source: Loan data from Federal Home Loan Bank Board of Chicago Survey (1973). See text.

Application of regression on principal components consists of three steps: (1) The method of principal components is applied to the independent variables. This transforms the data into uncorrelated indices (also known as factors) which are linear combinations of the twelve economic independent variables (see Exhibit 5-A-2). The results also guide the determination of the appropriate number of such indices needed to adequately explain the information contained in the variables. (2) Scores are computed on these indices for each of the zip code areas. (3) The economic indices and race (WHITE) are analyzed via regression.

Some type of variable reduction procedure is needed in the analysis because of the high collinearity among the independent variables. As opposed to dropping individual variables for substantive, subjective and/or mathematical considerations (usually based on pairwise correlations or partial correlations, see page 75 ), indices which are based on *all* the economic variables are utilized. These indices are designed to contain most of the information in the variables (in the sense of explaining variance in the economic variables).

There are two ambiguities involved in this method. The first is determining the number of indices to retain. The standard approach, which is followed here, is to keep all factors with eigenvalues greater than 1 (i.e., in this case, explain more than $1/12 = 8$ percent of the total variance of the twelve variables). A second ambiguity concerns the interpretation of the indices that are computed. This latter issue is not of concern here because the analysis does not focus on the economic variables per se but only in controlling for them as efficiently as possible.

A further issue concerns factor rotation. This procedure is usually applied in conjunction with principal components analysis. Rotation is not utilized here for while it modifies the individual factors into a new set of uncorrelated factors, it does not influence the effect of the total group of factors. Consequently, the summary findings in the regression, as R-squared, and the influence of race will not change if the rotation step is omitted.

RESULTS OF THE PRINCIPAL COMPONENTS ANALYSIS

Application of principal components to the twelve economic variables, the full regression case, yields three factors with eigenvalues above 1. The three factors account for 44, 25 and 12 percent of the variance, respectively, for a total of 81 percent. Each variable is well explained by the three factors except, possibly, for VACANT. This finding confirms a fairly high amount of redundancy among the twelve economic variables (see Exhibit 5-A-2).

Scores for each of the zip code areas were computed on each of these three factors. These scores were then used in lieu of the economic variables themselves in the regressions.

Chapter Five indicated that the log form of the loan measures was the appropriate dependent variable. Exhibit 5-A-3 indicates the correlations among the log loan measures, WHITE and the three factors. (While this exhibit shows only the 7273 correlations, the 7172 correlations are similar.) Exhibit 5-A-4 shows the results of the regression on WHITE and the factors. *WHITE is significant at the .001 level.* Controlling for the economic influences in factor form does *not* detract from the statistical importance of race.

Residual plots indicate that no further transformations appear necessary.

EXHIBIT 5-A-3

CORRELATIONS BETWEEN LOAN VARIABLES, FACTORS AND WHITE

|  | Log MU7273 | Log MS7273 | Factor 1 | Factor 2 | Factor 3 | White |
|---|---|---|---|---|---|---|
| Log MU7273 | 1.00 | .88 | .21 | .64 | .46 | .78 |
| Log MS7273 | .88 | 1.00 | .27 | .23 | .58 | .81 |
| Factor 1 | .21 | .27 | 1.00 | .00 | .00 | .29 |
| Factor 2 | .64 | .23 | .00 | 1.00 | .00 | .33 |
| Factor 3 | .46 | .58 | .00 | .00 | 1.00 | .64 |
| White | .78 | .81 | .29 | .33 | .64 | 1.00 |

*Source:* Loan data from Federal Home Bank Board of Chicago Survey (1973). See text.

EXHIBIT 5-A-4

REGRESSIONS ON PRINCIPAL COMPONENTS

Dependent Variable: Log MU7273
$S_{yx}$ = .73
$R^2$ = .77

| Independent Variables | b | Partial Correlation | F | Significance |
|---|---|---|---|---|
| White | .024 | .57 | 23.56 | .001 |
| Factor 1 | .096 | .12 | .76 | — |
| Factor 2 | .682 | .65 | 36.35 | .001 |
| Factor 3 | .197 | .19 | 1.93 | — |

Dependent Variable: Log MS7273
$S_{yx}$ = .71
$R^2$ = .66

| Independent Variables | b | Partial Correlation | F | Significance |
|---|---|---|---|---|
| White | .025 | .61 | 28.55 | .001 |
| Factor 1 | .078 | .10 | .54 | — |
| Factor 2 | −.004 | .01 | .01 | — |
| Factor 3 | .155 | .16 | 1.26 | — |

*Source:* Loan data from Federal Home Loan Bank Board of Chicago Survey (1973). See text.

LOG-LOG MODELS

A further check on the adequacy of the models and the viability of the corresponding conclusions was performed by using logs of the independent variables in the regressions.

Economic variables are sometimes asymmetric, a condition that may lead to nonsensical or spurious results in regressions. The asymmetric trait generally associated with variables of this type is addressed by log or similar transformations.

The models used in this check involve the thirteen basic independent variables (race [WHITE] and the twelve economic variables) and the dependent variables, Log MU7273 and Log MS7273. The first model logs only the dependent variables, e.g., MU7273, MS7273 (see Exhibits 5-A-5). The second logs the dependent variables and three economic independent variables (VALUE, INCOME, and RENT). The remaining economic variables are left untouched since the value, income and rent indicators are more prone to the asymmetric problem (see Exhibit 5-A-6). The third regression is on the logs of all independent variables (see Exhibit 5-A-7).

*The three sets of regressions are almost identical.* To illustrate, in the log MU7273 regressions, $R^2$ ranges from .82 to .85 and the F-statistics for the regression and for the racial variable (WHITE) are all significant at the .001 level. Finally, the partial correlations for race (WHITE) of .55, .57 and .59 indicate that race is a reasonably strong predictor of loans when economic variables are controlled. For log MS7273, $R^2$ ranges from .71 to .76, the F-statistics for the regression are all significant at the .001 level as are the F-statistics for WHITE. The partial correlations for WHITE of .58, .60, .61 are also reasonably strong in the MS7273 regressions. (The residual plots in all three cases appear satisfactory so that no further transformations of the predictor variables are necessary.) These findings are similar to those in Chapter Five. The analysis in this chapter therefore does not appear to depend on a particular handling or transformation of the race or control variables.

THE INFLUENCE OF DEMAND

Chapter Five discussed loan *selection* criteria and how these variables could influence loan distribution by zip code area. Inter-area loan demand is another possible determinant; mortgage volume can be expected to be higher in neighborhoods with high loan demand, and conversely, areas with low demand should have a lesser loan volume. Can the variations in the Chicago area loan volume (MU7172, MU7273, MS7172, MS7273) be explained by differentiations in demand?

The optimal approach for measuring demand would be to compute actual requests for either conventional or private financing. Such data are not

## EXHIBIT 5-A-5

## LOG MU7273 AND LOG MS7273 FULL REGRESSION EQUATION RESULTS

**Dependent Variable:** Log MU7273, Mean = 1.55, S = 1.47

**Independent Variables:** Full Regression Equation
**Sample:** Chicago
**Sample Size:** 54 (Zip Code Areas)

| Regression Equation | $R^2$ | $S_{YX}$ | F | Significance[1] |
|---|---|---|---|---|
| | .85 | .65 | 17.78 | .001 |

| Independent Variable | b | Partial Correlation | F | Significance[2] |
|---|---|---|---|---|
| UNEMPL | −.47 | −.40 | 7.54 | .01 |
| VACANT | −.16 | −.30 | 4.08 | .05 |
| PERSONU | −.21 | −.27 | 3.14 | — |
| VALUE | −.08 | −.08 | .23 | — |
| SAME65 | .01 | .01 | .00 | — |
| RENT | .03 | .04 | .08 | — |
| AGE55 | −.11 | −.18 | 1.45 | — |
| AGEHOUS | .19 | .22 | 2.06 | — |
| OWN | .66 | .44 | 9.60 | .01 |
| INCOME | −.30 | −.22 | 2.10 | — |
| PROF | .26 | .30 | 4.04 | — |
| CROWD | .40 | .33 | 4.77 | .05 |
| WHITE | .56 | .57 | 19.53 | .001 |

**Dependent Variable:** Log MS7273, Mean = 2.48, S = 1.17

**Independent Variables:** Full Regression Equation
**Sample:** Chicago
**Sample Size:** 54 (Zip Code Areas)

| Regression Equation | $R^2$ | $S_{YX}$ | F | Significance[1] |
|---|---|---|---|---|
| | .76 | .66 | 9.77 | .001 |

| Independent Variable | b | Partial Correlation | F | Significance[2] |
|---|---|---|---|---|
| UNEMPL | −.47 | −.32 | 4.66 | .05 |
| VACANT | −.18 | −.27 | 3.11 | — |
| PERSONU | −.33 | −.33 | 4.78 | .05 |
| VALUE | −.03 | −.02 | .01 | — |
| SAME65 | −.02 | −.02 | .01 | — |
| RENT | −.09 | .09 | .33 | — |
| AGE55 | −.10 | −.08 | .24 | — |
| AGEHOUS | .17 | .16 | 1.09 | — |
| OWN | .30 | .17 | 1.19 | — |
| INCOME | −.31 | −.18 | 1.39 | — |
| PROF | .35 | .32 | 4.54 | .05 |
| CROWD | .55 | .35 | 5.53 | .05 |
| WHITE | .79 | .61 | 23.43 | .001 |

1. Degrees of freedom equal 13 and 40.
2. Degrees of freedom equal 1 and 40.

*Source:* Loan data from Federal Home Loan Bank Board of Chicago Survey (1973). See text.

## EXHIBIT 5-A-6

## LOG MU7273 AND MS7273 REGRESSIONS WITH LOGS OF SPECIFIED ECONOMIC VARIABLES

**Dependent Variable: Log MU7273**
 Syx = .67
 F = 16.53   Significance[1] = .001
 R² = .84

| Independent Variable | b | Partial Correlation | F | Significance[2] |
|---|---|---|---|---|
| UNEMPL | −.50 | −.38 | 6.84 | .05 |
| VACANT | −.15 | −.28 | 3.43 | — |
| PERSONU | −.21 | −.26 | 2.91 | — |
| LOG VALUE | −.06 | −.06 | .15 | — |
| SAME 65 | .01 | .01 | .01 | — |
| LOG RENT | −.00 | −.00 | .00 | — |
| AGE 55 | −.14 | −.13 | .69 | — |
| AGE HOUS | .22 | .25 | 2.77 | — |
| OWN | .68 | .42 | 8.80 | .01 |
| LOG INCOME | −.33 | −.21 | 1.86 | — |
| PROF | .25 | .29 | 3.27 | — |
| CROWD | .35 | .27 | 3.27 | — |
| WHITE | .57 | .55 | 17.64 | .001 |

**Dependent Variable: Log MS7273**
 Syx = .67
 F = 9.35   Significance[1] = .001
 R² = .75

| Independent Variable | b | Partial Correlation | F | Significance[2] |
|---|---|---|---|---|
| UNEMPL | −.49 | −.31 | 4.25 | .05 |
| VACANT | −.18 | −.26 | 2.83 | — |
| PERSONU | −.33 | −.32 | 4.68 | .05 |
| LOG VALUE | −.01 | −.01 | .00 | — |
| SAME65 | −.01 | −.01 | .00 | — |
| LOG RENT | .06 | .05 | .11 | — |
| AGE55 | −.14 | −.11 | .45 | — |
| AGEHOUS | .21 | .19 | 1.51 | — |
| OWN | .30 | .16 | 1.08 | — |
| LOG INCOME | −.31 | −.16 | 1.07 | — |
| PROF | .35 | .32 | 4.47 | .05 |
| CROWD | .51 | .31 | 4.38 | .05 |
| WHITE | .79 | .60 | 21.97 | .001 |

1. Degrees of freedom equal 13 and 40.
2. Degrees of freedom equal 1 and 40.

*Source:* Loan data from Federal Home Loan Bank Board of Chicago Survey (1973). See text.

EXHIBITS 5-A-7

## LOG MU7273 AND LOG MS7273 REGRESSIONS WITH LOGS OF ALL ECONOMIC VARIABLES

**Dependent Variable: Log MU7273**
  Syx =    .72
  F    = 14.03  Significance[1] = .001
  R² =    .82

| Independent Variable | b | Partial Correlation | F | Significance[2] |
|---|---|---|---|---|
| Log UNEMPL | −.02 | −.02 | .01 | — |
| Log VACANT | −.02 | −.02 | .02 | — |
| Log PERSONU | −.18 | −.19 | 1.51 | — |
| Log VALUE | .24 | .20 | 1.64 | — |
| Log SAME65 | .37 | .39 | 7.04 | .05 |
| Log RENT | −.06 | −.07 | .19 | — |
| Log AGE 55 | −.09 | −.09 | .33 | — |
| Log AGE HOUS | .05 | .06 | .16 | — |
| Log OWN | .34 | .27 | 3.23 | — |
| Log INCOME | −.18 | −.11 | .52 | — |
| Log PROF | .03 | .04 | .06 | — |
| Log CROWD | −.10 | −.08 | .24 | — |
| Log WHITE | .62 | .59 | 20.90 | .001 |

**Dependent Variable: Log MS7273**
  Syx =    .72
  F    = 7.49  Significance[1] = .001
  R² =    .71

| Independent Variable | b | Partial Correlation | F | Significance[2] |
|---|---|---|---|---|
| Log UNEMPL | −.07 | −.04 | .07 | — |
| Log VACANT | −.03 | −.03 | .05 | — |
| Log PERSONU | −.18 | −.15 | .96 | — |
| Log VALUE | .29 | .19 | 1.47 | — |
| Log SAME65 | .39 | .34 | 5.06 | .05 |
| Log RENT | −.10 | −.09 | .31 | — |
| Log AGE 55 | −.04 | −.03 | .03 | — |
| Log AGE HOUS | .06 | .06 | .13 | — |
| Log OWN | −.17 | −.11 | .51 | — |
| Log INCOME | −.27 | −.14 | −.77 | — |
| Log PROF | .01 | .01 | .01 | — |
| Log CROWD | −.15 | −.10 | .37 | — |
| Log WHITE | .79 | .58 | 20.74 | .001 |

1. Degrees of freedom equal 13 and 40.
2. Degrees of freedom equal 1 and 40.

*Source:* Loan data from Federal Home Loan Bank Board of Chicago Survey (1973). See text.

available in Chicago or most other communities. (Recent disclosure regulations in California and other jurisdictions yield some information on loan demand.)

The next best strategy is to consider housing turnover as indicated by transfers in title. This computation is particularly difficult in Chicago, however, given its cumbersome county title record. Even with a better title system, it would be extremely laborious to calculate turnovers on a zip code area from the county record which shows transfers on a parcel by parcel basis.

Rather than abandoning the evaluation of demand because of data inadequacies, this study decided to pursue an analysis with information available from the 1970 Census, Fifth Count. The following three variables are rough proxies of loan demand:

1. *SAME 65*—the percent of area residents living in same unit in 1965.
2. *YRBLT*—the percentage of units constructed 1965-1970. (The Census lists various years—1965-1970, 1960-1964, 1950-1959—but the percentage constructed in the latest cohort [1965 to 1970] is employed here.)
3. *YRMOVE*—the percentage of residents who moved into their unit 1968 to 1970. (The Census lists various years, but this analysis uses the percentage who moved in the latest cohort—1968 to 1970.)

All three variables can serve as rough indicators of demand; the lower SAME65, the higher YRBLT, and the higher YRMOVE, most likely the greater the demand for loans. Low SAME65 reveals less turnover, higher YRBLT indicates greater new construction, and high YRMOVE reflects higher turnover. Can these demand proxies help explain variations in loan volume by Chicago neighborhoods?

To answer this question, a correlation matrix between the four loan volume indicators (log MS7172, log MS7273, log MU7172, log MU7273) and SAME65, YRBLT and YRMOVE was computed. The results are in Exhibit 5-A-8.

SAME65* has a significant (at the .05 level) correlation with all four loan measures while YRMOVE is significantly correlated with both MU variables. (The rest of the correlations are not significant.) SAME65 and YRMOVE are thus potentially important in explaining loan volume. But do they add any information not contained in the economic variables already considered?

At minimum, SAME65 and YRMOVE should be examined controlling for INCOME, VACANT and OWN. (The latter three indicators were used in the reduced regression equation.) When this

---

*While SAME65 has already been considered as one of twelve economic control variables (see Exhibit 5-4), it is considered in more detail in this section.

EXHIBIT 5-A-8

CORRELATIONS BETWEEN DEMAND AND LOAN VARIABLES[2]

|         | MU7172 | MS7172 | MU7273 | MS7273 |
|---------|--------|--------|--------|--------|
| SAME65  | .58[1] | .29[1] | .61[1] | .29[1] |
| YRBLT   | .07    | .21    | .07    | .21    |
| YRMOVE  | −.55[1]| −.24   | −.57[1]| −.22   |

[1]Significant at the .05 level, 2-tailed test
[2]All the loan variables are in log form.

*Source:* Loan data from Federal Home Loan Bank Board of Chicago Survey (1973). See text.

minimal set is controlled, none of the twelve partial correlations (3 demand variables by 4 dependent loan variables) is significant at the .05 level (or even the .10 level). In other words, demand (at least rough proxies of demand) are either poor predictors of loans granted or are collinear with economic variables. In either case, demand is not a strong independent influence on loans granted.

One surprising finding of this section is the fact that YRMOVE is negatively correlated with loan volume while logic would suggest a positive correlation.

The following factor may explain this negative correlation. Higher turnover in Chicago neighborhoods is often found in black areas. YRMOVE is negatively correlated with WHITE (−.45). MU and MS are negatively correlated with YRMOVE for YRMOVE is partially and incidentally a racial variable and lenders are avoiding black neighborhoods—the very areas with the highest YRMOVE values. The finding that YRMOVE is negatively correlated with MU-MS (albeit it is not always significant or important from a correlation standpoint) further suggests the finding that race influences underwriting.

## Notes

1. Illinois Legislative Investigating Commission, *Redlining-Discrimination in Residential Mortgage Loans* (Chicago: Legislative Investigating Commission, 1975), pp. 12-13.

2. *Ibid.,* p. 4.

3. *Ibid.*

4. *Ibid.,* p. 15.

5. *Ibid.,* pp. 15-16.

6. U.S. Postal Service, *ZIP Code Geographic Guide* (Washington, D.C.: Government Printing Office, 1976), p. 61.

7. Ron Abler, "ZIP-Code Areas as Statistical Regions," *The Professional Geographer,* Vol. 22, No. 5 (September 1970), p. 273.

8. *Ibid.*

9. *Ibid.*

10. *Ibid.,* p. 270.

11. See Abler, "ZIP-Code Areas as Statistical Regions."

12. U.S. Department of Commerce, Social and Economic Statistics Administration, "Data Access Descriptions - 1970, Census Fifth Count for Zip Codes, Counties and Smaller Areas," *DAD* No. 36 (Washington, D.C.: Government Printing Office, 1974), p. 1.

# Micro Data Analysis

## Introduction

Chapter Five examined macro data (areal loan, racial and economic information) and discovered a racial influence. But underwriting considers a further dimension, the economic strength of the mortgage applicant (e.g..income, assets, job history, etc.). This chapter analyzes this dimension, considering micro data (socio economic characteristics of mortgage loan applicants and disposition of loan requests) to test if race is a statistically significant criteria in evaluating loan requests. It utilizes survey results made available from the Comptroller of the Currency. The chapter first evaluates this information source and transforms it to a form most suitable for analysis. The discussion then considers and applies a number of statistical tests to examine the importance of race. The analysis considers whether race is a statistically significant variable after controlling for an applicant's economic profile. It concludes that race is a significant, independent influence.

## Data Base

The Comptroller of the Currency Survey C is part of the larger Fair Housing Lending Practices Pilot Project initiated by the federal financial regulatory agencies. Survey C began in November 1974 and finished six months later.[1] One hundred and fifty-two financial institutions (both thrift and non-thrift) in six disparate SMSAs (Bridgeport, Connecticut; Cleveland, Ohio; Memphis, Tennessee; Montgomery, Alabama; Topeka, Kansas; and Tucson, Arizona) were asked to participate. Each received copies of the Survey C form and instructions on how to complete the questionnaire. (The Survey C Equal Housing Lender Form is summarized in Exhibit 6-1.)[2] The survey instrument was designed to collect detailed information on the loan applicant, the property to be mortgaged (hereafter called subject property), and the disposition of each applicant.

During the survey period, participating lending institutions completed the survey forms in response to all inquiries about, or requests for, housing loans.[3] These forms were to be completed with respect to secured loans (conventional and FHA/VA) for purchasing a dwelling (including a condominium or cooperative). Specifically excluded were home improvement, repair, and maintenance loans, and second mortgages.

While the institutions were required to submit the form, individual applicants were requested, but not required, to fill it out.[4] Applicants could decline to complete part or all of the form. In this event, the interviewing (loan) officer was to complete the form for the applicant using his or her (the officer's) best judgement and whatever information was available from the institution's files. Certain questions (e.g., applicant's race and sex) typically could be completed by the loan officer while others would present greater difficulties.

During the six-month period of the survey, approximately 18,000 forms were returned to the Comptroller of the Currency. However, only about 12,700 of these were completed properly, fully and legibly, and hence were usable.

Survey C indicated that nonwhites were denied loans far more frequently than whites; 23 percent of the nonwhite applicants were rejected compared to 15 percent for whites. This nonwhite-white differentiation raises the question of *why* this occurs—are nonwhites denied because of their race or because of their weaker economic position?

## SURVEY C: DATA ADVANTAGES AND DISADVANTAGES

Exhibit 6-1 shows the data solicited by the Comptroller. There is substantial financial, social, and racial information on the applicant (race, income, work history, debt, assets), but less on the property to be mortgaged (purchase price, owner occupied or not).

The Survey C data that was released do not reveal zip code or Census tract location and hence areal characteristics cannot be examined. There are other defects. While lending institutions were asked to submit a form for prescribed credit applications, their compliance was not monitored by the Comptroller. Additionally, the instructions for filling out the forms were

EXHIBIT 6-1

INDEPENDENT RACIAL AND ECONOMIC VARIABLES:
EXPLANATION AND EXPECTED/ACTUAL RELATIONSHIPS

| Type of Data | Individual Variables as shown on Comptroller Form | Recoded Individual Variables | Explanation | Expected relationship with Loan Disposition if Racial Effect is not Present | |
|---|---|---|---|---|---|
| Lender Data | 1. Lender Name | INST - Thrift vs. non-thrift | Type of financial institution | Not applicable (NA) | NA |
| Regional Data | 2. Standard Metropolitan Statistical Area where the lender is located | SMSA - NE vs. other | Regional location | Not applicable | NA |
| Disposition | 3. Loan application disposition (approved or denied) | DISP - Accept (A) or reject (B) | Self explanatory | Not applicable | NA |
| | 4. Applicant race: Asian, Black, White, Spanish Descent, American Indian, Other | ETH - Nonwhite (NW) or white (E) | Self explanatory | No relationship | Positive with white, negative with nonwhite |
| | 5. Applicant sex: male or female | SEX - Male (A) or female (B) | Self explanatory | No relationship | Positive with male (see Text) |
| Applicant Racial and Economic Characteristics | 6. Applicant marital status: married, single, divorced, or widowed | MAR - Married (B) or not currently married (ACD) | Self explanatory | No relationship | Positive with married |
| | 7. Applicant gross annual income | INCO - Low (A $0-10,000, Moderate (B $10-15,000) High (DE $15,000+) | Wealth of applicant; Ability to afford home | Positive relationship | Positive |
| | 8. Applicant employment history | YEA - Marginal (AB 0-1 yrs) Light (1-5 yrs) Extensive (5+) | "stability"; future likelihood to afford home | Positive relationship | Positive with longer YEA |
| | 9. Spouse's employment history (Number of yrs. at present occupation) | YES - Same as for YEA | Same as for YEA | Positive relationship | No relationship |

(cont'd)

## EXHIBIT 6-1 (cont'd)

| | | | | |
|---|---|---|---|---|
| **Applicant and Economic** | 10. Applicant outstanding debt | DEBT - Low (A $0-5,000), Moderate (BC $5-20,000), High (DE $20,000+) | Added financial obligations to homeownership | Positive relationship | Positive |
| | 11. Applicant monthly debt payment | DBPY - Low (A $0-100 monthly) Moderate (BCD $100-$500 mo.) High (EF over $500 mo.) | See DEBT | Negative relationship (see Text) | Negative |
| | 12. Applicant assets etc. | ASSET - Low (AB $0-$10,000) Moderate (CDF $10-$60,000) High ($60,000+) | Wealth, ability to save, margin for future payment | Positive relationship | Positive |
| **Loan Data** | 13. Amount of loan requested | AMT - Low (ABCD $0-$15,000) Moderate (E $15-$25,000) High (F $25-35,000) Very High (GHIJ $35,000+) | LVR can be derived to show borrower's equity and lender's exposure | Negative relationship | Negative |
| **Property/ Neighborhood Data** | 14. Purchase price of subject property | PURPR - Low (ABC $10-$20,000). Moderate (D $20-$30,000). High (E $30-$50,000). Very High (FG $50,000) | Quality amenity, and market of mortgage property | Positive relationship | Positive |
| **Property Data** | 15. Will subject property be owner occupied (Yes or No) | OO - Owner occupied (A). not owner occupied (B) | Objective or purchase, homeownership versus investment | Positive relationship (with owner occupied) | No relationship |
| **Relative Economic Data** | | BURDEN - High (A greater than 7 times income) Low (Less than 7 times income) | Burden of paying for house | Negative relationship | Negative |
| | | LVR - High (A 0-100% LVR) Moderate (B 70-90% LVR) Low (below 70% LVR) | Amount of down payment (inverse of LVR) and lender exposure | Negative relationship | Negative |

*Source:* Comptroller of the Currency, *Fair Housing Lending Practices Pilot Project Survey C Approach* (Washington, D.C.: Comptroller of the Currency, July 1975).

not always followed. Some loan officers decided on their own such procedures as to how assets should be calculated (gross or net) and whether or not outstanding debt includes the mortgage being considered. Finally, many forms had blank, invalid, or inconsistent information. The N/A (non-applicable) response for loan dispositon (appropriate for pending loan decisions) was used inconsistently.

The Comptroller of the Currency carefully checked the forms it received. Forms were eliminated if many answers were blank or if the answers were inconsistent, questionable (loan amount higher than purchase price, for example), or illegible. This careful editing led the Comptroller to drop over 5,500 forms or about 30 percent of those received; approximately 12,700 forms were deemed usable for analysis.

The administrative defects of Survey C added to the fact that areal data are not available detracts from the definitive character of the data source. It is used here, however, for the sample, conceptual and analytic reasons explained in Chapter Four. Survey C is a large mortgage data sample, encompassing six SMSAs. Its comprehensive coverage of different regions and types of cities (i.e., older Northeast central city and newer Sunbelt locations) is virtually unique and minimizes the risk of bias. Survey C does not suffer from questions of standardization and demand "noise." It does not list loan volume (which raises loan demand and loan standardization questions), but rather loan acceptance and rejection rates.

Survey C shows detailed loan applicant data such as income, assets, debt payments, job records, etc. It allows probing for the significance of race and economics of specific applicants and thus complements the neighborhood analysis of Chapter Five.

*Categorizing and Refining the Survey C Data.* The original Survey C data were categorized into different nominal (male versus female, for example) and ordinal categories (i.e., income categories: $0-$5,000; $5,001-$10,000; $10,001-$15,000; $15,001-$25,000; and over $25,000. See Exhibit 6-1). To simplify the analysis and to make the data categories more meaningful, the numerous ordinal distinctions were grouped into larger classification categories shown in Exhibit 6-1 (Column 3). Recoding was based on several factors:

° *Discussions with lenders.* Lenders, given the available data, were asked to isolate significant thresholds or "break-points." To illustrate, lenders suggested that three logical categories of employment history might be "light" (applicant employed up to one year), "moderate" (employed one to five years), and "extensive" (employed five years or more).

° *Logical group agglomerations.* Some examples include combining the five nonwhite categories (Black*, Spanish descent, American Indian, Asian

*Blacks comprise roughly one-half of the nonwhite group.

and others) into one group (nonwhite) and combining the presently unmarried subcategories (single, divorced, and widowed).

° *Size considerations.* Wherever logic permitted, subcategories were defined with a sensitivity to their size—they should not be very large or very small relative to the other groups.*

*Creating Relative Economic Variables.* While recoding the Survey C information makes it more processable, the Comptroller data, in its present form, suffer from being absolute; they refer to the absolute dollars of income, debt, assets, etc. Relative relationships are in many instances more revealing (see Chapter Two) — how does income compare to housing loan expenditure (housing expenditure-to-income ratio); how large is the mortgage compared to the home's purchase price (LVR)?

Fortunately, the Comptroller's raw data lends itself to formulating ratios. For instance, a housing expense-to-income ratio can be computed from the Comptroller's informaton on applicant loan amount**and annual income. Loan amount can be converted to an annual dollar cost for principal and interest by assuming a loan term and interest rate.   Dividing this annual expenditure by annual income yields the housing expenditure-to-income ratios (coded BURDEN). Since many different BURDENs are derived (one for each matched income and loan amount converted to annual cost), the last step was to group the many BURDENs into different, broader BURDEN categories. Two***housing expense-to-income or BURDEN groups were formed: high and low.

Six other relative economic groups were formed in the same way. All are listed and explained below but only two of them were retained for analysis for reasons that will shortly be described. (see page 113)

*Intercorrelation of Absolute and Relative Economic Variables* The relative economic variables, while important, suffer from two shortcomings. First, they are rough approximations, for exact data are lacking on all the variables used to create the different ratios. Converting mortgage amounts to annual cost figures, for example, requires assumptions concerning exact loan size (e.g., the midpoints of the different loan amount intervals—

---

*Attention to size is especially important when data are analyzed via chi-square analysis, for this technique cannot readily be used if there are few cases in each variable subcategory.

**Since the loan amounts were shown on a cohort basis ($25,000 to $35,000; $35,000 to $45,000, etc.), loan amount midpoints were used ($30,000 and $40,000 in the two cases cited above) to compute annual costs.

***These groups were formed taking into consideration the same factors as those used in recoding the basic Comptroller data.

## PRELIMINARY LIST OF RELATIVE ECOMONIC VARIABLES

| Variable | Code | Description |
|---|---|---|
| Loan-to-value ratio | LVR | The size of the loan compared to the purchase price; the higher the LVR, the greater the underwriting risk. |
| Burden of "carrying mortgage | BURDEN | The required annual mortgage payment compared to annual income; the higher the burden, the greater the underwriting risk. |
| Mortgage-to-debt ratio | MGTDR | The size of the mortgage compared to the size of the existing debt; the higher the MGTDR, the greater the underwriting risk. |
| Mortgage payment-to-debt payment burden | MPDP | The size of the mortgage payments, compared to the existing debt payments; the higher the MPDP, the greater the underwriting risk. |
| Income-to-purchase price ratio | IPPR | The relationship of annual income to the total purchase price; the higher the IPPR, the lower the underwriting risk. |
| Reserves-to-commitment ratio | RCR | Relationship of assets to the home purchase price; the higher the RCR, the lower the underwriting risk. |
| Existing debt burden | EXDB | Relationship of existing debt payments to existing income; the higher the EXDB, the greater the underwriting risk. |

$30,000 for the $25,000 to $35,000 group, for example), and loan term and interest rate. Secondly, there is the question of intercorrelation; since the relative variables are based on the Comptroller's absolute data, it would not be surprising if a high intercorrelation existed between many relative and absolute variables. Given an overlap between the absolute and relative variables, the absolute variables would be chosen for they are more exact.

To check the overlap, an intercorrelation matrix of the absolute and relative economic variables (see Exhibit 6-2) was constructed. Of the seven relative variables, all, with the exception of LVR and BURDEN, are highly intercorrelated with the absolute economic variables.* Some examples: there is a .99 gamma between MGTDR and DEBT, a .85 gamma between MPDP and DEBT, a −.84 gamma between IPPR and PURPR, a −.94 gamma between RCR and ASSET, and a .99 gamma between EXDB and DBPY. Given these high interrelationships, very little would be gained from adding MGTDR, MPDP, IPPR, RCR, and EXDB. LVR and BURDEN are retained, however; not only are the two net additions (their intercorrelations with the absolute Comptroller variables are lower), but they are key underwriting considerations. LVR indicates lender exposure/borrower equity, while BURDEN shows the borrower's ability to support the loan indenture on the subject property.

*The measure of relationship or correlation used is gamma.

EXHIBIT 6-2

INTERCORRELATION MATRIX OF ABSOLUTE AND RELATIVE ECONOMIC
VARIABLES[1]

| ABSOLUTE ECONOMIC VARIABLES | RELATIVE ECONOMIC VARIABLES | | | | | | |
|---|---|---|---|---|---|---|---|
| | LVR | BURDEN | MGTDR | MPDP | IPPR | RCR | EXDB |
| INCO | −.07 | −.72 | −.03 | .02 | .32 | .26 | −.08 |
| YEA | −.12 | −.12 | .21 | .16 | .03 | .35 | .15 |
| YES | −.02 | −.38 | −.06 | −.03 | .27 | −.01 | −.12 |
| DEBT | .00 | −.08 | .99 | .85 | .10 | .69 | .89 |
| DBPY | .14 | −.11 | .74 | .95 | .23 | .47 | .99 |
| ASSET | −.21 | −.07 | .37 | .21 | .14 | −.94 | −.26 |
| AMT | .54 | .49 | −.34 | −.33 | −.61 | −.10 | .03 |
| PURPR | −.30 | .28 | −.19 | −.26 | −.84 | .00 | .02 |
| OO | .01 | .52 | .74 | .64 | .73 | .84 | .50 |

[1]The measure of correlation used is gamma.

Source: Comptroller of the Currency, Fair Housing Lending Practices Pilot Project Survey C Approach (Washington, D.C.: Comptroller of the Currency, July 1975).

Exhibit 6-1 summarizes the Comptroller of the Currency information as used by the analysis. It includes unrefined nominal Comptroller data (i.e., male versus female), recoded survey information (i.e., nonwhite versus white), and the LVR and BURDEN relative economic variables.

## Data Analysis Strategy

The null hypothesis that race does not play a role in urban loan underwriting is tested via chi square analysis.

The Comptroller of the Currency survey clearly shows that nonwhite applicants are rejected more frequently than white applicants (nonwhites are rejected 23 percent of the time compared to 15 percent for whites. See Exhibit 6-3). If chi square analysis shows that this difference is still significant after controlling for economic characteristics (personal and property), the null hypothesis is rejected. This outcome would support the eco-race model.

The null hypothesis is examined in a four-step procedure which separates racial versus economic factors to see whether or not race is still influential.

Step 1. The success of nonwhites versus whites in obtaining mortgages is examined to see whether nonwhites are in fact receiving significantly fewer mortgages. Step 1 is termed the social mortgage variation analysis.

Step 2. The fact that nonwhites are obtaining fewer mortgages may be due to economic reasons. To analyze this possibility, the economic factors associated with loan acceptance or rejection are examined. Step 2 is termed the economic mortgage variation analysis.

*Step 3.* How do whites versus nonwhites fare with respect to the economic variables isolated in Step 2? Step 3 analyzes the economic status of nonwhites versus whites. It is called the social group economic status analysis.

*Step 4.* Can the economic distinctions between whites versus nonwhites explain the variation in their loan acceptance-rejection rates? Controlling for differences in their economic status, Step 4 examines loan acceptance of nonwhites versus whites. It is called here the economic legitimacy of rejection analysis.

Step 1 sets the stage for the analysis by considering whether minorities are at a disadvantage in securing a loan. The wide disparities in the Comptroller's white versus nonwhite loan acceptance rates strongly suggest statistical significance. What accounts for the difference? Is the black-white variation due to economics or race? Step 2 examines how whites versus blacks fare according to the identified important economic loan variables. Finally, Step 4 evaluates whether the key white versus nonwhite economic status differences can explain the variation in the white versus nonwhite loan acceptance rate.

## Step 1—Social Mortgage Variation Analysis

Exhibit 6-3 shows that nonwhite loan applicants are rejected over 50 percent more frequently than whites; the former are denied loans 23 percent of the time as compared to 15 percent for the latter. The difference in frequencies yields a chi-square value of 65.6 which is significant at the .001 level.

More important is the level of association between disposition (DISP) and race (ETH). Exhibit 6-4 shows a gamma of .27 between these two variables.[5] At first glance this seems insignificant—gammas at the .2 to .3 level are not considered strong. On a relative basis, though, .27 is quite high, compared to the association of other variables.

The significance of the .27 value is highlighted in Exhibit 6-4 which shows the simple intercorrelation among all variables considered by this study. Gamma is the measure of correlation used. The low correlations of all the variables with DISP are immediately evident; most gammas (with DISP) are at the .1 to .2 level—barely meaningful. (The correlations of all the variables with loan disposition [DISP] are highlighted in column 1.) This weakness may be due to a number of factors. No one characteristic in fact may exert a very large influence on DISP. And, since areal effects are not measured, a whole influential dimension is not entering the analysis. "Noise" from poor survey administration also may affect the results.

Race's (ETH) .27 correlation with DISP is the highest simple correlation. It is at least 50 percent larger than the gamma of any other variable with DISP. Besides race (ETH), INCO (.17 correlation), ASSET (.14 cor-

EXHIBIT 6-3

## SOCIAL GROUP LOAN VARIATION BY RACE, MARITAL STATUS AND SEX[1]

*1) Disposition (DISP) by Race (ETH)*

|  |  | DISP | | |
|---|---|---|---|---|
|  |  | Accept | Reject |  |
| ETH | White | 9618 (85.3%) | 1653 (14.7%) | 11271 |
|  | Nonwhite | 1088 (77.0%) | 325 (23.0%) | 1413 |
|  |  | 10706 | 1978 | 12684 |

*II) Disposition (DISP) by Marital Status (MAR)*

|  |  | DISP | | |
|---|---|---|---|---|
|  |  | Accept | Reject |  |
| MAR | Married | 9187 (84.8%) | 1652 (15.2%) | 10839 |
|  | Not Married | 1500 (82.1%) | 326 (17.9%) | 1826 |
|  |  | 10687 | 1978 | 12665 |

*III) Disposition (DISP) by Sex of Applicant (SEX)*

|  |  | DISP | | |
|---|---|---|---|---|
|  |  | Accept | Reject |  |
| SEX | Female | 1462 (83.0%) | 299 (17.0%) | 1761 |
|  | Male | 9236 (84.6%) | 1680 (15.4%) | 10916 |
|  |  | 10698 | 1979 | 12677 |

[1] Row percentages are indicated.

*Source*: Comptroller of the Currency, *Fair Housing Lending Practices Pilot Project Survey C Approach* (Washington, D.C.: Comptroller of the Currency, July 1975).

relation), and BURDEN (.12 correlation) have reasonably strong correlations with loan disposition. Nonwhites seem clearly to be at a disadvantage in terms of obtaining a mortgage. (This differentiation may be due to economic variations, an influence examined later.)

Is it *race*, however, that distinguishes the nonwhite loan applicant? A significantly higher share of nonwhite loan applicants are currently unmarried and a significantly higher share of nonwhite loan applicants are female. Since both currently unmarried (single, divorced, widowed) and female loan applicants are rejected more frequently than their married, male counterparts (see Exhibit 6-3), it is possible that the higher failure rate of nonwhites is a reflection of their marital status and sex profile.[6]

Appendix 6-A considers these interrelationships. It concludes that despite the confounding of racial, social, and marital relationships, race can still be distinguished as a separate effect.

## Step 2—Economic Mortgage Variation Analysis

Is the minority financing shortfall due to race or economic status? To answer this question, the economic variables associated with loan acceptance or rejection must first be analyzed.

Empirical analysis of the Comptroller data reveals that successful loan applicants have stronger economic backgrounds and/or are seeking loans that pose less exposure for the lender. Individual variables are explained below.

1. *Income (INCO) has the highest association with DISP.* Few high or middle income individuals have problems in obtaining financing. Exhibit 6-5 shows that 86 percent of high income loan applicants, 83 percent of middle income applicants, and 77 percent of low income applicants receive mortgages. These differences are significant and there is a gamma of .17 between DISP and INCO. Income is important for it represents the primary source of loan repayment. It also is associated with other positive traits (i.e., stability, "seriousness", ability to accumulate assets, etc.).

2. *Assets (ASSET) are positively associated with loan disposition.* High asset applicants are more successful in securing credit (see Exhibit 6-5). After INCO, ASSET has the highest correlation (gamma = .14) with DISP (see Exhibit 6-6). Assets indicate an ability to accumulate wealth through saving or through access to inherited wealth—features which reduce lender risk.

3. *Purchase price (PURPR) is associated positively with loan disposition.* Purchasers of more expensive homes are more successful in obtaining mortgages. PURPR has a relatively high association with DISP (gamma = .11, see Exhibit 6-6). The purchase price measures subject property and neighborhood quality; all things being equal, the more expensive the home,

## EXHIBIT 6-4

### INTERCORRELATION MATRIX: SURVEY C ECONOMIC AND RACIAL DATA[1]

| | DISP | ETH | SEX | MAR | INCO | YEA | YES | DEBT | DBPY | ASSET | AMT | PURPR | OO | LVR | BURDEN |
|---|---|---|---|---|---|---|---|---|---|---|---|---|---|---|---|
| **DISP** | 1.00 | .27 | .06 | .09 | .17 | .06 | .05 | .08 | .13 | .14 | .05 | .11 | .00 | .11 | .12 |
| **ETH** | .27 | 1.00 | .13 | .16 | .13 | .01 | .28 | .06 | .03 | .24 | .12 | .24 | .08 | .16 | .07 |
| **SEX** | .06 | .13 | 1.00 | .74 | .41 | .05 | .23 | .19 | .21 | .10 | .24 | .19 | .13 | .09 | .16 |
| **MAR** | .09 | .16 | .74 | 1.00 | .63 | .07 | .87 | .36 | .35 | .31 | .39 | .36 | .11 | .09 | .26 |
| **INCO** | .17 | .13 | .41 | .63 | 1.00 | .28 | .43 | .48 | .41 | .63 | .64 | .64 | .32 | .07 | .72 |
| **YEA** | .06 | .01 | .05 | .07 | .28 | 1.00 | .06 | .30 | .21 | .37 | .09 | .19 | .46 | .12 | .12 |
| **YES** | .05 | .28 | .23 | .87 | .43 | .06 | 1.00 | .04 | .00 | .03 | .02 | .01 | .03 | .02 | .38 |
| **DEBT** | .08 | .06 | .19 | .36 | .48 | .30 | .04 | 1.00 | .92 | .67 | .24 | .28 | .64 | .00 | .08 |
| **DBPY** | .13 | .03 | .21 | .35 | .41 | .21 | .00 | .92 | 1.00 | .39 | .21 | .14 | .53 | .14 | .11 |
| **ASSET** | .14 | .24 | .10 | .31 | .63 | .37 | .03 | .67 | .39 | 1.00 | .38 | .59 | .64 | .21 | .07 |
| **AMT** | .05 | .12 | .24 | .39 | .64 | .09 | .02 | .24 | .21 | .38 | 1.00 | .85 | .36 | .54 | .49 |
| **PURPR** | .11 | .24 | .19 | .36 | .64 | .19 | .01 | .28 | .14 | .59 | .85 | 1.00 | .42 | .30 | .28 |
| **OO** | .00 | .08 | .13 | .11 | .32 | .46 | .03 | .64 | .53 | .64 | .36 | .42 | 1.00 | .01 | .52 |
| **LVR** | .11 | .16 | .09 | .09 | .07 | .12 | .02 | .00 | .14 | .21 | .54 | .30 | .01 | 1.00 | .48 |
| **BURDEN** | .12 | .07 | .16 | .26 | .72 | .12 | .38 | .08 | .11 | .07 | .49 | .28 | .52 | .48 | 1.00 |

[1]Measure of association used is gamma.

Signs (+ or -) are not indicated in this matrix because some variables are nominal. See text and Exhibit 6-6 for positive and negative indication.

*Source:* Comptroller of the Currency, *Fair Housing Lending Practices Pilot Project Survey C Approach* (Washington, D.C.: Comptroller of the Currency, July 1975).

## EXHIBIT 6-5

## LOAN DISPOSITION BY INCO, ASSET, AND LVR ECONOMIC CATEGORIES[1]

*I) Disposition (DISP) by INCOME (INCO)*

| | | DISP Accept | Reject | |
|---|---|---|---|---|
| | High | 6702 (86.1%) | 1085 (13.9%) | 7787 |
| INCO | Moderate | 2985 (83.5%) | 590 (16.5%) | 3575 |
| | Low | 982 (76.7%) | 298 (23.3%) | 1280 |
| | | 10669 | 1973 | 12642 |

*II) Disposition (DISP) by Assets (Asset)*

| | | DISP Accept | Reject | |
|---|---|---|---|---|
| | High | 2089 (86.0%) | 339 (14.0%) | 2428 |
| ASSET | Moderate | 6194 (85.7%) | 1032 (14.3%) | 7226 |
| | Low | 2408 (79.9%) | 607 (20.1%) | 3015 |
| | | 10691 | 1978 | 12669 |

*III) Disposition (DISP) by Loan-to-Value Ratio (LVR)*

| | | DISP Accept | Reject | |
|---|---|---|---|---|
| | High | 1484 (80.7%) | 356 (19.3%) | 1840 |
| LVR | Moderate | 6089 (84.9%) | 1079 (15.1%) | 7168 |
| | Low | 2894 (86.2%) | 463 (13.8%) | 3357 |
| | | 10467 | 1898 | 12365 |

[1]Row percentages are indicated.

*Source*: Comptroller of the Currency, *Fair Housing Lending Practices Pilot Project Survey C Approach* (Washington, D.C.: Comptroller of the Currency, July 1975).

## EXHIBIT 6-6
### ECONOMIC MORTGAGE VARIATION AND SOCIAL GROUP ECONOMIC STATUS ANALYSIS

| Variable | Relationship with DISP | Correlation of Variable with DISP | Relationship with ETH | Correlation of Variable with ETH | Risk of Nonwhite Loan Applicants Compared to White Applicants in Terms of Given Economic Variable |
|---|---|---|---|---|---|
| INCO | Positive. As INCO increases, DISP improves | .17 | Negative. Nonwhites earn less. | -.13 | Higher |
| ASSET | Positive. As ASSET increases, DISP improves. | .14 | Negative. Nonwhites have fewer assets. | -.24 | Higher |
| PURPR | Positive. | .11 | Negative. Nonwhites buy less expensive homes. | -.24 | Higher |
| AMT | Positive. | .05 | Negative. Nonwhites seek smaller loans. | -.12 | Higher |
| LVR | Negative. As LVR decreases, DISP improves. | -.11 | Positive. Nonwhites seek higher LVR loans. | .16 | Higher |
| BURDEN | Negative. | -.12 | Positive. Nonwhites have higher burdens. | .07 | Higher |
| DEBT | Positive. | .08 | Negative. Nonwhites have less debt. | -.06 | Higher |
| DBPY | Negative. | -.13 | Not significant. | — | Equal |
| YEA | Positive. | .06 | Not significant. | — | Equal |
| YES | Not significant. | — | Positive. Nonwhite spouses are employed longer. | .28 | Lower, but YES is not significant. |
| OO | Not significant. | — | Negative. Nonwhites have a higher occupancy rate. | -.08 | Lower, but OO is not significant. |

*Source:* Comptroller of the Currency, *Fair Housing Lending Practices Pilot Project Survey C Approach* (Washington, D.C. Comptroller of the Currency July 1975).

the better its condition, the more lavish its amenities, and the more desirable the neighborhood environment (in terms of public services, capital infrastructure, "market desirability," etc.). It is no wonder that underwriters favor higher PURPR.

4. *The amount of the requested loan (AMT) is also positively correlated with DISP.* This relationship is not surprising for AMT is highly associated with PURPR (.85 correlation). AMT is therefore also a rough proxy for subject property condition and amenity, as well as neighborhood quality. AMT, though, is more weakly related to DISP (.05 correlation) than PURPR, for LVR influences PURPR. AMT can be relatively high when PURPR is low when the borrower seeks highly leveraged (high LVR) financing.

5. *The loan-to-value ratio is negatively associated with DISP.* Low LVR applicants are more successful in obtaining loans (see Exhibit 6-6). Lenders view high LVR loans with disfavor for it means they will have a larger outstanding loan (for a given price home) and the borrower will have less equity and, presumably, a weaker attachment to his house.

6. *High (financial) BURDEN loans are rejected more frequently that low BURDEN loans* (see Exhibit 6-6). The influence of BURDEN on DISP is comparable to LVR (in terms of their gamma correlation with DISP). BURDEN's negative influence is self-explanatory.

After INCO, ASSET, PURPR, AMT, LVR, BURDEN and DEBT/DBPY (soon to be examined), which all have relatively strong relationships with DISP, the other remaining variables are largely much weaker. YEA is minimally associated with DISP and YES is not a significant influence.

7. *The size of debt (DEBT) has a mild, positive (gamma = .08) relationship with DISP.* Loan applicants who have secured credit in the past, as shown by the debt they owe, are more likely to receive a mortgage. In contrast, individuals with higher debt payments (DBPY) are less likely to obtain a mortgage; DBPY is correlated negatively (gamma = $-.13$) with DISP.

The relationship of DEBT and DBPY with DISP is seemingly contradictory; DEBT and DBPY are clearly related so why do the two have an opposite impact on DISP? We suggest the following explanation. DEBT is more strongly influenced by wealth (INCO and ASSETS) than by DBPY — an individual has to be wealthy to be able to go into debt. Wealth (INCO and ASSET) is in turn positively associated with DISP. DEBT is viewed positively by underwriters for it is a surrogate of wealth. DBPY is viewed more negatively, for it is much more weakly associated with wealth. (The affluent can secure more favorable terms for their DEBT.) DBPY also directly shows the additional financial obligation on the mortgager — a burden that may make him default on his loan. These reasons possibly lead underwriters to view DEBT more favorably than DBPY.

8. *The number of years the applicant has been employed (YEA) is another influence, albeit far less important than INCO.* (About 18 percent of those with a relatively limited employment history are rejected compared to 14 percent of those with the longest job history.) While DISP is correlated with YEA, the correlation is very weak (gamma = .06). The slight association should be interpreted in view of our data. Employment is almost certainly more important than indicated here, but the crucial consideration is not the number of years employed but rather the type of employment (professional versus service, for example). Survey C does not give job type information and this omission likely explains YEA's weakness.

9. *The number of years the spouse of an applicant has been working (YES) has no significant bearing on loan disposition.* This finding might reflect lender practice to either not count a spouse's income (in most cases, a working wife), or to substantially discount it. (The Equal Credit Opportunity Act now prohibits treating a spouse's economic contribution any differently than that of the principal wage earner.) In sum, the analysis reveals distinct economic variations between successful and unsuccessful loan applicants.

## Step 3—Social Group Economic Status Analysis

How do nonwhites fare with respect to the economic variables isolated in Step 2? If minorities are economically weaker, then economics may explain why nonwhite applicants are rejected more frequently than whites; if similar economically, then race would seem to influence DISP.

Exhibit 6-7 compares the profile of white versus nonwhite loan applicants for important economic variables (INCO, ASSET, and LVR). Nonwhites have significantly lower incomes and lower assets. They owe significantly less debt, but do not have significanlty less debt payments. Their length of employment is not significantly different from that of whites. Nonwhites purchase significantly less expensive homes than whites. They seek smaller mortgages in terms of the total loan, but more highly leveraged (high LVR) loans. While their mortgages are smaller, nonwhites have a higher housing BURDEN. (See Exhibit 6-6.)

1. *Income* - Black* mortgage applicants are less affluent than white applicants; 16 percent of the former group have low incomes compared to 9 percent for the latter. Conversely, 57 percent of black applicants have high incomes compared to 62 percent for whites. These differences are significant and are relatively strong (gamma = −.13). Lower nonwhite mortgage applicant income reflects lower nonwhite income in general; even more mobile and affluent minorities, those seeking to purchase a house, are still poorer

---

*Note: Black and nonwhite are used interchangeably.

EXHIBIT 6-7

ECONOMIC CHARACTERISTICS OF WHITE AND NONWHITE MORTGAGE
APPLICANTS
(INCO, ASSET AND LVR)[1]

*I) Ethnicity (ETH) by INCOME (INCO)*

| | | ETH Nonwhite | White | |
|---|---|---|---|---|
| | High | 800 *56.9%* | 6985 *62.2%* | 7785 |
| INCO | Moderate | 386 *27.5%* | 3189 *28.4%* | 3575 |
| | Low | 220 *15.6%* | 1059 *9.4%* | 1279 |
| | | 1406 | 11233 | 12639 |

*II) Ethnicity (ETH) by Assets (Asset)*

| | | ETH Nonwhite | White | |
|---|---|---|---|---|
| | High | 184 *13.0%* | 2245 *20.0%* | 2429 |
| ASSET | Moderate | 757 *53.5%* | 6565 *57.5%* | 7322 |
| | Low | 473 *33.5%* | 2542 *22.6%* | 3015 |
| | | 1414 | 11352 | 12766 |

*III) Ethnicity (ETH) by Loan-to-Value Ratio (LVR)*

| | | ETH Nonwhite | White | |
|---|---|---|---|---|
| | High | 279 *20.6%* | 1559 *14.2%* | 1838 |
| LVR | Moderate | 772 *57.1%* | 6396 *58.1%* | 7168 |
| | Low | 302 *22.3%* | 3053 *27.7%* | 3355 |
| | | 1353 | 11008 | 12361 |

[1]Column percentages are given.

*Source*: Comptroller of the Currency, *Fair Housing Lending Practices Pilot Project Survey C Approach* (Washington, D.C.: Comptroller of the Currency, July 1975).

than their white counterparts. Nonwhites' lower income increases their underwriting risk.

2. *Assets* - Nonwhite applicants have significantly lower assets (see Exhibit 6-7). The gamma between ETH and ASSET (−.24) is much higher than that between ETH and INCO (−.13). Nonwhite applicants have fewer assets because they earn less and there is less wealth within the minority community for the applicant to inherit or to draw upon in other ways. Nonwhites' lower ASSETS, like their lower INCO, increases the risk of granting loans to minorities.

3. *Purchase Price, Loan Amount and LVR* - Nonwhites purchase significantly less expensive homes because they are poorer and cannot afford more expensive dwellings. Discrimination also may play a role; nonwhites are steered away from more exclusive and expensive areas. To the extent that PURPR is a proxy of subject property and neighborhood condition/desirability,* then nonwhites are purchasing more modest properties in less desirable areas—traits that increase nonwhite loan risk.

Since nonwhites purchase less expensive homes, it is not surprising that they request smaller loans. (There is a −.12 correlation between AMT and ETH.) Nonwhites' lower AMT is a negative underwriting feature for AMT is positively correlated with DISP. This difficulty is compounded because nonwhites seek higher LVR** loans: 21 percent of nonwhites seek high LVR mortgages compared to 14 percent for whites. There is a relatively high correlation of .16 between ETH and LVR. Nonwhites understandably seek the high LVR financing because they have fewer means with which to purchase a home (i.e., their ASSETS are disproportionately lower), but in seeking these leveraged mortgages they increase risk of default.

4. *BURDEN* - Nonwhite loan applicants have a significantly higher BURDEN (see Exhibit 6-6). Since they have much lower incomes than whites, yet repay only a slightly smaller principal (AMT) than whites, their BURDEN has to be higher. A higher BURDEN is another risk-increasing trait of nonwhite loan applicants.

5. *Debt and Debt Payments* - Nonwhites have a significantly lower debt than whites. (The −.06 correlation of ETH and DEBT is relatively weak,

---

*This discussion assumes that PURPR serves as a similar proxy of neighborhood and property condition/desirability for *both* white and nonwhite homebuyers. Empirical evidence shows that "blacks pay more" than whites for similar housing.[7] Consequently, our assumption gives the black applicant PURPR a greater weight than it deserves.

**Nonwhites' higher LVR explains why the correlation between ETH and AMT (−.12) is much smaller than the (−.24) correlation of ETH and PURPR. While nonwhite loan amount is lower than white loan amount, the former is not lower by a margin commensurate with the white-nonwhite disparity in home purchase price, for nonwhites purchase their homes with high LVR mortgages.

however). Their lower wealth has proved an obstacle to obtaining credit. Discrimination is another possible impediment. Past discrimination barring nonwhites from credit has restricted their opportunity to develop a credit history—a record needed for obtaining future credit. Historical racial discrimination in financing may possibly perpetuate a cycle of credit difficulty.

While nonwhites have a lower debt, their debt payments are similar to white payments. (There is not a significant relationship between DBPY and ETH.) White-nonwhite DBPY parity, despite the former's larger DEBT, may be due to differences in the *cost* of credit. (Nonwhites may pay more for credit than whites.) Another explanation is nonwhites' disporportionate use of consumer credit which is relatively expensive compared to other types of loans.

6. *Employment History* - There is no significant difference in the job history of nonwhite versus white loan applicants (see Exhibit 6-6). The reader must remember, however, that the employment record is limited to the length of employment, not its type — a most important consideration.

The one area of nonwhite economic superiority is not given significant weight. A much larger share of the spouses of nonwhite loan applicants have been employed for a substantial amount of time. The correlation of ETH and YES (.28) is also relatively quite high (see Exhibit 6-6). The extra economic strength, resulting from the higher YES of nonwhite mortgage applicants, might help compensate for some of the nonwhite economic weaknesses, but a spouse's input traditionally has been discounted—YES is not significantly correlated with DISP.

In sum, the analysis indicates that nonwhite loan applicants have different economic characteristics and pose higher underwriting risks than their white counterparts. Do these higher risks explain why nonwhite applicants are rejected more frequently? Step 4 addresses this question. First, social-economic loan relationships are examined in greater detail.

## A Brief Examination of the Dynamic Interaction of Social-Economic Loan Relationships

The previous two sections examined the simple influences of certain economic variables on loan disposition. It only touched upon some serial or interactive relationships of the individual variables themselves. The following section presents a possible perspective in the social-economic loan dynamic (see Exhibit 6-8 for graphic illustration).

Three important social and economic characteristics—ETH, INCO, and ASSET—affect the type of home purchased, required financing, and ultimately, whether a loan request is accepted or rejected. INCO and ASSET, the wealth variables, are closely related (gamma = .63); income helps generate assets and assets are needed to earn income. Employment history

EXHIBIT 6-8

PRELIMINARY ANALYSIS OF SOCIAL-ECONOMIC LOAN RELATIONSHIPS

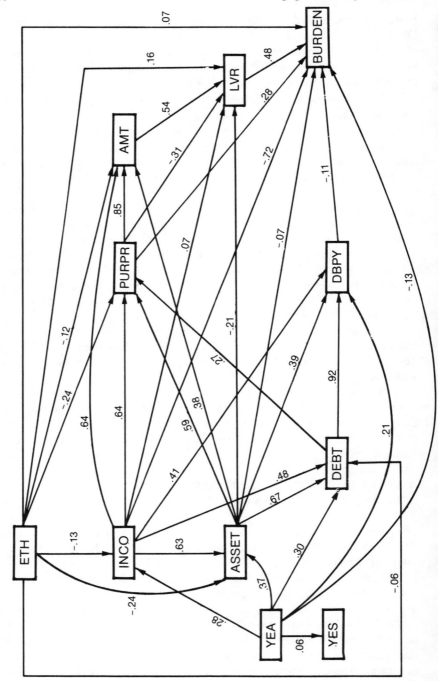

(YEA) influences both INCO and ASSET but much more weakly than the interaction of the two.

ETH also is related to wealth. Nonwhites earn less income and have far fewer assets to draw upon (there is a negative correlation of −.13 between ETH and INCO and a negative correlation of −.24 between ETH and AS-SET). The inferior nonwhite economic status is itself a product of racial and economic influences (exogenous factors not shown in the model), such as possible discrimination that keeps blacks from better-paying jobs.

Wealth (INCO and ASSET) affects the ability to secure credit. The more affluent have found it easier to obtain loans. (There is a .67 correlation between ASSET and DEBT and a .48 correlation between INCO and DEBT.) Race also affects the ability to secure credit, but its influence is far weaker (a negative .06 correlation between ETH and DEBT). Race's negative effect is again a product of discrimination and nonwhites' inferior economic position.

DEBT, in turn, influences DBPY, but factors exogenous to our model are playing a role. The exogenous influence is seen in the fall of wealth's influence on DBPY compared to DEBT.* While there is a .67 correlation between ASSET and DEBT, the correlation between ASSET and DBPY drops to .39. The exogenous influence is probably credit terms—how much is the debt costing and over how long a period must it be repaid. The more affluent may have more debt, but are repaying this debt at more favorable terms. This cost differential explains the drop in correlation between wealth (INCO and ASSET) and DBPY as compared to DEBT.

Wealth influences the quality of dwelling and neighborhood. The affluent have the means and access to purchase the most expensive homes in the most exclusive areas. (There is a .64 correlation between INCO and PURPR and a similar .59 correlation between ASSET and PURPR.) Nonwhites, in contrast, make do with less expensive housing. (There is a negative .24 correlation between ETH and PURPR.) Dual influences possibly are playing a role here again. Nonwhites do not have the wealth to buy more expensive dwellings and even when they do, they are sometimes precluded by discriminatory practices from buying more expensive houses in certain areas.

Purchase price is the strongest influence on loan amount (.85 correlation): higher-priced homes are financed with larger loans. LVR has a strong intervening affect on the PURPR and AMT relationship, however. Expen-

---

*It is interesting to note that the decline in correlations is much steeper for AS-SET and DBPY (versus ASSET and DEBT) as compared to INCO and DBPY (versus INCO and DEBT). This suggests that the ability to secure favorable loan repayment terms is more a function of accumulated wealth (ASSET) rather than current wealth (INCO) — or it may reflect different purchases and financing arrangements.

sive houses may be financed with relatively small loans (if LVR is low), or conversely less expensive dwellings may be bought with relatively large loans (if LVR is high).

LVR is the second strongest influence on AMT (.54 correlation); all things held equal, AMTs are higher with high LVRs. The wealthy do not rely on high LVR loans. (There is a negative correlation between ASSET and LVR and a very weak positive correlation between INCO and LVR.) They have the means to make larger downpayments and the houses they purchase often are not suitable for very high LVR loans.* Nonwhites, in contrast, favor the high LVR mortgages (there is a correlation of .16 between ETH and LVR). Not having the means to make large downpayments, they need the highly leveraged loans.

Those relying on high LVR financing pay a price for avoiding a sizeable downpayment since their interest and amortization costs are higher. These payments are more onerous because a larger principal is being repaid and usually at a higher interest rate as rates go up with LVR. These added expenditures contribute to the BURDEN of homeownership. (There is a .48 correlation between LVR and BURDEN.) Nonwhites have a higher BURDEN, for not only are their incomes lower but they can purchase single-family dwellings only with high LVR financing. The affluent, in contrast, have a low BURDEN for their incomes are higher and they use moderate LVR loans.

All of the variables—ETH, INCO, ASSET, AMT, LVR, BURDEN, etc.—are related to DISP: their individual strengths have been examined in Step 2. INCO, ASSET (wealth) and ETH are especially important predictors of DISP (see Exhibit 6-6). Not only do they have the highest simple correlations with DISP, but they are also associated with the network of other variables (PURPR, AMT, DEBT, etc.) that in turn also are considered by underwriters.

What is race's (ETH) independent effect; is it significant controlling for the primary measures of wealth (INCO and ASSET) as well as the secondary economic considerations (i.e., PURPR, LVR, etc.)? This question is addressed in step 4.

## Step 4—Economic Legitimacy Of Rejection Analysis

An approach to examining ETH's effect is to consider DISP by ETH controlling for:**(1) the economic variables that are significant in terms of

---

*FHA/VA offers the highest LVR mortgages (up to 100 percent LVR), but FHA/VA loans may not be suitable for expensive houses because of loan size limitations or other restrictions.

**The justification for not considering the full range of economic variables including many relative economic criteria has already been explained.

loan disposition; and (2) those variables where nonwhites pose a significantly higher risk. Exhibit 6-6 indicates that INCO, ASSET, PURPR, AMT, LVR, BURDEN and DEBT satisfy these two criteria, while DBPY, YEA, YES and OO do not. Even as large a sample as that afforded by the Comptroller's survey does not allow the retention of these seven economic controls. This analysis considers four economic characteristics: INCO, ASSET, LVR and PURPR. These four are retained and AMT, BURDEN and DEBT are deleted for the following reasons.

1. INCO, ASSET, LVR and PURPR all have a relatively high association (gamma is .10 or greater) with both ETH and DISP.

2. From a substantive perspective, the four variables are quite important. INCO and ASSET are good measures of an individual's economic status. LVR reveals the level of risk associated with the requested loan and PURPR gives some indication of house and neighborhood quality.

3. It would be redundant to include all seven economic variables for some are highly intercorrelated, e.g., there is a gamma of .72 between BURDEN and INCO. While two of those that are retained (ASSET and PURPR) are also highly correlated with INCO, the correlations are slightly smaller and they offer the substantive advantages just discussed.

Once deciding to retain four economic characteristics, it is important to decide how to incorporate these controls. One possibility is to consider the six-way table of DISP x ETH x INCO x ASSET x LVR x PURPR. This table contains 432 cells (2x2x3x3x3x4) or equivalently a 2x2 table of DISP by ETH for each of 108 economic conditions (e.g., one condition is high INCO, high ASSET, low LVR and low PURPR; another is high INCO, high ASSET, low LVR and high PURPR, etc.).

This approach is problematical, however. The economic variables are highly correlated, and consequently there are many empty or near-empty cells at various "extreme" or atypical points. (For instance, there are no applicants, white or nonwhite, in the low INCO, high ASSET, high LVR and low PURPR group. There are eleven other completely empty economic groups along with other groups with few applicants.) The legitimacy of chi-square procedures is suspect in this situation since there will be many low expected values for some of the hypotheses we want to test. Furthermore, even if the basic test is valid, it becomes very difficult to compute the appropriate degrees of freedom under the conditions discussed above.

One way to address the problem of low expected frequency cells is to do separate analyses on the ETH by DISP tables for all the economic groups that have sufficient sample size. This procedure offers the advantages of being straightforward in computation,* and is specific in result—it indicates where significant results are found (e.g., in high LVR cases). At the same time the subtable strategy suffers from serious disadvantages:

1. It is difficult to compare the subtables because they contain different sample sizes.

2. With the multitude of tests that would be done, some spurious results are expected in using standard levels of significance.

3. Doing individual tests on subtables has a significant "price" in terms of power since it is impossible to use the complete sample in one test. (Power considerations are especially important if the effects are not large, as is likely here.)

4. The results, when using subtables, are difficult to summarize either from a statistical or substantive perspective.

## Log Linear Analysis and Selection of Appropriate Analysis Subgroups

It is possible to avoid some of the drawbacks of individual 2 x 2 table analyses by utilizing such techniques as the Mantel-Haenszel statistic and log-linear analysis. These approaches are explained in detail later, but both consolidate the individual economic variable into a combined economic index labeled ECONOMICS** (e.g., consolidated INCO, ASSET, PURPR and LVR). After forming ECONOMICS, it is important to consider how many (of the 108) economic subgroups, i.e., levels of ECONOMICS, should be retained for testing and estimation. For the sake of completeness, we would like to keep all the groups that had loan applicants, but the numerical requirements of the tests employed compel a more conservative strategy.

Two approaches are therefore followed; these are labeled Set I and II. In Set I all economic groups where there is at least one white loan applicant and one nonwhite loan applicant are retained. Set II is more conservative. It retains all economic groups where there are at least ten whites and ten non-whites and there are no zeros in the 2 x 2 ethnicity by disposition table*** (see Exhibit 6-9 for details****).

Almost all the 12,277 people (12,277 is the number of people for whom there was information on all six variables considered here) are contained in the 81 groups of Set I. Although almost 14 percent of the sample size is lost

---

*Some results using a subtable analysis strategy are discussed in Appendix 6-A.

**ECONOMICS is thus considered a nominal scale with 108 categories.

***The "no zero" property is useful in some estimation procedures and is indirectly beneficial for chi-square tests.

****Two other sets were considered: Set I with the additional requirement of no zeros in the table, and Set II without the no zero requirement. Analysis of these sets yielded similar results to those reported in the text.

EXHIBIT 6-9

SELECTION OF APPROPRIATE ANALYSIS SUBGROUPS

|        | No.<br>Groups | Total<br>n | %<br>(of 12,277) |
|--------|---------------|------------|------------------|
| Set I  | 81            | 12,203     | 99.4             |
| Set II | 40            | 10,565     | 86.1             |

EXHIBIT 6-10

LOAN DISPOSITION (DISP) BY ETHNIC GROUP (ETH):
FREQUENCY TABLE[1]

|       |          | DISP | | |
|-------|----------|------|------|--------|
|       |          | *Accept* | *Reject* | |
| ETH   | *White*    | 9,348 (9,255)[2] | 1,591 (1,684) | 10,939 |
|       | *Nonwhite* | 1,039 (1,132)    | 299 ( 206)    | 1,338  |
|       |          | 10,387 | 1,890 | 12,277 |

*Note:* $X^2$ = 55.70, p < .001; $\gamma$ = .26
[1]For respondents with information on INCO, ASSET, LVR and PURPR.
[2]Expected frequencies are given in parentheses.

EXHIBIT 6-11

LOAN DISPOSITION (DISP) BY ETHNIC GROUP(ETH):
PERCENTAGE TABLE

|       |          | DISP | | |
|-------|----------|------|------|-------|
|       |          | *Accept* | *Reject* | |
| **ETH** | White    | 85.5 | 14.5 | 100.0 |
|       | Nonwhite | 77.7 | 22.3 | 100.0 |

*Source:* Comptroller of the Currency, *Fair Housing Lending Practices Pilot Project Survey C Approach* (Washington, D.C.: Comptroller of the Currency, July 1975).

in Set II, there are still more than 10,500 applicants considered there—a quite comfortable number for the analysis.

In sum, the analysis focuses on DISP x ETH x ECONOMICS tables of dimensions 2x2x81 in Set I and 2x2x40 in Set II. It follows a five step strategy:

1) Is ETH significant when controlling for ECONOMICS? The Mantel-Haenszel statistic is used to examine the existence of an effect due to ethnicity.
2) Does the ethnicity effect (if any) interact with ECONOMICS, i.e., does the strength of ethnicity (as a predictor of DISP) vary over the different economic groups? This question is examined via log-linear analysis.
3) If race is a significant variable, how strong is its effect? This question is tackled by first estimating the gamma averaged over the economic groups and then considered more directly by estimating the difference between a white being accepted for a mortgage loan and a nonwhite being accepted.
4) Are sex and marital status confounding variables in the race-disposition correlation? The sex and marital status effects can be partialled out by considering each of the four sex-marital status groups separately. (See Appendix 6-A for specification of groups.) In three of the groups, there does not exist sufficient sample size for detailed analysis. For the fourth group, married males, the multistep analytic approach is carried out.

IS THERE AN EFFECT DUE TO ETHNICITY?

Exhibit 6-3 considered DISP by ETH for the entire sample. This test was conducted before isolating those economic variables that are significantly related to DISP. At this last stage of the analysis, it is appropriate to consider DISP by ETH for those cases in which all the significant economic data are available (see Exhibits 6-10 and 6-11.)

Exhibit 6-10 reveals that similar results are obtained—nonwhites are rejected at a significantly higher rate (exhibits 6-3 and 6-10 are almost identical). But the same question remains: is the result spurious, due to economics; do the nonwhites receive too few loans because they are disproportionately poor, or is there an ethnicity effect even after economics has been controlled? This question can be addressed via the Mantel-Haenszel statistic.

In 1959, Nathan Mantel and William Haenszel examined the incidence of pulmonary carcinoma among various age and occupation subgroups.[8] They used chi-square analysis and found statistically significant variation among some of the subgroups they examined (e.g., housewives, 45-50 years old). Mantel-Haenszel considered the need for an overall statistical measure.[9]

> The problem of overall measures of relative risk and statistical significance still remains. A reasonable overall significance test which has power for alternative hypotheses,where there is a consistent association in the same direction over the various sub-classifications between the disease and a study factor, is provided by relating the summations for the discrepancy between observation and expectation to its variance.

The two researchers developed a weighted chi-square summary statistic which is now called the Mantel-Haenszel statistic. Mantel refined and explained the technique in 1963,[10] but this summary statistic received little attention outside of the epidemiological field.

A 1975 article in *Science* by P.J. Bickel, E.A. Hammel and J.W. O'Connell spurred more popular interest in summary contingency table analysis.[11] The article, considering whether there was sex bias in Berkeley graduate admissions, has particular relevance to our search for mortgage racial discrimination.

The three researchers first examined the percentage of males versus females who were admitted to the university. The rejection rate was significantly higher for females, thereby prompting a preliminary conclusion that sex bias existed. Bickel *et al.* reasoned, however, that since individual departments accepted or rejected applicants (and departments differed in their rejection rate), it would make more sense to examine the behavior of each individual department. They considered intra-departmental admission patterns and found a mixed outcome; some departments admitted a disproportionately higher number of males while others admitted a higher share of females. Bickel *et al.* discussed that such a varied pattern seemed inconclusive:[12]

> (in) examining 85 separate departments at the same time for evidence of bias we are conducting 85 simultaneous experiments, and in that many experiments the probability of finding some marked departures from expected frequencies just by chance is not insubstantial.

The *Science* analysis of sex bias is directly analogous to this study. A chi-square test has revealed that black mortgage applicants are rejected more frequently than white applicants — an outcome similar to the overall higher rejection rate of females applying to Berkeley. Like Bickel *et al.*, this analysis concluded that the summary distinction could be misleading and therefore examined critical subcategories. The evaluation of mortgage disposition for the 81 economic subgroups is similar to considering admissions for 85 graduate departments. As in the case of the sex bias study, this monograph is confronted with the task of interpreting a finding of significant differences among *some* of the subgroups being examined. Is the outcome of racial (or sexual) variation among certain subgroups statistically significant or can this outcome be merely due to chance?

Bickel chose the Mantel-Haenszel statistic to answer this question. This study opts for a similar approach for two reasons. First, the statistic is extremely powerful—reducing all the observations (in Bickel's case 12,763 and in our case 12,277) into a one degree of freedom test.* This allows for the detection of small effects at standard levels of significance. Second, the statistic gives, as a byproduct, an estimate of the excess number of whites given loans (which is equivalent to the deficit in the number of nonwhites given loans). This byproduct is a concrete, absolute measure that gives some sense of the race effect.

The Mantel-Haenszel statistic itself is calculated as follows. For the $i^{th}$ level of economics the following tables can be derived (see Exhibit 6-12).

EXHIBIT 6-12

MANTEL—HAENSZEL TABLE DERIVATION

|          | accept | reject |
|----------|:------:|:------:|
| white    | $a_i$  | $b_i$  |
| nonwhite | $c_i$  | $d_i$  |

total $= N_i = a_i + b_i + c_i + d_i$

The cell of interest is the one containing the number of whites accepted for a loan.** The expected frequency under independence of ethnicity and disposition is

$$E_i = (a_i + b_i) \times (a_i + c_i) / N_i$$

where $N_i$ is the total number of applicants in this $i^{th}$ group. The variance of the frequency under independence is

$$Var_i = (a_i + b_i) \times (a_i + c_i) \times (c_i + d_i) \times (b_i + d_i)$$

The difference between the observed number, $a_i$, and the expected number, $E_i$, summed over the 81 economic groups is

$$\Sigma \ (a_i - E_i) = DIFF$$

In our case, DIFF is the deficit (if negative) or excess (if positive) in the number of whites accepted for loans. The Mantel-Haenszel statistic is

$$X^2 = \frac{(DIFF)^2}{\Sigma \ Var_i} \quad \text{with df} = 1$$

---

*It is not necessary to use the more conservative Set II data, for the Mantel-Haenszel statistic is valid for Set I data.

**The choice of cell to work with is unimportant. The results are identical with any of the three other cells used as the base.

Bickel applied the Mantel-Haenszel statistic and concluded that the sexual variation among the subgroup departments was not significant: Berkeley's graduate admissions program was not guilty of racial bias.

Our analysis suggests that a racial bias does exist. The Mantel-Haenszel statistic for the Set I data is 40.2 which is significant at the .001 level. Race is significantly associated with the disposition of the loan after economics has been controlled. DIFF is 80, thus 80 too many whites (or 80 too few nonwhites) were given loans than would be expected if ETH and DISP were independent given ECONOMICS.

It is interesting to compare the controlled results of Mantel-Haenszel with the uncontrolled results in Exhibit 6-10. In the latter case the chi-square was 55.70 and the excess number of whites accepted was 93. (See exhibit 6-10: 93 = 9348 − 9255 = 1132 − 1039). Thus, when controlling for economics, the ethnicity effect is diminished, but is still significant.

THE INTERACTION OF ETH WITH ECONOMICS

The Mantel-Haenszel statistic reveals the existence of a significant ethnicity effect when the results from each of the economic tables are pooled. However, information has been lost by pooling; does the ethnicity effect vary significantly across the economic groups? If yes, then ethnicity interacts with economics and the effect of ETH on DISP is not universal; it may even disappear in some cases, e.g., high INCO. It is important, then, to consider the effect of ECONOMICS, especially in regard to its interaction with ETH. To do this log-linear analysis will be utilized.

Log-linear analysis is a direct extension of the chi-square test of independence in a two-way table to tests in multi-way tables. These multi-way cross tabs contain one dependent variable and several predictor variables. Log-linear analysis can be used to test many potential hypotheses of interest including:

1) independence of the dependent variable and the whole group of predictor variables;
2) conditional independence of one predictor variable and the dependent variable given the other predictor variables;
3) the interaction between two or more of the predictor variables.

(In this context, the statement that a predictor variable has no effect is equivalent to saying that it is conditionally independent of the dependent variable given the other predictor variables.)

Mechanically, log-linear analysis consists of fitting the data to various sets of parameters representing main effects and interactions* of the predictor variables. After fitting the model which is appropriate for the hypothesis

---

*These parameters have similar interpretations to those in analysis of variance.

of interest, the expected frequencies under this model and the observed frequencies are compared with a chi-square statistic. For instance, to test the conditional independence of ETH and DISP given ECONOMICS, the parameters representing the main effect of ETH and the parameters representing the interaction of ETH and ECONOMICS are set to 0 before the data is fit.

The results of the log-linear analysis are in Exhibit 6-13.

The analysis indicates that ethnicity and economics are significant in both sets of data. This ETH effect does not significantly vary across economic conditions; there is no significant interaction between economics and ethnicity at standard levels of significance. (This is especially the case in Set II data where the assumptions of the chi-square statistics are more reasonable.)

In sum, the finding that ETH is significant is similar to the Mantel-Haenszel results. Additionally, by disproving a significant ECONOMICS by ETH interaction, the log-linear analysis confirms that little is gained by looking at the separate (by levels of ECONOMICS) 2 x 2 tables of DISP x ETH in analyzing the ETH effect.

## HOW STRONG IS THE RACIAL EFFECT?

Since ethnicity's effect on disposition does not vary significantly over the economic groups, it is reasonable to use a pooling technique to get an overall measure of gamma. (Pooling would not be justified if the relationship varied widely for the economic groups since the pooled gamma in that case could be a combined function that is not representative of any table.)

EXHIBIT 6-13

LOG-LINEAR ANALYSIS RESULTS

| I) Using Set I data | | | |
|---|---|---|---|
| Effect | df | $X^2$ | Significance |
| ETH[1] | 81 | 137.3 | .001 |
| ECONOMICS | 160 | 332.5 | .001 |
| ETH x ECONOMICS | 80 | 81.5 | .13 |
| II) Using Set II data | | | |
| Effect | df | $X^2$ | Significance |
| ETH[1] | 40 | 94.2 | .001 |
| ECONOMICS | 78 | 185.7 | .001 |
| ETH x ECONOMICS | 39 | 40.2 | — |

[1]This is the hypothesis that DISP is conditionally independent of ETH given ECONOMICS. Similarly, the ECONOMICS effect is conditional on ETH.

The pooled gamma is a weighted average of the individual gammas at the various level of ECONOMICS, where the weight is the denominator of the gamma at that level. This pooled gamma is called a partial coefficient by Davis.[13]

The pooled (or partial) gamma is .24 for the Set I data and .25 for Set II (see Appendix 6-A for calculations). These results are almost identical to the original gamma of .26 derived from the simple 2 x 2 cross tab of DISP by ETH (see Exhibit 6-10). In sum, the relationship between disposition and ethnicity remains reasonably strong when economics has been controlled: ECONOMICS does not explain the association between ethnicity and disposition.

A graphical summary of the gammas (for Set II data) is given in Exhibit 6-14. The gamma for each group is plotted against the group's sample size. In interpreting the graph, it is important to remember that:
1) Gamma is greater than zero only if the proportion of whites accepted is greater than the proportion of nonwhites accepted.
2) The results of the test for interaction between race and economics imply that the gamma does not vary significantly among the points in the graph.

The gammas range from −.57 to .85 across the 40 groups contained in Set II. High INCO, high ASSET, medium PURPR and low LVR is the economic cluster with the smallest sample size (38) in Set II. Its gamma is .20. The group with the largest sample size (1503) is high INCO, medium ASSET, medium PURPR and medium LVR. Its gamma is .43.

Exhibit 6-14 indicates that 80 percent (32 of 40) of the gammas are greater than 0. Approximately half (19 of 40) of the gammas are greater than or equal to .25—the pooled gamma estimate. The graph illustrates the reasonably tight distribution of gammas around the summary value. The extreme individual points are found in the smallest sample sizes where greater heterogeneity is expected.


ESTIMATION OF THE DIFFERENCE IN A WHITE
VERSUS A NONWHITE BEING ACCEPTED FOR A LOAN

A further insight into the strength of race is afforded by examining the variations in the chance that whites versus nonwhites have in obtaining a loan. The absolute race effect (the probability of a white being accepted for a loan minus the probability of a nonwhite being accepted) is estimated to be .078* from the pooled table, but this is a "raw" estimate that does not control for economics.

---

*See Exhibit 6-11. .078 = .855 − .777

EXHIBIT 6-14

GRAPHICAL SUMMARY OF GAMMAS

PLOT: GAMMA (DOWN) — BY ECONOMIC GROUP SIZE* (ACROSS)

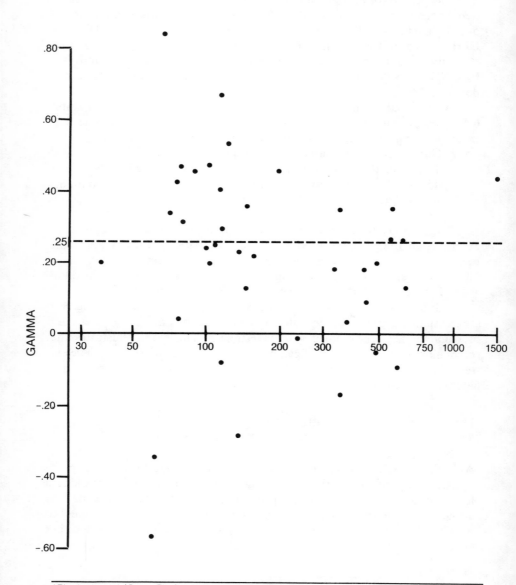

*The horizontal (Group Size) axis is on a log scale.

To partial out the economic effect, a pooled, weighted estimate will be computed—as was done with gamma. First the race effect, along with its variance, can be estimated* for each economic category. This estimated race effect is then weighted by the reciprocal of its estimated variance. (This is a standard method of weighting as, for instance, in weighted least squares.)

The weighted estimation procedure is most applicable when the estimated race effect is approximately normally distributed and a good estimate of its variance is available. This condition is likely not satisfied for some of the groups in Set I because of small sample size. The instability of the variance estimates is especially troublesome.

A partial remedy is to add .5 to all the frequencies in the table. (This has been suggested by Goodman in related contexts.[14]) This .5 addition is followed for the Set I estimation. The fairly rigorous sample size restrictions of the tables in Set II guarantee reasonable estimation with no adjustments. Adding .5 to Set I frequencies and retaining the Set II frequencies yields the results shown in Exhibit 6-15.

Exhibit 6-15 reveals that race is not a very strong effect in an absolute sense. Whites' acceptance rate for mortgage loans is about 6 percent higher than nonwhites' acceptance ratio. Since the estimated effect is more than five standard errors above zero,** statistical significance is assured at all reasonable levels. The introduction of an economic control has only slightly attenuated the estimated race effect from .078 to .06.

### EXHIBIT 6-15

### ESTIMATES OF THE RACE EFFECT

| | Estimate | Standard Error |
|---|---|---|
| Set I (+.5) | .059 | .011 |
| Set II | .062 | .012 |

*The variance estimate used is the standard one for the difference of two independent proportions.
**Another way to pool the individual race effects is to take a simple (instead of weighted) average. A simple average yields an unbiased estimate of the race effect but is usually less precise than the weighted estimate. For comparison, the simple averages were slightly higher (around .070) than the weighted averages reported in Exhibit 6-15.

EXHIBIT 6-16

RACE EFFECT BY ECONOMIC STATUS

PLOT: RACE EFFECT (DOWN) BY ECONOMIC GROUP SIZE * (ACROSS)

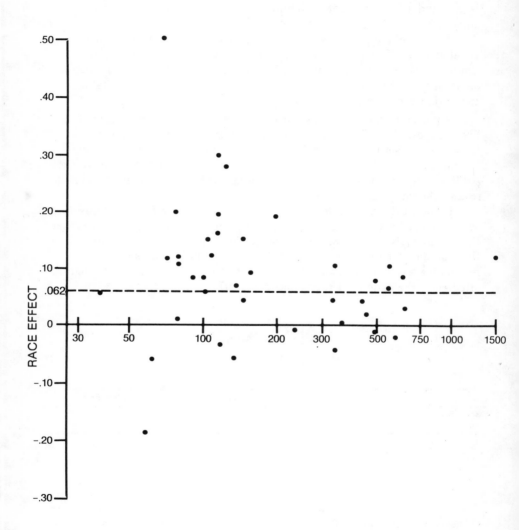

*The horizontal (Group Size) axis is on a log scale.

Exhibit 6-16 graphically summarizes the estimated race effects for each of the clusters in Set II. As in the gamma analysis, 32 of the 40 points are positive.* Here 23 of the 40 points are above .062, the weighted estimate.

The estimated race effects range from −.186 to .300. For the smallest economic cluster (high INCO, high ASSET, medium PURPR and low LVR) the estimated effect is .057. The group with the largest sample size (high INCO, medium ASSET, medium PURPR, and medium LVR) has an estimated effect of .120. Interpretation of these results is similar to that discussed for the individual gamma analysis.

### EXHIBIT 6-17

### LOAN DISPOSITION FOR MARRIED MALES

**I) Disposition (DISP) by Race (ETH) Frequency Table**

DISP

|  |  | Accept | Reject |  |
|---|---|---|---|---|
| ETH | White | 7312(7242) | 1212(1282) | 8524 |
|  | Nonwhite | 798(868) | 223(153) | 1021 |
|  |  | 8110 | 1435 | 9545 |

$$X^2 = 41.48 \quad P < .001$$
$$gamma = .26$$

**II) Disposition (DISP) by Race (ETH) Percentage Table**

DISP

|  |  | Accept | Reject |
|---|---|---|---|
| ETH | White | 85.8 | 14.2 |
|  | Nonwhite | 78.2 | 21.8 |

**III) Economic Set Information**

|  | *No Groups* | *n* | *% (of 9545)* |
|---|---|---|---|
| Set I | 75 | 9487 | 99.4 |
| Set II | 32 | 7840 | 82.1 |

*Note:* Expected frequencies under the hypothesis of independence are given in parentheses.

*Source:* Comptroller of the Currency, *Fair Housing Lending Practices Pilot Project Survey C Approach* (Washington, D.C.: Comptroller of the Currency, July 1975).

---

*As with gamma, a positive value means that the proportion of whites accepted is greater than the proportion of nonwhites accepted. A negative value means nonwhites were favored.

SEX-MARITAL STATUS EFFECT ON LENDING

All the analyses thus far have pooled the 12,277 sample into one group in order to work with the largest sample size possible. This strategy raises the possibility of confounding race, sex and marital status effects. Is the significance of race due to different sex-marital status profiles of whites and nonwhites? This question is tackled by analyzing the subsample of married males only.

Of the original sample of 12,277 people, 9,545 (77.7 percent) are married males. With this large a sample the complete procedure discussed previously (e.g., significance of ETH/importance of ETH) can be undertaken.

The data for married males is shown in Exhibit 6-17.

The Mantel-Haenszel statistic for married males (for Set I data) is 29.14 which is significant at the .001 level. This value, (29.14), is just slightly less than 78 percent of the original Mantel-Haenszel statistic (40.16) for the whole sample. The attenuation reflects, at least partially, the linear relationship of chi-square and sample size (9545/12227 = .78)

The strength of ETH is seen in other ways. Under the assumption of independence of ETH and DISP given ECONOMICS, 59 fewer male-married-nonwhites (equivalently 59 too many whites) were accepted for loans than would be expected when controlling via Mantel-Haenszel. This differential compares with the deficit of 70 nonwhite loans in the whole table for married males when not employing this test and is almost three-quarters of the 80 differential for the full sample (i.e., all loan applicants) — almost identical to the differences in respective sample sizes.

Applying log-linear analysis to the male-married cluster yields similar results to those derived from the full sample. (Compare Exhibits 6-13 and 6-18.) In all cases ethnicity given economics is significant and vice-versa. The only difference between the full sample and married males is the somewhat stronger evidence of a ETH-ECONOMICS interaction in the latter case. In fact, for married males, the interactions are significant at the .10 level. This may need more study in the future to determine how the race effect varies with level of economics.

The estimate of gamma for the male-married set, when pooled over the economic groups, is .22 for Set I and .25 for Set II. These values are almost identical to the gamma of .26 yield by the complete (non-control) white male table and show that ethnicity is a reasonably strong predictor of disposition when economics are controlled.

The "absolute" race effect for married males is shown in Exhibit 6-19. The uncontrolled effect for married males is .076 (.076 = .858 − .782, see Exhibit 6-17.) This measure drops to approximately .06 when economics is controlled. The estimated race effect is statistically significant (it is about

## EXHIBIT 6-18

### LOG-LINEAR ANALYSIS FOR MARRIED MALES

| | ECONOMIC SET I | | |
|---|---|---|---|
| **Effect** | **X²** | **df** | **Significance** |
| ETH | 119.5 | 75 | .001 |
| ECONOMICS | 294.8 | 148 | .001 |
| ETH x ECONOMICS | 91.5 | .74 | .095 |
| | ECONOMIC SET II | | |
| **Effect** | **X²** | **df** | **Significance** |
| ETH | 71.4 | 32 | .001 |
| ECONOMICS | 143.3 | 62 | .001 |
| ETH x ECONOMICS | 42.1 | 31 | .088 |

## EXHIBIT 6-19

### ESTIMATE OF THE RACE EFFECT FOR MARRIED MALES

| | **Estimate** | **Standard Error** |
|---|---|---|
| Set I (+ .5) | .061 | .012 |
| Set II | .055 | .014 |

four standard errors above 0) but about ten percent weaker than that yielded for the total sample (compare Exhibits 6-15 and 6-19) for Set II data while essentially equal for Set I data.

In sum, the analysis of the married-male subsample reveals largely comparable* results, though slightly weaker in terms of the racial effect, to those of the full sample. This outcome suggests that the relationship between DISP and ETH is partially due to sex and marital status differences of whites and nonwhites, but confirms the major conclusion that race is a factor in loan disposition.

---

*When, if applicable, adjusted for sample size.

# Appendix 6-A: Additional Data and Analysis

This appendix considers:
1. Simple contingency table analysis of the racial effect on underwriting.
2. Calculation of the pooled gamma (detailed analysis).
3. Estimation of the race effect (detailed analysis).
4. Contingency table analysis of the sex and marital status effect.

## The Race Effect Examined Via
## Simple Contingency Table Analysis

Chapter Six examined the influence of race controlling for economic variables via log linear analysis and the Mantel-Haenszel procedure. Can similar results be obtained utilizing "simple" two-way contingency tables?

The significance of race can be evaluated by considering DISP by ETH controlling for economic variables for which nonwhites have a lower economic status than whites; to that degree, the nonwhites may be higher risks. Chapter Six discusses that INCO, ASSET, PURPR and LVR should be considered as controls. INCO and ASSET will be entered first, for the two constitute the most significant wealth influences. Not only do they have the highest correlations with DISP, but they are highly correlated with ETH (see Exhibit 6-7). Entering INCO and ASSET says in effect that we shall look at the variation in loan outcome by race first controlling for the two strongest economic influences. After INCO and ASSET, LVR and PURPR are entered as controls.

Exhibit 6-A-1 shows an interesting progression. Racial distinctions are found when income is controlled (1st level control). In other words, high, middle, and low income nonwhites are denied loans significantly more often than their white counterparts. Mixed results are obtained when income and assets are controlled (2nd level control). In most cases there are no significant racial distinctions among the nine subgroups.* This outcome is not universal, however. Racial distinctions are found among three subgroups (those having High INCO, Moderate ASSETS; Moderate INCO, Low ASSETS; and Low INCO, Low ASSETS). In these cases, nonwhites are denied loans at a significantly higher rate.

Similar results are obtained when purchase price is added to the income and asset controls (3rd level control), and at the fourth level entry, when LVR is added as a control (see Exhibit 6-A-1). In the overwhelming number of cases race is not significant, but the DISP by ETH differences do not disappear entirely. Racial distinctions are found among certain subgroups, such as those having low income and assets and those who purchase less expensive homes with low LVR mortgages. The correlation between DISP and ETH is fairly high among these smaller subgroups. (Gamma equals .85 for the low INCO, low ASSET, low PURPR and low LVR subset, for example).

In sum, DISP does vary significantly by race when economic variables are controlled, but only for isolated subgroups. This result is seemingly contradictory to the stronger racial presence detected in Chapter Six. It may be due to the sample size of the subsets. The individual table analysis in this appendix suffers from a sample size deficiency problem. The race effect found in Chapter Six is not large and is therefore difficult to isolate in subtables, each of which contains a relatively small number of loan applicants. Stronger results are shown in Chapter Six because the log-linear and Mantel-Haenszel tests are able to pool the results from all the tables in an appropriate manner. Even though many of the subtables do not show that ETH is significant, log-linear is sensitive to a consistent tendency for whites to be accepted more readily for loans. This tendency is strong enough to imply an overall race effect.

## Regional Variations

Is lender behavior uniform? There are at least theoretical reasons why regional distinctions might exist. Northeastern cities have experienced some of the most dramatic racial and economic shifts in the post World War II

---

* 3 INCO subgroups times 3 ASSET subgroups.

EXHIBIT 6-A-1
DISP BY ETH CONTROLLING FOR INCO, ASSET, PURPR AND LVR

| DISP BY ETH: | CONTROL | CONTROL SUBGROUPS | SIGNIFICANT (CHI SQUARE) | CORRELATION (GAMMA) |
|---|---|---|---|---|
| 1st Level Control | Income (INCO) | High Income | Yes | .24 |
| | | Moderate Income | Yes | .29 |
| | | Low Income | Yes | .27 |
| 2nd Level Control | Income & Assets (INCO & ASSET) | High Income, High Assets | No | — |
| | | Moderate Income, High Assets | No | — |
| | | Low Income, High Assets | No | — |
| | | High Income, Moderate Assets | Yes | .31 |
| | | Moderate Income, Moderate Assets | No | — |
| | | Low Income, Moderate Assets | No | — |
| | | High Income, Low Assets | No | — |
| | | Moderate Income, Low Assets | Yes | .31 |
| | | Low Income, Low Assets | Yes | .35 |
| 3rd Level Control | Income, Assets & Purchase Price (INCO, ASSET & PURPR) | High Income, High Assets, Very High Purchase Price | No | — |
| | | Moderate Income, High Assets, Very High Purchase Price | No | — |
| | | Low Income, High Assets, Very High Purchase Price | No | — |
| | | High Income, Moderate Assets, Very High Purchase Price | No | — |
| | | Low Income, Moderate Assets, Very High Purchase Price | No | — |
| | | High Income, Low Assets, Very High Purchase Price | No | — |
| | | Moderate Income, High Assets, High Purchase Price | No | — |
| | | Low Income, Low Assets, Very High Purchase Price | No | — |
| | | High Income, High Assets, High Purchase Price | No | — |
| | | Moderate Income, High Assets, High Purchase Price | No | — |
| | | Low Income, High Asset, High Purchase Price | No | — |
| | | High Income, Moderate Assets, High Purchase Price | Yes | .31 |
| | | Moderate Income, Moderate Assets, High Purchase Price | No | — |
| | | Low Income, Moderate Assets, High Purchase Price | No | — |
| | | Low Income, Moderate Assets, High Purchase Price | No | — |
| | | High Income, Low Assets, high Purchase Price | Yes | .38 |
| | | Moderate Income, Low Assets, High Purchase Price | No | — |

EXHIBIT 6-A-1 (Cont'd)

DISP BY ETH CONTROLLING FOR INCO, ASSET PURPR AND LVR

| DISP BY ETH: | CONTROL | CONTROL SUBGROUPS | SIGNIFICANT (CHI SQUARE) | CORRELATION (GAMMA) |
|---|---|---|---|---|
| | | Low Income, Low Assets, High Purchase Price | No | — |
| | | High Income, High Assets, Moderate Purchase Price | No | — |
| | | Moderate Income, High Assets, Moderate Purchase Price | No | — |
| | | Low Income, High Assets, Moderate Purchase Price | No | — |
| | | High Income, Moderate Assets, Moderate Purchase Price | No | — |
| | | Moderate Income, Moderate Assets, Moderate Purchase Price | No | — |
| | | Low Income, Moderate Assets, Moderate Purchase Price | No | — |
| | | High Income, Low Assets, Moderate Purchase Price | No | — |
| | | Moderate Income, Low Assets, Moderate Purchase Price | No | — |
| | | Low Income, Low Assets, Moderate Purchase Price | No | — |
| | | High Income, High Assets, Low Purchase Price | No | — |
| | | Moderate Income, High Assets, Low Purchase Price | No | — |
| | | Low Income, High Assets, Low Purchase Price | No | — |
| | | High Income, Moderate Assets, Low Purchase Price | Yes | .57 |
| | | Moderate Income, Moderate Assets, Low Purchase Price | No | — |
| | | Low Income, Moderate Assets, Low Purchase Price | No | — |
| | | High Income, Low Assets, Low Purchase Price | No | — |
| | | Moderate Income, Low Assets, Low Purchase Price | Yes | .35 |
| | | Low Income, Low Assets, Low Purchase Price | Yes | .38 |
| 4th Level Control | Income, Assets, Purchase Price & Loan to Value Ratio (INCO, ASSET, PURPR &LVR) | 108 Subgroups (3 INCO x 3 ASSET x 4 PURPR x 3 LVR) Most were not significant; some exceptions include: | | |
| | | High Income, Moderate Assets, Moderate Purchase Price, Medium LVR | Yes | .43 |
| | | High Income, Moderate Assets, Low Purchase Price Medium LVR | Yes | .68 |
| | | Low Income, Low Assets, Low Purchase Price,Medium LVR | Yes | .54 |
| | | Moderate Income, Low Assets, Low Purchase Price, Low LVR | Yes | .85 |

*Source:* Comptroller of the Currency, *Fair Housing Lending Practice Pilot Project Survey C Approach* (Washington, D.C.: Comptroller of the Currency, July 1975).

era. More muted changes occurred in other areas, especially the "Sunbelt" region. Have the dramatic Northeastern transitions increased the sensitivity of lenders in this region toward race as an underwriting criteria? Are Northeastern financial institutions more hesitant to give loans to nonwhites, given the frequent and rapid racial and economic shifts they have witnessed?

The existence of regional variations in underwriting, at least in terms of the racial (ETH) influence, can be tested by examining the Comptroller's data. The Comptroller lists the SMSAs where the sample loans are granted. Two are in the Northeast while the remainder are outside the Northeast. The possible presence of variations in lender behavior by region can be examined by comparing DISP and ETH for the Northeast and outside the Northeast locations.

Regional variations were evaluated as explained above and a null finding was reached. Lenders in the Northeast and outside this region behave in a similar fashion.

## Calculation of the Pooled Gamma

Besides the method of pooling gamma used in the text, two other techniques were developed and used by the authors. Since no one method of pooling gamma is universally accepted, it is instructive to use several approaches, hoping that each produces a similar number. Although the three techniques (see below) will generally yield similar results, they will not necessarily do so.

The three methods used (Davis' and the two in this appendix) produced pooled gammas of about .25. (The results were .23, .25, and .26.) The results are robust — not dependent on a particular mode of analysis.

The two methods developed in this appendix are based on the relationship of the odds ratio (or relative risk), commonly called R, and gamma. Gamma can be considered to be a standardized version of R. The R-gamma relationship can be explained as follows:

Given a table

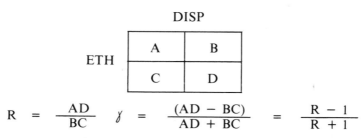

$$R = \frac{AD}{BC} \qquad \gamma = \frac{(AD - BC)}{AD + BC} = \frac{R - 1}{R + 1}$$

it is easily seen that $\gamma$ is a monotone increasing function of R. So $\gamma$ takes the measure R, which takes values from 0 to infinity, and transforms it into the interval $(-1, 1)$.

The appendix utilizes methods for estimating an R that is pooled over many groups and then transforms this pooled R into a gamma. As with Davis' method, these methods are based on schemes which weigh the results in the individual tables by functions of the sample sizes in the tables. The "simpler" technique is shown below. The calculation assumes that the $i^{th}$ table has specified frequencies:

DISP

|     | | |
| --- | --- | --- |
| ETH | $A_i$ | $B_i$ |
| | $C_i$ | $D_i$ |

Total in this table is $N_i = A_i + B_i + C_i + D_i$

$$\text{pooled gamma} = \frac{\Sigma (A_i D_i - B_i C_i) / N_i}{\Sigma (A_i D_i + B_i C_i) / N_i}$$

A more "detailed" method is based on weighting the

$R_i = \dfrac{A_i D_i}{B_i C_i}$ in each table by its estimated variance

$$S_i = \frac{1}{A_i} + \frac{1}{B_i} + \frac{1}{C_i} + \frac{1}{D_i} \quad (10).$$

Thus R pooled $= (\Sigma R_i / S_i)/(\Sigma 1 / S_i)$. (This method can be applied only when all the tables have no zero frequencies.) This pooled R is then transformed into the pooled gamma via the formula shown above.

## Calculation of the Difference in a White Versus a Nonwhite Being Accepted for a Loan

In this appendix, the details for computing the pooled estimate of a white versus a nonwhite being accepted for a loan are presented.

As mentioned in Chapter Six, the procedure used is based on weighted least squares. This technique weights the estimate from each individual table by the reciprocal of its variance.

Graphically, assume that the table for the ith economic cluster is:

DISP

| | | Accept | Reject |
| --- | --- | --- | --- |
| ETH | W | $A_i$ | $B_i$ |
| | NW | $C_i$ | $D_i$ |

The probability of a white being accepted, say, $W_i$, is estimated by $A_i/(A_i + B_i)$. For a nonwhite, $NW_i$ is similarly defined. Thus, the estimate of the race effect in this economic group is $W_i - NW_i$. The estimated variance of $W_i - NW_i$ is

$$V_i = \frac{W_i \times (1 - W_i)}{(A_i + B_i)} + \frac{NW_i \times (1 - NW_i)}{(C_i + D_i)}$$

Finally, the pooled estimate of a white versus a nonwhite being accepted for a loan is

$$(\Sigma(W_i - NW_i)/V_i)/(\Sigma 1/V_i).$$

## A Further Examination of the Sex-Marital Influence

Chapter Six considered the interactive effect of economics, race, sex-marital status and loan disposition. This subject is examined further below.

The race versus sex-marital status impact is clouded because of the relationship between these variables. Is the higher rejection rate of nonwhites a function of their race or does it reflect their marital status and/or sex discrimination? A higher share of nonwhite loan applicants (in the Comptroller survey) are currently unmarried (18 percent versus 14 percent for whites), and a higher share of nonwhite loan applicants are female (17 percent versus 14 percent for whites, see Exhibit 6-A-2). Since both currently unmarried (single, divorced, widowed) and female loan applicants are rejected more frequently than their married, male counterparts (see Exhibit 6-3) the fact that nonwhites find it harder to secure credit may reflect their marital status and/or sex, not their race.

Three chi-square tests were employed to examine the interactive affects of race, marital status, and sex (see Exhibit 6-A-3). The first examined loan disposition (DISP) by race (ETH), controlling for marital status (MAR) and sex (SEX). In effect, we were considering DISP by ETH for four subgroups of loan applicants; female married, male married, female currently unmarried, and male currently unmarried. The two other tests looked at DISP by MAR controlling for ETH and SEX, and DISP by SEX controlling for ETH and MAR.

The analysis suggests the predominance of ETH as compared to MAR and SEX. DISP differed significantly by ETH for all subgroups, except female married applicants. The result is interesting for it shows that while nonwhite, male, married applicants are rejected more frequently than their white counterparts, nonwhite, female, married applicants are not treated significantly differently than white females. This outcome may be due to the

### EXHIBIT 6-A-2

### SEX AND MARITAL STATUS BY RACE[1]

*I) Sex by Race (ETH)*

|  | | SEX | | |
|---|---|---|---|---|
|  | | Female | Male | |
| ETH | White | 1522 (13.5%) | 9741 (86.5%) | 11263 |
|  | Nonwhite | 238 (16.9%) | 1172 (83.1%) | 1410 |
|  | | 1760 | 10913 | 12673 |

*II) Marital Status (MAR) by Race (ETH)*

|  | | MAR | | |
|---|---|---|---|---|
|  | | Married | Not Married | |
| ETH | White | 9682 (86.0%) | 1571 (14.0%) | 11253 |
|  | Nonwhite | 1153 (81.8%) | 256 (18.2%) | 1409 |
|  | | 10835 | 1827 | 12662 |

1. Row percentages are indicated.

*Source*: Comptroller of the Currency, *Fair Housing Lending Practices Pilot Project Survey C Approach* (Washington, D.C.: Comptroller of the Currency, July 1975).

key economic role often played by females in the black family. A nonwhite, female, married applicant may apply for a loan where she has stronger economic credentials than her husband. The combination of her economic strength and the fact that she is married appear to be adequate for putting her on par with married white females, at least as far as underwriters are concerned. The marriage factor is extremely important when looking at nonwhite female applicants. While married nonwhite females are rejected 17 percent of the time (about the same as the 16 percent rejection rate for married white female applicants), currently unmarried black females are rejected at a 30 percent rate — almost double the percentage for currently unmarried white female applicants (16 percent). The correlation between DISP and ETH (.37) is highest when dealing with currently unmarried females. (It is weakest with the female married subgroup.)

The overall influence of ETH on DISP stands in contrast to both the relationship of MAR and DISP controlling for ETH and SEX and the relationship of SEX and DISP controlling for ETH and MAR. DISP varies significantly by MAR only for nonwhite females. It is possible that the stiff barriers encountered by females who are nonwhite (there is a .36 correlation between DISP and MAR for this subgroup) is an important reason why DISP varies significantly by marital status.

EXHIBIT 6-A-3

## EXAMINING THE SEPARATE RELATIONSHIPS OF RACE, MARITAL STATUS, AND SEX WITH LOAN DISPOSITION

| Two Primary Variables, Examined | Controls | Control Sub-groups | Significant Difference Between Primary Variables[1] | Correlation[2] |
|---|---|---|---|---|
| DISP By ETH | MAR and SEX | Female married | no | — |
| | | Male married | yes | −.27 |
| | | Female currently unmarried | yes | −.37 |
| | | Male currently unmarried | yes | −.30 |
| DISP by MAR | ETH and SEX | Nonwhite females | yes | −.36 |
| | | White females | no | — |
| | | Nonwhite males | no | — |
| | | White males | no | — |
| DISP by SEX | ETH and MAR | Nonwhite married | no | — |
| | | White married | no | — |
| | | Nonwhite, currently unmarried | no | — |
| | | White, currently unmarried | no | — |

[1]As shown by chi-square test.
[2]As shown by gamma value.

Source: Comptroller of the Currency, Fair Housing Lending Practices Pilot Project Survey C Approach (Washington, D.C.: Comptroller of the Currency, July 1975).

The variation of DISP by SEX disappears completely when controlling for MAR and ETH. This probably reflects the fact that SEX is relatively not as strongly associated with DISP as ETH and MAR (see Exhibit 6-A-3).

It is important to realize the tentative nature of these conclusions. First, they are a product of a selected statistical strategy (such as using a .05 significance level). Accepting a larger margin of error would have yielded significant MAR differences and a significant variation by SEX.

More important is the timing of the Controller survey and the changing nature of loan applicants. The "typical" mortgage applicant in years past was a white married male. Females or unmarried loan applicants were a rarity; of the few that sought credit, many were possibly black — a reflection of the strong role played by the female in the black family. Given this strong overlay of race (ETH) onto the MAR and SEX characteristics, race dominates as the significant consideration, as compared to MAR and SEX. It is not that marital status and sex have no bearing, but rather that in the particular sample (Comptroller survey) these variables are overwhelmed by a racial impact.

The analysis of the married male subgroup in Chapter Six provides strong evidence for the hypothesis that a sex and/or marital status effect, if it exists at all, is of a smaller order of magnitude than the ethnicity influence. When the results of the married males alone are compared to the total group, we should see a significant change if sex and/or marital status were important. Instead, the Mantel-Haenszel statistic (when adjusted for sample size), the estimated gamma between ethnicity and disposition, and the probability of a white versus a nonwhite being accepted for a loan are all similar.

## Notes

1 Comptroller of the Currency, *Fair Housing Lending Practices Pilot Project Survey C Approach* (Washington, D.C.: Comptroller of the Currency, July 14, 1975), pp. II.1.
2. *Ibid.*, p. II.5.
3. *Ibid.*, p. II.4.
4. *Ibid.*
5. Gamma equals $(P - Q)/(P + Q)$ where P is the number concordant pairs while Q is the number of discordant pairs. See Norman H. Nie *et al., Statistical Package for the Social Sciences* (New York: McGraw Hill, 1975), p. 228.
6. See Ketron Inc., *Women in the Mortgage Market: Statistical Methods and Tables for Use in Appraising the Stability of Women's Income* (Washington, D.C.: Government Printing Office, 1976), p. 27.
7. See Kain and Quigley, *Housing Markets and Racial Segregation.*
8. Nathan Mantel and William Haenszel, "Statistical Aspects of the Analysis of Data from Retrospective Studies of Disease," *Journal of the National Cancer Institute,* Vol. 22 (1959), pp. 719-48.
9. *Ibid.*, p. 734-35.
10. Nathan Mantel, "Chi-square Test with One Degree of Freedom: Extensions of the Mantel-Haenszel Procedure," *Journal of the American Statistical Association,* Vol. 50 (1963), pp. 690-700. See also Yvonne M.M. Bishop *et al., Discrete Multivariate Analysis: Theory and Practice* (Cambridge, Mass.: MIT Press, 1974), pp. 146-148; Rupert Miller, "Combining 2x2 Contingency Tables" in *Biostatistics Case Book,* Vol. I, Technical Report #21, (Stanford University, June 14, 1976).
11. Peter J. Bickel; Eugene A. Hammel; and J. William O'Connell, "Sex Bias in Gradual Admissions: Data from Berkeley," *Science,* Vol. 187 (February 7, 1975), pp. 398-404.
12. *Ibid.*
13. James Davis "A Partial Coefficient for Goodman and Kruskal's Gamma" *Journal of the American Statistical Association*, Vol. 62 (1976), pp. 189-193; James Davis,"Hierarchical Models for Significance Tests in Multivariate Contingency Tables: An Exegesis of Goodman's Recent Papers," in *Sociological Methodology 1973-74,* Herbert Costner, editor.
14. L.A. Goodman, "A General Model for the Analysis of Surveys," *American Journal of Sociology,* Vol. 77 (1972), pp. 1035-86; L.A. Goodman, "The Analysis of Multidimensional Contingency Tables: Stepwise Procedure and Direct Estimation Methods for Building Models for Multiple Classifications," *Technometrics,* Vol. 13 (1977), pp. 13-61; L.A. Goodman, "Multivariate Analysis of Qualitative Data: Interactions Among Multiple Classifications," *Journal of the American Statistical Association,* Vol. 65 (1970), pp. 226-256.

Section **III**
*Summary*

Chapter 7
# Perspective and Policy Implications

---

## Introduction

This chapter summarizes the findings of the study and attempts to place the conclusions in appropriate perspective. The discussion broadens the focus away from a narrow statistical testing of the racial influence in lending to a more general evaluation of what has been discovered, how the results relate to existing theory, and the policy applications of the conclusions.

## Summary of Findings

The study examined the urban financing problem. It first described the manifestations of the financing difficulty and then discussed the many influences on the credit crunch (multidimensional model of the urban financing problem). The multidimensional model isolated two factors — race and economics — that have been the subject of intense recent debate. These influences were discussed in terms of two models: economic and eco-race. To better conceptualize the economic versus eco-race debate, the study suggested a mortgage distribution model.

The macro and micro analyses reveal *that race is independently a statistically significant influence on lenders.* The Chicago study indicates that the racial composition of the neighborhood has a significant relationship with the volume of loans given to an area. The WHITE independent variable is significant in explaining some of the variation in the dependent loan volume measures (MS7172, MS7273, MU 7172, MU7273) even after

157

controlling for economic variables. The analysis of the Comptroller of the Currency survey indicates that the race of a mortgage applicant has an independent, statistically significant effect on loan disposition. Significant differences are found in the outcome (accept or reject loan) of white versus minority loan applicants, even after controlling for economic characteristics.

## Statistical and Conceptual Framework of Findings

It is important to be cognizant of some of the study's shortcomings. In general, there is a problem in using any statistical technique to explore complex, multifaceted problems and interactions.[1] There is an added difficulty in considering race and economics, for the two are so intertwined. Furthermore, the conceptualization and definition of the variables that are considered in underwriting and the delineation of neighborhoods (i.e., on a zip code base) are fraught with difficulty because so little is known about actual field level underwriting and neighborhood demarcation practices. The models presented by this study to consider the influence on lending are clearly preliminary attempts suggesting important variables rather than polished schema fully reflecting the complexity of urban underwriting.

The micro and macro data analyzed in this monograph have certain deficiencies. While more current surveys (usually mandated by federal or state disclosure statutes) are often not much more revealing, the Chicago and Comptroller information sets are somewhat dated. Both are incomplete; neither yields a full neighborhood, property or personal borrower profile, and loan demand data are lacking. Both rely on Census data, a source which suffers from certain deficiencies, especially when used for mortgage studies (see Chapter Three). There is an added question with reference to the appropriateness of the Chicago survey; while the neighborhood racial economic cleavages that characterize this city are duplicated in other large, older urban centers, do they typify cities in general? Finally, is a zip code location (or Census tract) an appropriate spatial reporting area with which to study neighborhood lending?

It is also important to remember that race and economics are only two of the many influences on the urban financing problem. The multidimensional model discussed in Chapter One isolated additional geographic, business velocity, and other considerations. Discrimination and economic conditions may indeed be two reasons why there is a credit shortfall, but they are only two of many factors. White residents of older urban areas, not subject to racial bias, may still encounter difficulty in securing credit for such reasons as lenders favoring suburbs or particular urban neighborhoods.

The study has not considered the influence of possible spatial redlining — the denial of loan to an area because of area and not as a function of neighborhood economics or racial characteristics. The reader should be cognizant, however, of the difficulty of isolating such spatial preference; who will define this area and how can the areal factor be isolated from intertwining racial and economic characteristics, especially since the designated location will usually not be coterminous with zip code or Census tract locations.

The dynamic of time and changes over time is another factor not discussed by the analysis. The multidimensional and economic/eco-race models show relationships at one point and do not indicate feedback influences. They suggest that geographic, economic and racial factors (independent variables) influence the supply of credit (dependent variable). Over time a serial dynamic is likely in which the credit shortfall will affect some of the independent variables. To illustrate, a reduction in mortgage availability (dependent variable) will in turn catalyze continued housing deterioration (independent variable).

The serial effects are not incorporated for the data did not allow for longitudinal, empirical analyses. The Chicago survey, while showing loan patterns over a two-year period, was not suitable for showing serial influences because:

1. Loan data were given only for a short span (2 years).
2. The two-year period was consecutive, thus not allowing for an adequate "spread" to see loan volume changes over time.
3. The 1970 Census, the source of the economic and social neighborhood profiles, was not sensitive to the neighborhood changes induced by varying credit availability.

The omission of time analysis does not invalidate the conclusions. Were race merely incidental to economic characteristics, then race would never be significant even when considering economic-racial loan relationships at *one* point in time. It would be a different matter if economics alone and not race could explain credit variation for that would raise the issue of isolating prior discriminatory policies which could have affected present economic conditions.

In sum, this study's analysis has shortcomings endemic to statistical social science research in general and specific deficiencies arising from choice of sample, analytic strategy, etc. This discussion is not meant to discredit the findings, but rather to alert the reader to these issues. The analysis of redlining and the question of race versus economic underwriting is just beginning. Extensive ongoing research by the Harvard-MIT Joint Center and others (see Appendix 3-A) will throw further light on the causes of the unequal distribution of credit in urban and suburban areas.

## Theoretical Framework of Findings

THE CONTINUING DEBATE OVER THE INFLUENCE OF RACIAL
DISCRIMINATION

The 1960's saw an outpouring of studies documenting the disadvantaged economic position of minorities and the racial discriminatory barriers they faced.[2] The National Advisory Commission on Civil Disorders reflected the spirit of these analyses when it reported "our nation is moving toward two societies, one black, one white — separate and unequal."[3]

Increased efforts were taken in the 1960s to remove minority racial barriers and to upgrade minority economic status. New legal safeguards were provided by constitutional amendments prohibiting discrimination in voting, housing, etc. Existing civil rights statutes were meaningfully enforced for the first time. A score of programs — "Grey area," Model Cities, War on Poverty — were established to address the housing, employment and social problems of minorities.

These policies met some success; "Jim Crow" discrimination in the South, especially barriers to voting and access to public facilities, have largely been removed. Blacks have made substantial gains in other areas such as educational attainment (i.e., the percentage completing high school has increased). But while improvements have been made, the real significance of the changing economic and social profile of minorities (and implicitly the continued presence and nature of discrimination) has been the subject of debate over the last decade.[4] While Ben Wattenberg and Richard Scammon, for example, reported that "it is clear the American Negro is winning his fight — certainly not as fast as he wishes to win it but winning it nonetheless,"[5] Sar A. Levitan concluded that black economic equality with whites was "still a dream."[6] Social scientists have debated which criteria are the most meaningful for showing change in social position and how should shifts be best interpreted (i.e., absolute versus relative changes in black economic attainment).

The debate over black status and discrimination, ongoing for the past decade, has recently been intensified by the publication of *The Declining Significance of Race*[7] by William Wilson. This author traces three periods of racial relations in the United States: preindustrial (the 17th to late 19th century), industrial (the late 19th century to World War I), and modern industrial (post World War II). An unyielding racial-caste system existed in the first period. In the second, black-white boundaries were not as rigid, but nonetheless blacks were subject to pervasive racial oppression. In the last period racial barriers were much less important:[8]

> Race relations in the United States have undergone fundamental changes
> in recent years, so much so that now the life chances of individual blacks
> have more to do with their economic class position than with their day-to-

day encounters with whites . . . In short, whereas the old barriers portrayed the pervasive features of racial oppression, the new barriers indicate an important and emerging form of class subordination.

Wilson does not argue that racism is no longer a barrier, but rather that class, namely the economic position of minorites, is "more important than race in determining black life chances in the modern industrial period."[9] Minorities, as well as underclass whites, are seen as suffering from similar pervasive and destructive features of membership in the lowest economic class.

The Wilson thesis has been criticized by Kenneth Clark and others. Clark, for example, argues that "race is still the dominant factor in determining blacks' chances in life."[10] He cites the seminal inferiority of segregated education and the continued dependence of black progress upon white benevolence.

In a sense,Wilson supports the economic model of lender behavior — blacks experience problems in obtaining credit because of their economic (class) position.

This study's acceptance of the eco-race rather than the economic model of lender behavior suggests that racial discrimination, and not only economic or class considerations, acts as a barrier to minorites wishing to obtain credit.

Discriminatory barriers to obtaining credit are an especially significant impediment to nonwhite economic advancement. A credit crunch, by fostering neighborhood and housing decay, imperils existing minority living conditions and assets. It is economically deleterious in other ways as well. Studies by John Shelton, Henry Aaron and John Kain[11] have indicated that it is less expensive to own a house than to rent because of the generous tax benefits accorded to homeowners; racial discrimination in lending also affects future black economic status for it denies minorities an opportunity to increase their assets from the appreciation in home values:[12]

> Homeownership has clearly been the most important method of wealth accumulation for low and middle-income families in the current period . . . Home equities accounted for more than one-third of the wealth of all United State households earning between $10,000 and $15,000 . . . If . . . discrimination in urban housing markets has reduced black opportunities for home ownership, this limitation is an important explanation of the smaller quality assets owned by black households of each income level.

The cycle of poverty moreover perpetuates itself. If minorities cannot accrue assets from homeownership, then they will continue to encounter difficulties in purchasing a home since they will lack an adequate downpayment and may fail to gain credit approval. (Chapter Six indicated that assets, along with income, are two important individual underwriting variables.)

In sum, while race may be a lesser credit influence today than in years past, this study takes issue with the position that discrimination is no longer a major impediment to minority advancement.

RELATIONSHIP OF FINDINGS TO
THE EXISTING URBAN FINANCING LITERATURE

Chapter Four identified three groups of studies examining the urban financing problem: (1) political-economic; (2) minority housing opportunity; and (3) empirical economic and eco-race. While this study is closest to the empirical economic eco-race literature, its findings have certain implications for the other two categories of analyses.

The political-economic approach is, in part, a reaction to the inadequacy of the liberal conception of "freely working economic forces that would act rationally and with equal opportunity toward the greatest good of all."[13] This study suggests that credit allocation is not a purely rational, egalitarian process, but is subject to "irrational" racial policies. It is in terms of the acknowledgement and interpretation of the racial influence that the analysis differs from the political-economic view of "redlining." Harvey and other latter-day radical geographers have emphasized economic-class determinism;[14] ghettos and slums are the products of "usual" capitalist entrepreneurial behavior.[15] Racial discrimination is given very little attention and is interpreted in various ways: (1) discrimination is a consequence of economic exploitation to the extent that blacks are a source of cheap labor for industry; (2) discrimination is a deliberate policy fostered by the bourgeoisie to placate the white underclass (the white lumpenproletariat will feel more privileged compared to blacks despite their exploitation by the bourgeoisie) and to divide the white and black proletariat; and (3) racial segregation and bias is indeed a separate force from class segregation, but it is less important than class separation.

Our finding that race is a significant underwriting criteria suggests that the political economists should devote greater attention to racial influences. This is not to say that race is necessarily more important than class, or that it is impossible to separate race and class (as some British radical geographers have argued).* Race may indeed be just a corollary to economic exploitation (as explained above), but it still is an urban influence that deserves more discussion than has been given by the political economists.

The radical geographers themselves have recognized the need to consider other urban influences besides class.[16] John Campbell, for example, has suggested a typology of major and minor determinants of urban segrega-

---

*It is interesting to note the British Institute of Race Relations, the publisher of the journal *Race* changed the title of this periodical to *Race and Class*. The Institute argued that race could not be discussed independently from class.

*Race and Class* contains many articles on Third World exploitation and this focus may partially explain the added significance attributed to racial influences. We find a similar race-class consciousness in other Third World studies. See Peter Simmons "Red Legs: Class and Color Contradictions in Barbados," *Studies in Comparative International Development.* Vol. II (Spring 1976), pp. 3-24.

tion.[17] The major distinction concerns class, but there are also three minor influences: (1) segregation which results from the impact of recent migration; (2) racial segregation; and (3) segregation due to "differential residential utility functions of different types of people" (e.g., the elderly, women, etc.).[18]

RELATIONSHIPS OF FINDINGS TO
MINORITY HOUSING OPPORTUNITY LITERATURE

The study's findings and analysis are related to the "classic" minority housing opportunity studies in the sense that it updates their conclusions of a decade ago; while Grier, and Helper[19] documented instances of credit discrimination in the 1960's, this analysis indicates continued racial barriers in the 1970s.

The most recent and dynamic work in minority housing opportunity has been conducted by Kain and Quigley.[20] Their work represents a conceptual departure from the traditional housing and location theories of Von Thunen, Alonso and Muth. The traditional theorists stressed long-run equilibrium and avoided externalities and interdependence.[21] Kain and Quigley suggest that the housing stock is not characterized by long-term equilibrium, but is influenced by such "blips" as heterogeneity, durability and irregular spatial distribution. They stress the strong impact of non-market forces, especially racial discrimination.

In many respects, traditional housing theory is similar to the economic model of lender behavior. Both emphasize rational, economic forces; the city is formed according to immutable economic residential location decisions; credit is distributed according to objective and universal underwriting standards. The eco-race model, in contrast, is conceptually closer to Kain and Quigley's model of housing-location behavior in the sense that it too recognizes externalities and stresses the nonrational but nonetheless strong impact of race. The thesis that the eco-race model is more valid than the economic one is analogous to the Kain-Quigley departure from traditional general housing-location theory.

While conceptually similar, this analysis is not redundant to the Kain-Quigley approach but rather adds to the understanding of the process and internal dynamic of racial restrictions in housing. Kain-Quigley focus on the outcome of the housing market as evidence of internal racial restrictions. Bias is inferred if housing output is unevenly distributed in favor of whites (in terms of share of homeownership, cost of housing, or the opportunity to live in suburbs) and if these discrepancies cannot be explained by economic (income, family size, age, etc.) or attitudinal factors (i.e., blacks prefer to live with blacks).[22]

Kain and Quigley conclude from the outcome of the housing market that discrimination is a widespread barrier to improved housing opportunities for minorities. They do not elaborate on the *process* of discrimination, however, but rather mention some possible "supply restrictions", such as realtors steering blacks to black neighborhoods or lenders discriminating against minorities.

This study adds to the Kain-Quigley analysis by empirically documenting that one of the "supply restrictions" they suggest is indeed a statistically significant barrier. Discrimination in lending is very likely an important reason why Kain-Quigley find such patterns as a much lower homeownership rate for blacks versus whites. (It is interesting to note that other researchers are currently attempting to document and detail other discriminatory process mechanisms such as the declining availability of home insurance in minority areas.)

This study adds to the their research in other ways as well. It can address a question they raise concerning the ability of blacks to purchase homes, given their more limited assets. Kain and Quigley lack black asset data and thus cannot control for this important determinant of homeownership. They argue that this omission is tolerable because of two reasons: black income is related to black assets and they control for black income. Black assets reflect blacks' prior ability to purchase a home. Thus lower black assets are in part a proxy of past discrimination.

Howard Birnbaum and Rafael Wetson have examined the black asset question.[23] They obtained asset data from the Survey of Economic Opportunity and entered an asset variable into a similar multiple regression equation used by Kain-Quigley to control for the economic determinants of homownership. Birnbaum and Wetson similarly found that race was a significant influence, albeit that its importance was reduced when assets as well as income were entered into the regression model.

This monograph's micro analysis can add to the evaluation of the influence of assets and its importance in explaining minority homeownership potential. It confirms the Kain-Quigley argument that income and assets are highly intercorrelated (there is a .63 gamma between income and assets). It also shows that blacks' more limited assets cannot explain their lower rate of homeownership (at least in terms of access to credit) for there are significant racial variations in securing credit even after controlling for lower nonwhite assets.

The micro analysis adds to Kain-Quigley in still one other respect. They suggest that one possible explanation for lower black homeownership is the difference in the "taste" for homeownership, i.e., blacks may be less willing to shoulder the financial burden of owning a home.[24] Kain and Quigley debunk the cultural hypothesis by arguing that it is unlikely that such a difference actually exists. This study and the Birnbaum-Wetson analysis support the Kain-Quigley contention that blacks are not culturally less willing to purchase a home. Birnbaum-Wetson prove that at every income level blacks consistently invest a larger share of wealth in home as compared to other types of equity (car, stocks, bonds, etc.). The analysis of the

Comptroller of the Currency's survey reveals that black homeowners are willing to spend a larger share of their income for a house than whites. (BURDEN is significantly higher for minority loan applicants.) In sum, blacks are favorably inclined to invest in a home and are willing to assume a larger financial hardship to pay for their purchase.

RELATIONSHIP OF FINDINGS TO
RECENT ECONOMIC AND ECO-RACE STUDIES

Appendix 3-A identified numerous major empirical analyses conducted by Robert Schafer, George Benston and others. Some of these support the economic hypothesis, others the eco-race hypothesis.

It is difficult to compare studies. For example, this monograph utilizes zip codes as the spatial reporting base (in the Chicago survey) while most other analyses employ Census tracts. Zip codes and Census tracts both have strengths and weaknesses. Some zip codes are so large that they encompass several "neighborhoods"; the Census values averaged over a zip code may therefore not be representative of any of the contained "neighborhoods." On the positive side, the zip code loan rates are fairly stable since they are averaged over a relatively large group of housing units.

Analyses utilizing Census tracts offer complementary advantages/problems. The tracts are generally small enough so that they encompass homogeneous areas—"average" tract variables — characteristics are therefore more meaningful. But Census tracts may be too small a base for measuring mortgage loan frequency. In Hauser's study, for example, approximately 23 percent of the Census tracts received no loans, while another 27 percent were granted 1-5 loans.

The skewness in the Census loan measure, typified by the high concentration of zeroes, makes it difficult to utilize regression analysis. The stability of the Census loan measure is also an issue; since the number of mortgages granted per tract is often minimal, perturbations in local conditions can have a large relative effect. This disturbance affects the precision of regression analysis by adding random noise to the data. Finally, logarithms of the loan measures cannot be easily used for Census tract data because of the frequency of zeroes.

There are similarities and differences in the models and statistical approaches utilized in the different studies. This monograph as well as most other investigations (e.g. by Dingemans and Ahlbrandt), standardize loan volume measures. This standardization is not always done, however (see the Hauser and Hutchinson studies).

The method of analysis and interpretation—regression with t-tests and partial correlations—is generally similar in this and other analyses. Results do differ. The race effect is usually weaker in the studies involving Census tracts. The correlations between percentage nonwhite and loans in the

Hauser and Dingemans studies (.31 and .40, respectively) are lower than the correlation in this study. Hauser's partial correlation (when economics are controlled) is a substantively insignificant .12, while in the Dingemans study, race is the fourth variable entered into a stepwise regression and shows a weak effect. Ahlbrandt and Hutchinson do not give the original correlations of race and loans, but report generally statistically insignificant results for race in their regressions. Hutchinson also tests for curvature in the race effect, finding it to be insignificant.

Some of the recent studies have approached the loan distribution question by a "neighborhood extension" method. They compute an equation to predict the number of loans granted to neighborhoods receiving adequate credit. This equation is then applied to an allegedly redlined area. The redlining charge is contested if the predicted number of loans is less than or equal to the actual number of loans that are granted in the mortgage-short neighborhood.

The study has not followed a "neighborhood extension" strategy for two reasons. Predicting loans in the allegedly redlined areas typically involves extrapolation of the regression equation well beyond the range in which it was computed. (For instance, median income is usually much lower in the allegedly redlined areas than in the control neighborhoods.) To justify this extrapolation, one must assume that the regression equation is valid over a broader area than that for which it was computed—an assumption that is open to question and is not easy to justify (or refute). Even if the extrapolation is reasonable, the estimated error of the predicted value will be relatively high. (The estimated error of a predicted point increases as the magnitude of the independent values, used in the prediction, depart from the means of the variables in the control group.) Thus, even if the predicted dependent loan frequencies appear to signify that redlining does not exist, the standard error of the predicted value may be so large as to make the estimate barely meaningful.

## Policy Implications of the Findings

This study's major finding is the significance of race. The racial barrier should be met with vigorous enforcement of anti-discriminatory statutes. This strategy requires documentation of possible discrimination and a willingness to pursue vigorous executive and judicial action.

## Data Collection:
## Mortgage Disclosure

In May, 1975, the Home Mortgage Disclosure Act was signed into law by President Ford.[25] The stated purpose of the Act is to "provide the citizens and public officials of the United States with sufficient information to enable them to determine whether depository institutions are fulfilling their obligations to serve the housing needs of the communities and neighborhoods in which they are located."[26] This goal is to be attained through the disclosure of mortgage-lending information by certain financial institutions located within urban areas. The minimum information to be collected and made publicly available includes the number and dollar amount of residential mortgage and home improvement loans by geographic area, the breakdown between loans to owner-occupied versus absentee-owned housing, and whether the mortgage loans are FHA or VA insured.

In regulations issued in June 1976, the Federal Reserve Board specified the exact type of data and manner of presentation required of lending institutions (Exhibit 7-1). The regulations require institutions making any federally related mortgage loans to disclose aggregate data on number of loans and total loan amount with respect to mortgages and home improvement loans on single-family and multiple-unit dwellings. For the fiscal year ending June 1976, these data are to be reported for postal zip code areas and made publicly available by September 30, 1976. After the initial year, information is to be reported by Census tract, except for those counties not tracted (see Exhibit 7-1).

Much concern over the urban financing problem has also arisen at the state level, especially in California, Massachusetts and Illinois, where laws or administrative regulations attempt to combat the credit shortfall through mortgage disclosure. Several other states, notably New York, New Jersey, Michigan and Wisconsin, have enacted similar laws or rules (see Exhibit 7-1).

State disclosure requirements vary greatly. California has the most comprehensive reporting system. The following is required for each loan originated or puchased: race of applicant; Census tract; purpose (speculative construction, construction for owner, purchase of property, refinance, home improvement); type of property; number of units; loan amount; appraised value; selling price; interest rate; term-to-maturity; fees; discount; and whether or not the loan is a variable rate/federally insured mortgage. In addition, information on denied loans is collected as well as the status of verbal loan requests where a written application has not been completed.

More typical (and limited) are disclosure statutes that call for depository institutions to disclose the number and total dollar amount of mortgage loans originated or purchased by that institution. Loan data are to be listed for each zip code or Census tract and catalogued by type of loan (e.g., FHA-insured versus conventional).

## EXHIBIT 7-1

## A COMPARISON OF FEDERAL AND SELECTED STATE DISCLOSURE REQUIREMENTS

| *Jurisdiction:* | *Federal* | *California* |
|---|---|---|
| DISCLOSURE STATUTE, DIRECTIVE, OR BILL | Home Mortgage Disclosure Act of 1975, Title III of P.L. 94-200 | Admin. Code Title 10, Ch. 2 Sub. ch. 23. |
| WHO DISCLOSES | Depository institutions (savings and loan association, commercial bank, or credit union) with assets of $10 million or more located in an SMSA and making "federally related mortgage loans" | State-chartered savings and loan associations |
| WHICH MORTGAGES REQUIRE DISCLOSURE | "mortgage loan"—loan secured by residential real property or a home improvement loan | Loans secured by a lien or real estate |
| BREAKDOWN OF REQUIRED MORTGAGE DATA | I. Mortgage loan data (number and dollar amount) divided into two categories:<br><br>*originations*—loans originally made by the depository institution<br><br>*purchase loans*<br><br>II. Within each of these categories, the data must be segregated between loans on property located within the *relevant SMSA* (i.e., the SMSA where a home or branch office is located) and loans on property outside of the relevant SMSA. Each of these segregations must be further itemized to show the number of loans of total dollar amounts of different categories of mortgages (i.e., FHA and VA loans).<br><br>III. Loans located within the "relevant" SMSA must be further itemized by either census tract or zip code. | I. data on successful and unsuccessful loan applications including race of applications including race of applicant, purpose, type of property, loan amount, value of units of mortgaged property, loan interest rate, and loan terms<br><br>I. locations of successful and unsuccessful loan by Census tract |
| DISCLOSURE UNIT | By Census tract where readily available and reasonable costs are determined by the Federal Reserve, otherwise by zip code. The Board has tentatively decided to require disclosure by Census tract. | Census tract |
| DISCLOSURE MONITORING BODY | Federal Reserve | California Business and Transportation Agency |

EXHIBIT 7-1 (continued)

## A COMPARISON OF FEDERAL AND SELECTED STATE DISCLOSURE REQUIREMENTS

| *Jurisdiction:* | *Massachusetts* | *New York* |
|---|---|---|
| OTHER FEATURES | For institutions with offices in only one SMSA, data are to be made available at the home office and one branch office. A depository institution with offices in more than one SMSA would be required to make data available in at least one branch office in each SMSA.<br><br>The Board can grant exemptions to state-chartered institutions subject to local disclosure laws that are substantially similar to the federal requirements. | California has required some disclosures since 1964 in its Loan Register. |
| DISCLOSURE STATUTE, DIRECTIVE, OR BILL | Publication 8260-9-555-7-75 CR of the Massachusetts Commissioner of Banks | Supervisory Procedure G107 and appendices (February 18, 1976) |
| WHO DISCLOSES | State-chartered banks and credit unions having $20 million in deposits and having main offices located within the Boston SMSA. | State-chartered banks, trust companies, savings banks, and savings and loan associations with assets of $50 million or more. Disclosure is also required of national banks and federally chartered savings and loan associations located in New York. |
| WHICH MORTGAGES REQUIRE DISCLOSURE | Mortgages | Loan secured by a mortgage or other lien upon real property, whether residential or otherwise. |
| BREAKDOWN OF REQUIRED MORTGAGE DATA | I. Number of mortgages granted, average interest rate, outstanding balance, number of applications, average down payment, and number of foreclosures segregated by:<br>a. zip code areas for all cities and towns within the Boston SMSA<br>b. total for all other areas within Massachusetts<br>c. total for all out of state<br>d. Census tract areas for selected towns and cities.<br>II. Within each of these categories the data must be segregated by FHA/VA loans, non-FHA/VA loans, loans on all other buildings designed principally as residences, home improvement loans, and all other mortgages. | I. data on written mortgage application including:<br>a. SMSA census tract of the subject property on which a mortgage loan is sought<br>b. background data on mortgage applicant and property<br>c. disposition of application<br>d. reasons for denial or mortgage loan<br>II. data on financial institutions and other operations<br>III. disclosure of location of mortgage loan by zip code or census tract giving total number and aggregate amount of loan. Loans are to be segregated into various categories. |

## EXHIBIT 7-1 (continued)

### A COMPARISON OF FEDERAL AND SELECTED STATE DISCLOSURE REQUIREMENTS

| Jurisdiction: | Massachusetts | New York |
|---|---|---|
| DISCLOSURE UNIT | a. zip code<br>b. Census tract<br>c. in Massachusetts but outside Boston SMSA<br>d. outside Massachusetts | By Census tract for loans secured by property located within (and deposits received from) SMSAs; by zip code areas in the case of all other mortgage loans or deposits |
| DISCLOSURE MONITORING BODY | Massachusetts Commissioner of Banks | New York Banking Department |
| OTHER FEATURES | Deposit information is also required including the number and amount of savings. Time, new, and demand accounts must be segregated into zip code, Census tract, in state, and out-of-state categories. | A sample of deposits (number and amount) will be disclosed by either zip code or Census tract. Loan and deposit data are to be submitted in a computer readable format. |

A first-lien mortgage loan on 1-4 family residences that is federally-insured or an original loan that is insured or guaranteed by HUD or intended to be sold to FNMA, GNMA, GNMA or FHLMC.

Includes loans on single-family homes, residences from 1-4 families, and multifamily dwellings, loans on individual units of condominiums and cooperatives, and both secured and unsecured home improvement loans. Junior mortgages as well as senior mortgages would be covered and a participating interest in specific mortgage loans would be disclosed to the extent of the participation. A refinancing involving an increase in the unpaid principal amount would be considered a new mortgage.

The specific loan breakout includes: (a) originated or purchased FHA, FMHA, and VA loans; (b) originated or purchased mortgage loans made to mortgagors not residing in the mortgaged property; and (c) originated or purchased home improvement loans. Data for loans on multifamily dwellings (4 units or more) would be separately itemized, but would not require the loan breakout (i.e., FHA, home improvement) described above.

Includes applicant gross annual income, years at present employment, amount of outstanding debts, monthly debt payments, assets, amount of loan requested, purchase price of subject property, and whether subject property will be owner-occupied.

Includes type, size, total real estate loans and participation on properties located in and outside New York State, total number of construction loans, total number of FHA/VA loans and participations (segregated by in-house and outside servicing and location within and outside New York State), aggregate dollar amount of GNMA pass-throughs, etc.

Includes number of mortgaged properties presently under foreclosure action, value of purchase money mortgages, average rate of interest, average loan-to-value ratio. These data are to be further segregated into various categories such as conventional vs. FHA/VA, own vs. outside serviced loans.

*Note:* Federal and state disclosure requirements are frequently modified.
*Source:* Michael Agelasto and David Listokin, "Redlining in Perspective"; Donald Phares (ed), *A Decent Home and Environment: Housing Urban America* (Cambridge: Ballinger, 1977), Chapter 4.

MORTGAGE DISCLOSURE: EVALUATION

A major problem in conducting this study was the difficulty in securing adequate data. With the exception of the California, New York and perhaps Illinois disclosure statutes, the first wave of federal and state disclosure has not significantly improved the situation. The drawbacks can be evaluated by considering the general mortgage distribution model. To properly evaluate the credit crunch and the appropriateness of lender credit policies, loan demand and loan selection should be analyzed. The federal mortgage disclosure statute and most state legislation do not require any demand information. They ask that lenders list where they are making loans but do not require credit institutions to tabulate the requests for loans they have received.

In addition to avoiding the question of loan demand, the first wave of disclosure requirements gives an inadequate base for considering loan selection. While an analyst requires lender, property and neighborhood profiles, disclosure only shows neighborhood — the zip code or Census tract where loans are made. Most statutes do not require that lenders describe who applied for credit and the type of parcel that will stand as security for the loan — crucial information for determining whether lenders are following prudent underwriting standards or are unjustifiably disinvesting.

Federal and most state disclosure laws currently often provide an incomplete picture for examining or documenting cases of discrimination. More comprehensive statutes, which would yield demand and loan selection variables, are required. The California rules are a good model for future consideration.

## Civil Rights Enforcement

A logical choice for eliminating racial bias in lending is enforcement through litigation of existing civil rights statutes and guarantees. The basic provisions requiring federal financial regulatory agencies to act affirmatively to eliminate discrimination in lending are contained in Executive Order 11063.[27] This was issued in 1962 by President Kennedy to insure equal opportunity in federal-assisted housing. Title VI of the 1964 Civil Rights Act prohibits racial discrimination in other programs or activities receiving federal financial assistance.[28]

Executive Order 11063 and Title VI of the 1964 Civil Rights Act have long stood as *potential* weapons against discrimination in lending yet they were often not effective because the plight of mortgage-short areas had not been given the attention it receives today. Also, proving racial discrimination in predisclosure days was nearly impossible. And in the past, some of the federal financial regulatory agencies, who were charged with enforcing the safeguards, have adhered to a conservative outlook on financing.[29]

The Fair Housing Act of 1968, referred to as Title VIII, generally prohibits financial institutions that make real estate loans from discriminating.[30] Section 808(d) requires all federal agencies to implement their programs in a manner that would achieve the fair housing goal and to cooperate with the Secretary of HUD, who is charged with the overall responsibility for administering the program.[31]

*Laufman v. Oakley Building and Loan Company* is the first lawsuit under Title VIII involving discrimination in housing finance.[32] Robert Laufman brought a class action suit on behalf of all property owners residing in racially integrated or predominately black neighborhoods as well as prospective purchasers of homes in such areas. The suit charged that Oakley Building and Loan Company of Cincinnati had rejected loan applications for houses in a racially integrated neighborhood. The plaintiff averred that the loans were denied for racial reasons and this rejection violated civil-rights guarantees. Oakley retorted that the Civil Rights Act was not applicable.

In February 1976, the U.S. District Court for Southern Ohio ruled that a prospective homebuyer denied a loan because of neighborhood racial composition can bring action under Title VIII of the 1968 Civil Rights Act.[33] The court stated that redlining would violate Section 804 of the act, which prohibits discrimination in the provision of services relating to selling or renting a dwelling, as well as Section 805, which prohibits discrimination in the financing of housing. The *Laufman* ruling is important because it acknowledges civil rights litigation as a medium for fighting suspect lending practice.

Subsequent to *Laufman,* a number of other suits, such as the *Heinzeroth*[34] case, have been tried alleging racial discrimination in lending. And federal regulatory agencies such as the Federal Home Loan Bank Board have promulgated guidelines prohibiting lending discrimination based on individual/neighborhood race, sex, age or other suspect characteristics.[35]

An enforcement strategy to address the credit shortfall is a type of action that is likely to gain in popularity. The organizations that have been the most active in 'ighting the financing problem (i.e., the NCDH, NAACP, Urban League) have emphasized a litigation policy, much in the same way they have fought racial barriers in voting, employment, etc.

Litigation against racial bias in lending is likely to achieve the same slow progress that other civil rights enforcement efforts have attained. It is a strategy fraught with difficulty.

1. *It is difficult to prove discrimination in lending.* This study has shown some of the problems of documenting bias. The flaws in present disclosure statutes will perpetuate many of these difficulties.

2. *The courts have retreated in their support of active civil rights enforcement.* Many courts are now requiring a more stringent level of proof (i.e., intent to discriminate in zoning, not just discriminatory effect) and are hesitant to allow strong relief measures.

3. *Civil rights enforcement is a limited policy.* Racial barriers are only one restriction to minority and center city credit access. In the discussion of the conceptual framework other restraints such as geographical favoritism were mentioned. There is also the question of role. Even were discrimination eliminated, banks in many states would have no obligation to substantially invest in mortgages. An emerging vital question concerns the appropriate role and obligation of financial institutions; are lenders required to make certain public or quasi-benefit investments, that might not have the highest yield or lowest risk, solely because they are publically chartered institutions (the same question is currently being asked of FNMA and public pension funds)?

## Other Strategies to Address the Urban Financing Problem

Race is only one contributor to the urban financing shortfall and, hence, strategies that go beyond addressing just discrimination in lending should be considered.

The traditional approach for ameliorating the urban credit crunch has been for lenders to establish a pool of loans targeted for mortgage-short areas. Mortgage pools spread the risk of individual loans among the participating institutions so that no single lender is disproportionately penalized in the event of a bad loan.

This strategy has a long history. In 1954, the Voluntary Home Mortgage Credit Program (VHMCP) was established to facilitate lending in areas avoided by financial institutions and to encourage mortgage borrowing by minorities. An applicant rejected for an FHA-VA loan by two or more lending institutions could apply to a regional VHMCP office, which maintained a roster of cooperating banks. Mortgage applicants were then sent on a rotating basis to these institutions until accepted. The Federal government provided a small coordinating staff, office facilities, and advice.

A more recent effort was the life insurance industry's 1970 Urban Investment Program.[36] Over 140 life insurance companies made commitments to invest in inner city housing and job-creating opportunities. On a prorated basis according to their assets, the companies invested $2 billion in urban areas they normally avoided.

Many financial institutions have established urban pool and other supportive programs, such as mortgage review boards and special service corporations to rehabilitate properties. Some examples include the New York State pool and the Mortgage Review Board, the Community Participation

Corporation (CPC) in New York City, the Boston Urban Renewal Group, the Philadelphia and New Haven pools, the Philadelphia Mortgage Plan (The PMP is not a loan pool program, but rather is a federated effort by lenders to follow more realistic urban underwriting criteria.), the Savings Service Corporation in St. Louis, the Mortgage Opportunity Committee in Pittsburgh, the California Savings Associations Mortgage Company, Inc. and the Savings Associations Final Enterprises, Inc. in Washington, D.C.

These voluntary investment efforts have achieved some measure of success. The Urban Investment Program helped finance the construction or rehabilitation of over 60,000 units, and the New York State pool helped finance many of the Bedford Stuyvesant Restoration Corporation's initial housing efforts. The PMP has succeeded in granting over 4,000 mortgages in Philadelphia. CPC has sparked substantive renovation in many troubled multifamily buildings. Profit was one of the factors that prompted these investments, although the expected return on any of the loans proved less than what could be expected on comparable non-urban mortgages. Other important considerations were protection of sunk investments and to demonstrate to the public the social conscience of the business community.

To encourage further private urban lending, some jurisdictions have attempted to reduce lender risk, through such means as offering mortgage insurance. The Maryland Housing Fund offers up to 100 percent insurance coverage of single-family loans for Baltimore properties.[37] A number of other insurance programs, such as a Fresno, California effort[38] and more recently the Real Estate Mortgage Insurance Program (REMIC) in New York City,[39] have been developed.

The insurance strategy offers numerous advantages. Lenders will be more amenable to granting urban mortgages if their liability is reduced. Additionally, a considerable leverage results from the amount of insurance that is generated from a relatively small public investment. REMIC, for example, was capitalized with a $7.5 million reserve and this reserve is deemed sufficient to sustain $150 million in insurance coverage — a leverage ratio of 1:20.

Other combined public-private policy initiatives can encourage greater urban lending. The Neighborhood Housing Services (NHS) demonstrates the viability of such joint action. This program includes the High Risk Revolving Loan Fund which is established through grants from foundations, financial institutions, businesses, corporations, and more recently, the Urban Reinvestment Task Force. Individuals in the target communities denied conventional financing and considered unacceptable for loans by traditional lending institutions apply to NHS. A loan committee reviews the applications. If approved, the applicant is granted a loan from the High Risk Loan Fund at interest rates ranging from zero to market rate, depending on the particular financial circumstances. Bankable loans are referred to cooperating lenders, who are expected to be more sympathetic to granting financing as a result of the NHS's supportive activities. Local governments participate through programs designed to prevent neighborhood deterioration such as code enforcement and improving public facilities and services.

Special incentive programs to encourage innovative urban financing programs are also being explored. A prime example is the $2 billion Community Investment Fund (CIF) established by the Federal Home Loan Bank Board. The CIF advances lower cost loans to saving institutions initiating innovative financing and neighborhood supportive actions, such as loan counselling. To date about $400 million of the $2 billion fund has been credited to over 500 institutions.

## Conclusion

The discussed above is only a brief capsule of the steps being undertaken to both force and encourage increased urban lending. In part, civil rights groups are applying the same litigation strategy they have used in the areas of voting, equal employment opportunity, etc. In part, regulatory agencies are moving to force compliance with existing borrower safeguards and to provide incentives for increased lender activity. In part, lenders themselves are realizing that the cities offer a potentially viable market. The very rules or standards for lender activity in and responsibility towards urban neighborhoods are also changing; the Community Reinvestment Act, for example, requires financial institutions to file statements describing how they are serving the needs of host neighborhoods.

Clearly changes are occurring. Are these changes adequate? The ultimate resolution of the urban financing problem depends on the ability to address discrimination in lending and to improve urban housing and economic conditions. The twenty-five year struggle following the *Brown* decision attests to the difficulty of ensuring equal rights to minorities. The difficulties of revitalizing the urban economic base and housing stock needs no elaboration — it requires a massive national commitment that has yet to be forthcoming on an enduring basis.

There is no easy answer to the urban credit shortfall. This monograph has attempted to provide some framework for discussion and further research.

## Notes

1. John Madge, *The Tools of Social Science* (New York: Anchor Books, 1965); Abraham Kaplan, *The Conduct of Scientific Inquiry* (Scranton: Chandler, 1964).
2. See National Advisory Commission on Civil Disorders, *Report* (New York: E.P. Dutton, 1968).
3. *Ibid.*
4. John F. Kain and John M. Quigley, *Housing Markets and Racial Discrimination* (New York: National Bureau of Economic Research, 1975). See "Bibliography" pp. 377, 385.
5. Ben J. Wattenberg and Richard M. Scammon, *This U.S.A.* (Garden City, N.Y.: Doubleday, 1965), p. 297.
6. Sar A. Levitan *et al., Still a Dream — The Changing Status of Blacks Since 1960* (Cambridge: Harvard University Press, 1975).
7. William Julius Wilson, *The Declining Significance of Race* (Chicago: University of Chicago Press, 1978).
8. William Julius Wilson, "The Declining Significance of Race," *Society,* Vol. 15, No. 2 (January/February 1978), p. 56.
9. *Ibid.*
10. Kenneth B. Clark, "No. No. Race, Not Class is Still at the Wheel," *The New York Times,* March 22, 1978, p. A25.
11. John P. Shelton, "The Costs of Renting Versus Owning A Home," *Land Economics* Vol. 44, (February 1968), pp. 59-72; Henry Aaron, "Income Taxes and Housing," *American Economic Review,* Vol. 60, No. 5 (December 1970), pp. 789-806. Cited in Kain and Quigley, *Housing Markets and Racial Discrimination,* p. 148.
12. Kain and Quigley, *Housing Markets and Racial Discrimination,* p. 158.
13. P.L. Wagner, "Reflections on a Radical Geography," *Antipode,* Vol. 8, No. 3 (September 1976), p. 83.
14. Michael E. Stone, "The Housing Crisis, Mortgage Lending and Class Struggle," *Antipode,* Vol. 7, No. 2 (September 1973), pp. 9-21; David Harvey, "Revolution and Counter Revolutionary Theory in Geography and the Problem of Ghetto Formation," *Antipode,* Vol. 4, No. 2 (July 1977), p. 9.
15. *Ibid.*
16. John S. Campbell, "Libertarian Reactions to a Marxist View: Comment of David Harvey," *Antipode,* Vol. 4, No. 2 (July 1977), p. 21-25.
17. *Ibid.*
18. *Ibid.,* p. 24.
19. See Chapter Three of this monograph.
20. Kain and Quigley, *Housing Markets and Racial Discrimination.*
21. *Ibid.,* Chapter 2.
22. *Ibid.,* Chapters 3 and 5.
23. Harold Birnbaum and Rafael Wetson, "Homeownership and the Wealth Positions of Black and White Americans," *Review of Income and Wealth* Series 20, No. 1 (March 1974), pp. 103-119.
24. See also Edward C. Banfield, *The Unheavenly City Revisited* (Boston: Little Brown, 1974).
25. P.L. 94-200.
26. P.L. 94-200, Sect 302(b).
27. 27 Fed. Reg. 11527 (1962).
28. 42 U.S.C. Sec 2000(d) (1964).
29. U.S. Commission on Civil Rights. *The Federal Civil Rights Enforecement Effort: A Reassessment.*

30. 42 U.S.C. Sec. 3601-31 (1968).
31. Pub. L. 90-284, 82 Stat. 84.
32. Southern District of Ohio, Feb. 13, 1976, C-1-74-153.
33. *Ibid.*
34. See law review articles in Annotated Bibliography.
35. Bureau of National Affairs, *Housing and Development Reporter* Vol. 5, No. 4 (May 24, 1978) p. 1309.
36. Statement of American Life Convention and Life Insurance Association of America — $1 billion Urban Investment Program of the Life Insurance Business, in *Hearings on Financial Institutions and the Urban Crisis Before the Subcomm. on Financial Institutions of the Sen. Comm. on Banking and Currency,* 90th Cong., 2d Sess., p. 166 (1968); See C. Moeller, Jr., Economic Implications of the Life Insurance Industry's Investment Program in the Central Cities, *Journal of Risk and Insurance* Vol. 36 (1969), p. 93.
37. Arthur Goldberg, "Maryland's Housing Insurance Program: A Forerunner of Future State Activity," 5 *Urban Lawyer* Vol. 5 (1973), p. 524.
38. Fresno, Cal. Ord. 68-63, April 1968.
39. New York Assembly Act 7342-A March 6, 1973.

Section **IV**
*Annotated*
*Bibliography*

# Bibliography

Section Four is an annotated bibliography focusing on the literature published from 1970 to 1977. The bibliography is based on: (1) Council of Planning Librarians Exchange Bibliography (Number 890,1975) *The Urban Financing Problem* by Michael Agelasto and David Listokin; (2) an unpublished bibliography, "Disinvestment-Reinvestment" prepared by Michael Agelasto and David Listokin in 1976; and (3) a 1978 bibliographic survey prepared by Carl Horowitz, a research associate at the Rutgers University Center for Urban Policy Research.

Section Four is divided into three parts. The first annotates federal activity such as congressional hearings on the disinvestment problem and studies intiated by various federal departments such as the U.S. Commission on Civil Rights and the Department of Housing and Urban Development. The second part annotates state activity — hearings and studies conducted at the state level — as well as books, research reports and articles prepared by academicians, community groups and others. Part three is a non-annotated reference containing further materials on urban disinvestment and reinvestment.

It is important to realize that the bibliography is not a complete listing but rather is compiled to give the reader a sense of the growing urban financing literature.

FEDERAL ACTIVITY

Broyhill, James T. "Congressional Rural Caucus Budget," *Congressional Record,* Vol. 123 (March 10, 1977), H 1966-1970. Included in the

remarks of Congressman Broyhill is a discussion of the lending practices of financial institutions in rural areas and the problems of credit
shortfall in rural America.

Collins, Cardiss. "Redlining," *Congressional Record,* Vol. 122 (November
20, 1975), H 11510-11511. Remarks by Illinois Representative support
mortgage disclosure legislation.

Federal Deposit Insurance Corporation. "Inter-Agency Fair Housing Data
Evaluation Project," *Federal Register,* Vol. 39 (May 31, 1974), 19271.

Federal Home Loan Bank Board. 1971 Survey on Lending Practices, (1972).
Results of a questionnaire returned by 74 Savings and Loan Institutions indicate that 12 percent of their loan portfolio, on the average,
consists of loans in low-income or minority residents; 58 percent feel
redlining certain urban neighborhoods is not a problem; and 57 percent feel that a group of savings and loan institutions in a concerted
effort could make a significant impact in revitalizing deteriorated
neighborhoods.

―――."Non-Discrimination in Lending," *Federal Register,* Vol. 39 (April
3, 1974), 12110-12114.

―――. Office of General Council. "The Applicability of the Board's Non-
discrimination Regulation to the Practice of 'Redlining' by Federal
Home Loan Bank Board Member Institutions," Memorandum
(March 21, 1974). Redlining which has an unlawful discriminatory effect violates Section 528.2 (d). In each case, however, it will be necessary to resolve the factual question of whether a redlining pattern has
such an effect. Each loan application should be considered on the basis
of all relevant criteria, not simply on the basis of the security property.
Lenders who redline must show clear evidence that the practice is a
matter of business necessity and that no less dicriminatory means are
available to assure sound financial lending.

"Federal Loan/Deposit Disclosure Bill Introduced by Proxmire," *Housing
and Development Reporter,* Vol. 2 (April 7, 1975), 1143. Witnesses during the hearings included community groups, civil rights and public interest groups and mortgage lenders. The record includes testimony,
case studies of redlining and the response by the industry to the
criticism.

Federal National Mortgage Association. *Forum One-Mobilization of Private
Initiative for Inner City Residential Development.* Washington, D.C.,
September, 1973. This report overviews American housing programs
and problems. It analyzes past F H A redlining policies and subsequent reform efforts.

Federal National Mortgage Association. *Redlining.* Washington, D. C.:
Federal National Mortgage Association, 1976. This 40-page booklet
contains two essays: "Some Perspectives on Redlining," by Gordon E.
Nelson and "The Redlining of Neighborhoods by Mortgage Lending

Institutions and What Can Be Done About It," by Hilbert Fefferman. Nelson's article says: "Redlining and neighborhood decay go hand in hand, and although there are cases where lenders have failed to make good loans that should have been made, most redlining is based on sound business judgement relating to risks and return on investment." Fefferman writes: "No doubt many other cooperative mortgage financing arrangements could be worked out in different localities, by municipal or non-profit development corporations. What is needed to begin with is more realistic attention by the public sector and more sympathetic attention by the private sector to the mortgage credit problems of older neighborhoods."

Federal Reserve Board. *Regulations Implementing the Home Mortgage Disclosure Act of 1975.* Adopted June 9, 1976. (Available from Federal Reserve Board, 20 & Constitution Ave., S.W., Washington, D.C.)

U.S. Commission on Civil Rights, *Housing-1961. Commission on Civil Rights Report.* Washington, D.C.: U.S. Government Printing Office, 1961. This report examines racial discrimination in housing as practiced by private lenders and real estate brokers, as well as by various government agencies. It also analyzes steps taken and/or contemplated by various governmental agencies. The report contains an excellent summary of agencies regulating financial institutions and their stand on ending credit discrimination. See also U.S. Commission on Civil Rights. *Civil Rights Excerpts from the 1961 Commission on Civil Rights Report, Part VI.* Washington, D.C.: U.S. Government Printing Office, 1961.

————. *The Federal Civil Rights Enforcement Effort: One Year Later.* Washington, D.C.: U.S. Government Printing Office, 1971. This study is a follow-up analysis of an earlier report, *The Federal Civil Rights Enforcement Effort.* Among the areas examined are housing and the role of the F H A and the financial institution regulatory agencies in combatting dicrimination.

————. *The Federal Civil Rights Enforcement Seven Months Later.* Washington, D.C.: U.S. Government Printing Office, 1971. This report, in part, discusses the actions taken by the financial regulatory agencies to stop lending discrimination.

————. *Home Ownership for Lower Income Families.* Washington, D.C.: U.S. Government Printing Office, 1971. This report focuses on the racial and ethnic impact of the Section 235 low-income homeownership program established by the 1968 Housing Act. Chapter Three (of Part Three) discusses the past redlining policies effected by the F H A and recent reform strategies.

————. *Housing in Washington.* Hearings. Washington, D.C.: U.S. Government Printing Office, 1962. These hearings document the mortgage financing difficulties faced by blacks in Washington, D.C. The sources

of mortgage financing in the city are examined. Some brief attention is
also paid to the Voluntary Home Mortgage Cooperative Program
(VHMCP).

———. *Mortgage Money, Who Gets It?* Washington, D.C.: U.S. Government Printing Office, 1974. This is a case study of the problem of
mortgage financing in Hartford, Connecticut. It details where
mortgages are or are not available and the sources of such loans. The
report also makes recommendations for alleviating the urban
mortgage crunch. The report focuses on sex discrimination.

U.S. Congress, House, Committee on Banking, Currency and Housing.
*Depository Institutions Amendments of 1975.* H. R. 94-561. 94th Cong.,
1st sess., Oct. 10, 1975, Washington, D.C.: Government Printing Of-
fice, 1975. This report follows the June 1975 hearings held by the
House subcommittee on H.R. 10024, which was to become the 1975
Home Mortgage Disclosure Act.

———. Committee on Banking, Currency and Housing. Subcommittee on
Housing and Community Development. *Extension of Urban Riot
Reinsurance and Crime Insurance Programs.* Hearings. February 16,
1977. Washington, D.C.: Government Printing Office, 1977.

———. Committee on Banking, Subcommittee on Home Financing Prac-
tices and Procedures of the Committee on Banking and Currency. 91st
Congress, 1st session. *Financing of Inner-City Housing Part 1.*
Washington, D.C.: U.S. Government Printing Office, 1969.

———. Committee on Banking, Currency and Housing. *Home Mortgage
Disclosure Act.* Conference Report. H.R. 94-762, 94th Cong., 1st sess.,
Dec. 15, 1975. Washington, D.C.: Government Printing Office, 1975.

———. Committee on Banking, Currency and Housing. Sucommittee on
Housing and Community Development. *National Neighborhood
Policy Act.* Hearings, Sept. 9, 1976. Washington, D.C.: Government
Printing Office, 1976. 351-page hearings on three bills to create a
national commission on neighborhoods, H.R. 14756, H.R. 14361,
H.R. 15388 contain much discussion on redlining/disinvestment.

———. Committee on Banking, Currency and Housing. *National
Neighborhood Policy Act.* H.R. 94-1600. 94th Cong., 2d sess., Sept. 17,
1976. Washington, D.C.: Government Printing Office, 1976.

———. Committee on Banking, Currency and Housing. *The Rebirth of the
American City.* Hearings. 94 Cong., 2d sess., Sept. 20-24, 1976 (Part 1):
Sept. 27-Oct. 1, 1976 (Part 2); Appendix (Part 3). Washington, D.C.:
Government Printing Office, 1976. A number of witnesses testifying
at these hearings dicuss the problems facing neighborhoods unable
to secure adequate residential financing.

———. Committee on Banking and Currency. Subcommittee on Housing.
*The Residential Mortgage Financing Problem.* 92nd Cong., 1st sess.,
Washington, D.C.: Government Printing Office, 1971.

————. Committee on Government Operations. U.S. Cong. House. Committee Govt. Operations 92nd Cong. 2nd sess., *Defaults on F.H.A. Insured Mortgages.* Washington, D.C.: U.S. Government Printing Office, 1972. These hearings discuss F H A program abuses, including complaints of redlining in various urban neighborhoods and the adverse effect of such disinvestment.

————. Subcommittee on Civil and Constitutional Rights. 94th Congress, 2nd sess., March 9, 10, 11, 1976 (part 1) and September 22 and 30, 1976 (part 2). Washington, D.C.: U.S. Government Printing Office, 1976. These volumes, in exploring housing dicrimination in the U.S., touch on redlining.

————. Committee on the Judiciary. Subcommittee on Civil Rights Oversight. *Federal Government's Role in the Achievement of Equal Opportunity in Housing.* Serial No. 34. Washington, D.C.: U.S. Government Printing Office, 1972. These hearings discuss HUD's enforcement of Title VIII of the 1968 Civil Rights Act as well as other governmental agency efforts to eliminate discrimination in financing. Included are the results of a HUD survey administered to private financial institutions to determine their consideration of racial factors in mortgage lending.

U.S. Congress, Senate, Committee on Banking and Currency. Subcommittee on Financial Institutions. "Financial Institutions and Urban Crisis," 90th Cong., 2nd sess., September, 1968.

————. Committee on Banking, Housing And Urban Affairs. *Community Credit Needs.* Hearings. 95th Cong., 1st sess., March 23-25, 1977. Washington, D.C.: Government Printing Office, 1977.

————. Committee on Banking, Housing and Urban Affairs. *Enforcement of the Equal Credit Opportunity and Home Mortgage Disclosure Acts.* Second report. 94th Cong., 1st sess., March 1977. Washington, D.C.; Government Printing Office, 1977.

————. Committee on Banking, Housing and Urban Affairs. *Equal Opportunity in Lending.* Serial No. 69-574. Oversight on Equal Opportunity in Lending Enforcement by the Bank Regulatory Agencies. Hearings. March 11-12, 1976. Washington, D.C.: Government Printing Office, 1976.

————. Committee on Banking, Housing and Urban Affairs. *Fair Lending Enforcement by the Four Federal Financial Regulatory Agencies.* 94th Cong., 2nd sess., Senate Report 94-930, June 3, 1976. Washington, D.C.: U.S. Government Printing Office, 1976. The 19-page Committee report is critical of agency enforcement of Fair Housing laws and states that "no agency has adopted a racial record-keeping requirement to facilitate detection of discriminatory lending patterns by examiners as part of the normal examination routine."

—————. Committee on Banking, Housing and Urban Affairs. *Home Mortgage Disclosure Act of 1975.* 2 Vols. Hearings. 94th Cong., 1st sess., May 5, 6, 7, and 8, 1975. Washington D.C.: Government Printing Office, 1975. Witnesses during the hearings included community groups, civil rights and public interest groups and mortgage lenders. The record includes testimony, case studies of redlining, and the response by the industry to the criticism.

—————. Committee on Banking, Housing and Urban Affairs. *Home Mortgage Disclosure Act of 1975.* Senate Report 94-187. 94th Cong., 1st sess., June 6, 1975. Washington, D.C.: U.S. Government Printing Office, 1975. This report follows the May 1975 hearings held by the committee on S. 1281, and contains both majority and minority views on the proposed legislation, which was to become the 1975 Home Mortgage Disclosure Act.

—————. Committee on Banking, Housing and Urban Affairs, *Home Mortgage Disclosure and Equal Credit Opportunity.* Hearings. 94th Cong., 1st sess., (November 23, 1976.) Washington, D.C.: Government Printing Office, 1976.

—————. Committee on Banking, Housing and Urban Affairs. *National Neighborhood Policy Act.* 94th Cong., 2d sess., July 28, 1976. Washington, D.C.: Government Printing Office, 1976.

—————. Committee on Banking, Housing and Urban Affairs. *Neighborhood Preservation.* Hearings, 94th Cong., 2d sess. June 14, 1976. Washington, D.C.: Government Printing Office. This 245-page hearing record includes testimony by community groups, federal officials and others on S. 3554 National Neighborhood Policy Act, which was not enacted by Congress that year. Much information centers around the proposal to expand the neighborhood housing services program of the Federal Home Loan Bank Board.

—————. Committee on the Judiciary, Subcommittee on Antitrust and Monopoly. 92nd cong. 2nd sess., *Competitions in Real Estate and Mortgage Lending.* Part 1-Boston; Part 2A & 2B, Washington, D.C.: Government Printing Office, 1972. These hearings discuss abuses in F H A mortgage programs for low and moderate income families. They also present evidence of disinvestment in numerous areas,e.g., St. Louis, Central Brooklyn in New York City, etc. Some proposals are also made for increasing the volume of institutional financing in urban areas through such strategies as joint public/private lending efforts and cooperative bank pools.

U.S. Department of Housing and Urban Development. *Administrative Meeting on Redlining and Disinvestment as a Discriminatory Practice in Residential Mortgage Loans.* Washington, D.C.: HUD, 1976. The HUD Assistant Secretary for Fair Housing and Equal Opportunity received public testimony from about 25 witnesses in hearings held in

Philadelphia July 14-15-16, 1976. Lenders generally declined to attend, with most of the testimony given by academicians and members of community groups, and local officials. The transcript, with inserted material, was printed by HUD in unedited form, in two volumes.

————. *Housing in the Seventies.* Washington, D.C.: U.S. Government Printing Office, 1974. This report, the product of the HUD Housing Review Task Force, analyzes past governmental housing programs and evaluates various alternative future strategies. As part of its analysis, the report reviews housing finance (Chapter 3) and considers reform efforts in liberalizing F H A mortgage insurance to minimize negative impact.

————. U.S. Department of Housing and Urban Development, Office of the Assistant Secretary of Fair Housing and Equal Opportunity, *Women v. Housing: A Report on Sex Discrimination in Five American Cities,* Washington, D.C.: U.S. Government Printing Office, June, 1975. This is a final report on the testimony of several hundred men and women in public hearings and workshops in Atlanta, St. Louis, San Antonio, San Francisco and New York. It reveals that women have suffered extensive discrimination in applying for mortgage credit and recommends that the Federal government must take a stronger role in broadening the scope and enforcement of legislation with respect to sex discrimination in the mortgage market.

————. Office of Equal Opportunity. *Private Lending Institutions Question-naire: Initial Report on Returns,* (April 25, 1972). The questionnaire (OMB form 63-S7000) was distributed by the regulatory agencies to member institutions. 18,456 forms were analyzed representing a 91 percent return. The survey shows that 18 percent of savings and loan institutions in 50 cities with largest minority populations state they refuse to make loans in one or more areas with a high concentration of minority group members. Also, there is information on neighborhood characteristics considered by lenders in making loans.

U.S. Department of the Treasury. Comptroller of the Currency. "Real Estate Loan Activities. Notice of Commencement of Fair Housing Lending Practices Pilot Project," *Federal Register,* Vol. 39 (April 5, 1974). Announcement of the commencement of a recordkeeping experiment (June 1, 1974-November 30, 1974), in 18 Standard Metropolitan Statistical Areas, by the Federal Deposit Insurance Corporation, Comptroller of the Currency, Federal Reserve System, and Federal Home Loan Bank Board. Data, collected on three different forms used in different SMSAs, relate to race, income and zip code of mortgagor and price of property. The experiment was conducted to test the feasibility of nationwide recordkeeping requirements.

STATE ACTIVITY/REPORTS, JOURNAL ARTICLES AND BOOKS

Agelasto, Michael and David Listokin. *Redlining in Perspective: An Evaluation of Strategies to Deal with the Urban Financing Dilemma.* 1976. This 22-page paper was presented to the May 21, 1976 meeting of the American Real Estate and Urban Economics Association meeting in Washington, DC. It consists of sections taken from a larger report the authors prepared. The complete paper appears in *A Decent Home and Environment: Housing Urban America,* Don Phares (editor), Cambridge, Mass.: Ballinger, 1977.

Ahlbrandt, Roger S., Jr. "Credit Allocation Legislation No Answer to Redlining Controversy," *The Mortgage Banker,* Vol. 36 (Mar. 1976), 6-17. "The biases of lending officers, appraisers and realtors also enter into the decision-making process. To the extent that these people may be biased against a neighborhood, loan policies will be affected, and decline will be accelerated. However, the point cannot be overemphasized that financial institutions are just a part of the process. There is virtually no evidence that financial institutions begin the disinvestment process."

———. *Mortgage Lending in Pittsburgh.* Pittsburgh: Action-Housing, Inc., 1975. This 24-page study states "The analysis of mortgage lending in Pittsburgh shows that lenders make their decisions on the basis of the economic level of the neighborhood and its livability. Racial attributes of the neighborhoods alone do not account for differences in lending."

———. *Redlining: An Economic Phenomenon.* Pittsburgh: Action-Housing, Inc., Mimeograph. 1976. This 21-page article attempts to document the factors which influence mortgage lending decisions of financial institutions. Mortgage lending activity in the City of Pittsburgh is studied through the use of multiple regression analysis. Income and neighborhood variables, and not racial variables, are shown to be statistically significant in explaining lending behavior. The results argue for use of financial incentives directed through the market place, rather than regulation or credit allocation, to stimulate lending in declining neighborhoods.

Aleinikoff, T. Alexander. "Racial Steering: the Real Estate Broker and Title VIII," *Yale Law Journal,* Vol. 85 (May 1976), 808. "This (comment) analyzes racial steering practices and concluded that virtually all are unlawful under Title VIII. It argues that Title VIII's most far-reaching prohibition against steering is its 'colorblind' standard, which forbids real estate brokers from treating customers differently on the basis of race."

American Society of Appraisers. *Valuation,* Vol. 23, No. 2 October/November 1976 see Special Section, Part II, "Urban Disinvestment, Redlining and the Appraiser," pp. 138-229. This report contains a brief anthology of articles, statements, legislative enactments, and court decisions that pertain to the redlining issue. It includes a statement made on behalf of the American Society of Appraisers at the HUD Fair Housing Meeting in Philadelphia in July, 1976, the bill proposing the National Neighborhood Policy Act, and the opinion of the United States District Court in the *Laufman v. Oakley Building and Loan Company.*

Baltimore Department of Housing and Community Development, Home Ownership Development Program. *Home Ownership and the Baltimore Mortgage Market.* Baltimore, n.d. Using 1970, 1971, and 1972 data from Lusk's Maryland Real Estate Guide for Baltimore City and Baltimore County and 1970 Census data, this report studies mortgage activity by Census tract for difficult types of institutional lenders. It concludes that the center of the city is not serviced by conventional lenders and that different types of lenders concentrate their financing in different city neighborhoods.

Baptiste, Kim E. "Attacking the Urban Redlining Problem," *Boston University Law Review,* Vol. 56. (Nov. 1976), 989-1019. Law Review comment examines urban redlining and potential remedies. The author proposes a remedy involving regulation of branching, revamping the FHA insurance program, and establishment of local assigned-risk mortgage insurance pools.

Baum, Daniel Jay with Karen Orloff Kaplan. *Toward a Free Housing Market.* Coral Gables, Florida: University of Miami Press, 1971. This study analyzes an effort to expand housing opportunities. It describes some discriminatory financing practices and the obstacles to ending such policies.

Benston, George J., Daniel Horsky, and H. Martin Weingartner. *An Empirical Study of Mortgage Redlining,* New York: New York University, Graduate School of Business Administration, Salamon Brothers Center for the Study of Financial Institutions, Monograph No. 1978-5, 1978. Argues that redlining is essentially nonexistent. After providing a critique of the assumptions underlying previous redlining studies, this report examines the distribution of mortgage loans made to low-income neighborhoods in Rochester, New York. It concludes that when one controls for the demand for mortgages, the creditworthiness of borrowers, and the time elapsed over which lending practices are measured, the hypothesis that local mortgage lenders discriminate on the basis of neighborhood location is not supported.

Bentley, Allen and Angus Macbeth. "Mortgage Lenders and the Housing Supply." *Cornell Law Review,* Vol. 57 (1972), 149-177. Following a discussion of social and cultural factors influencing mortgage lending, the authors propose some strategies for improved financing.

Boyer, Brian. *Cities Destroyed for Cash.* Chicago: Follett Publishing Co., 1973. This book discusses some of the destructive import of inner city speculation and abuses in some of the F H A urban mortgage programs for low and moderate income homeowners.

Bradford, Calvin P. and Leonard S. Rubinowitz. "The Urban-Suburban Investment-Disinvestment Process: Consequences of Older Neighborhoods, *Annals of American Academy of Political and Social Science,* Vol. 422 (November 1975), 77-86. This article summarizes the work of the Urban-Suburban Investment Study Group, Center for Urban Affairs, Northwestern University, much of which was under- taken for the Governor's Commisssion on Mortgage Practices. The authors state that a relatively small number of private sector actors, in- cluding institutional investors, developers and mortgage bankers, have invested increasingly in large-scale developments on the suburban neighborhoods and that these investment decisions have significant negative impacts on older, middle class neighborhoods which are struggling to remain viable. Stating that it is appropriate that there be public intervention to assure an adequate flow of capital into these neighborhoods, the authors suggest several approaches including regulation and subsidy.

California, Department of Savings and Loan. *Fair Lending Report No. 1, Vols. I & II,* October, 1977 and *Report No. 2, October, 1978.* These are the first in a series of public Fair Lending Reports prepared pursuant to California State regulations that went into effect in 1976. Report No. 1 analyzes the mortgage lending practices of State-charterd sav- ings & loan associations. Volume I concentrates upon the investiga- tion of potential regulatory violations by lenders and the action taken toward any lender found to violating the regulations, while Volume II considers geographical lending patterns of savings & loan associations in nine California counties. Volume II reports that lenders pursue a policy of rish aversion; that conscious geographically-based disinvest- ment is prevalent. The report, however, rejects the contention that out- right discrimination is practiced by the lenders against blacks on the basis of their race.

"Can Associations Save the Inner City?," *Savings and Loan News* (March 1970), 34-40. This article discusses the problems of disinvestment and reviews reform strategies that can be effected by savings and loan in- stitutions, such as establishing service corporations and taking an equity position in urban housing efforts.

Case, Frederick, (Editor). *Inner-City Housing and Private Enterprise.* New York: Praeger, 1972. One of the few comprehensive analyses of the problems of urban lending, this book is based on studies conducted in cities throughout the country. Among the topics discussed are the housing needs, borrowers and lenders, and lending territory of the inner city, and the dynamics of the urban housing market. Some unpublished reports from which the Case study is derived include:

George Bloom and Thomas Lemon, *Housing the Underhoused in Inner-City Indianapolis, Indiana.*

Carl Tschappat and Joe Lee, *Housing the Underhoused in Atlanta, Georgia.*

Marshall Minich et. al., *Housing the Underhoused in Fresno, California.*

Frederick Case et. al., *Housing the Underhoused: The California Studies.*

William Grigsby et. al., *Housing and Poverty in Baltimore, Maryland.*

George Sternlieb et. al., *Housing Costs and Housing Restraints.*

Center for New Coporate Priorities (The National Task Force on Credit Policy) *Where the Money Is—Mortgage Lending.* Los Angeles County, 1975. Analysis of mortgage lending data for Los Angeles County, as collected by the California Savings and Loan Commissioner for state-chartered savings and loan institutions by Census tract. Sample data from January to May 1974 show few loans made in inner city Los Angeles.

Center for Urban Affairs, Northwestern University. *The Role of Lending Practices in Older Urban Neighborhoods: Institutional Lenders, Regulatory Agencies and their Community Impacts.* prepared by the Urban-Suburban Investment Study Group for the Illinois Housing Development Authority, 1975. This extensive volume surveys economic factors, community issues, and alternative policies of the disinvestment-reinvestment process. The Chicago area is the focus of the Study Group, but national issues are covered as well.

Center for Urban Studies of the University of Illinois, Urban-Suburban Investment Study Group. *Redlining and Disinvestment as a Discriminatory Practice in Residential Mortgage Loans.* Prepared by U.S. Department of Housing and Urban Development, Office of Assistant Secretary for Fair Housing and Equal Opportunity, June, 1977. Part I of this report is a summary of the HUD Administrative Meeting on Redlining and Disinvestment conducted in Philadelphia in 1976. Part II is an overview of redlining issues, including government regulatory authority, the FHA insurance program, racial biases in appraisal in older, racially-changing neighborhoods, and the response of the public sector to the redlining issue. Part III consists of the Study Group's own legal and administrative recommendations.

Chatterjee, Lata, David Harvey and Lawrence Klugman. *F.H.A. Policies and the Baltimore City Housing Market.* Prepared by The Center for Metropolitan Planning and Research, The Johns Hopkins University, Baltimore, Maryland: April, 1974. This analysis reviews the changing role of the F H A , the various sources of mortgages in different Baltimore neighborhoods, and problems resulting from existing financial practices. The report suggests changes needed in F H A policies and practices and other reforms to increase the flow of mortgages to urban neighborhoods.

Chicago Commission on Human Relations. *Selling and Buying Real Estate in a Racially Changing Neighborhood.* Chicago, Illinois: (June 14, 1962). This report focuses on the prevalence of non-institutional mortgages, i.e., land contracts, in racially changing areas. It follows the sequence of transfers and discusses the varieties and sources of mortgages used in these transactions.

Cincotta, Gale and Randy Vereen, *Regulatory Agencies and the Redlining and Disinvestment Process: A Report* Prepared for U.S. Department of Housing and Urban Development Report, 1974. Like the 1976 Naparatek-Cincotta study, this report is basically an overview of redlining issues. Additionally, however, this report presents disclosure data on mortgage loans in Chicago and a history of the activities of local anti-redlining organizations in that city.

Clearinghouse on Corporate Responsibility. *A Report on the 2 Billion Urban Investment Program of the Life Insurance Business.* New York, 1973. One of numerous publications by the Clearinghouse on Corporate Responsibility on corporate urban investment, this report analyzes why the life insurance industry decided to effect its Urban Investment Program. It discusses what investments were made and how they have fared.

Coalition of Neighborhoods. *Housing Analysis in Oakley, Bond Hill and Evanston, January 1960-April 1974 - Financial Investment Patterns.* Cincinnati, Ohio: June 1974. These studies examine the source of lending money in three Cincinnati neighborhoods. Local institutions invest less in the black and mixed areas and are not sponsoring Federally guaranteed loans in these neighborhoods. Non-conventional monies in the sampled communities come from out-of-town lending institutions.

Courant, Paul Noah. *Economic Aspects of Racial Prejudice in Urban Housing Markets.* Unpublished Ph.D. dissertation. Princeton University, 1974. This thesis discusses some economic theories for lender disinvestment behavior.

Daniel, Edwin C. "Redlining," *Journal of Housing,* Vol. 32 (Sept: 1975), 441-444. "One older neighborhood after another in urban areas has fallen victim to the red pencil of financial institutions but Congress is moving to expose discriminatory home lenders so depositors may boycott them."

D.C. Commission on Residential Mortgage Investment. *Housing Finance in Washington, D.C.: A Strategy for Change, 1976.* This 168-page report finds that a "large, untapped demand for home mortgage loans throughout many sections of the city east of Rock Creek Park . . . while loans by local banks and S&Ls have decreased significantly in

these areas." The six-member Commission was chartered by the D.C.
city council and spent two years investigating charges of mortgage-
lending discrimination.

————. *Residential Financing Practices in the District of Columbia* (May 6,
1976). This 35-page preliminary report offers recommendations
designed to increase lending opportunity in the District and describes
the Commission and its activities.

D.C. Public Interest Research Group. *Redlining: Mortgage Disinvestment in
the District of Columbia.* Washington, D.C.: 1975. This report, which
examines the lending activity of 15 Washington savings and loan institutions using Lusk's *Real Estate Directory* data for 1972, 1973 and
1974, identifies a pattern of disinvestment in several inner neighborhoods.

Davis, Irving. *Current Problems in Financing Older Homes in Fresno.*
Fresno, Cal.: Fresno State College, School of Business, Bureau of
Business Research and Service, Study No. 22, September 1968. The
author examines selling prices and mortgage data in Fresno, California and evaluates the relationship between age of structure and loan
terms.

Devine, Richard with Winston O. Rennie and N. Brenda Sims. *Where the
Lender Looks First: A Case Study of Mortgage Disinvestment in Bronx
County.* Prepared for the National Urban League, 1974. This study
traces the pattern of disinvestment of Bronx banks from that borough.
Through regression analysis, it attempts to show that financial institutions have in recent years reacted to racial-social changes in the Bronx
by selectively refusing to grant new or refinanced mortgages. The
report offers suggestions for various public policies to increase the
flow of mortgages to urban areas including the establishment of a
Land Preservation Bank. The study reviews the literature focusing on
the disinvestment dilemma.

Dingemans, Dennis et. al. *Redlining and the Geography of Residential
Mortgage Loans in Sacramento.* Davis, Cal.: University of California
at Davis, Department of Geography, 1977. This study analyzes home
mortgage loans made in 120 Census tracts of the Sacramento SMSA
during 1976. It indicates a clear pattern of disinvestment in low-
income, Sacramento neighborhoods.

Downie, Leonard, Jr. *Mortgage on America.* New York: Praeger, 1974. Sections of the study analyze the adverse effects of some of the F H A
low- and moderate-income housing programs and of real estate
speculation in the inner city.

Duncan, Marcia, Edwin T. Hood and James L. Neet. "Redlining Practice,
Racial Resegregation, and Urban Decay: Neighborhood Housing Services as a Viable Alternative," *Urban Lawyer,* Vol. 7 (Summer 1975),
510-539. The article examines federal laws prohibiting housing dis-

crimination and several court cases involving their enforcement. It discusses Neighborhood Housing Services as a possible solution to arresting urban decay.

Education/Instruction, Inc. *Redlining— Fair Housing At Its Worst In Hartford, Connecticut.* Hartford, Ct.: Education/Instruction, Inc., 1977. This 22-page report, Number 9, dated February 7, 1977, is one of a series of reports issued by this public interest group. "This report will analyze the mortgage loan data recently required to be disclosed by federal law. Through the Federal Deposit Insurance Corporation (F.D.I.C.), we have also obtained deposit figures by bank branches for the Capitol Region which for the first time provides the public with the comparison necessary to demonstrate a huge cash flow from the urban poor to support the investment opportunities of the racially segregated and wealthy suburbs."

"Exploring Some Answers to Redlining," *Planning,* Vol. 42 (October 1976), 7-8. "Urban decay cannot be blamed solely on financial institutions that redline; federal and state policies on cities also are at fault. This was the consensus of the participants at a conference on redlining held in early September in Chicago."

Fahey, Noel. "Lending Discrimination? Look at the Facts," *Savings and Loan News,* Vol. 97 (August 1976), 60-64. Article examines certain "myths" by presenting "facts" from the 1970 housing census data on lending patterns by savings and loan associations.

Gold, Andrew J. *A Report to the State Banking Commissioner Regarding "Redlining" and Home Mortgage Disclosure.* (January 1977). This 77-page report states that "The Home Mortgage Disclosure Act of 1975 does not contain enough information to permit a determination as to whether or not banks are redlining . . . The State Banking Department needs to define what is and what is not acceptable as appraisal and underwriting criteria . . . The Legislature in conjunction with the Commissioner should set up a study commission to investigate many of the possible remedies to redlining in particular and to urban disinvestment in general."

Grant, Richard. "Inner City Rehabilitation and the Savings Association: A Successful Case History," *Federal Home Loan Bank Board Journal* (November 1971), 15-21. This article discusses the successful urban mortgage financing program effected by a New York City bank to encourage housing rehabilitation.

Gray, Robert. "Funding High Risk Loans in Low-Income Areas," *The Mortgage Banker* (November 1970), 108-118. This article discusses various strategies for increasing the volume of low cost loans in urban areas.

Green, R. Jeffery and George von Furstenburg. "The Effects of Race and Age of Housing on Mortgage Delinquency Risk," *Urban Studies,* (December 1975), pp. 85-89. The authors examine the association between neighborhood racial composition and mortgage delinquency risk. Using 160 wards in Allegheny County in the Pittsburgh SMSA including the central city proper as a test case, they conclude that "the age of structure variables are at least as effective in explaining mortgage delinquency risk as the neighborhood racial characteristic variables."

Grier, George and Eunice, *Equality and Beyond*. Chicago: Quadrangle Books, 1966. As part of its analysis of housing discrimination, this study documents F H A. redlining practices and early reform strategies that were contemplated.

Grigsby, William and Louis Rosenburg. *Urban Housing Policy*, New Brunswick, New Jersey: Center for Urban Policy Research, 1975. This study of Baltimore, which discusses inner city disinvestment, states that the dearth of mortgage capital is one critical factor in the declining inner city market. The credit squeeze forces out-migrating families to sell at depressed prices, denies homeownership opportunities to many families who could afford to make purchases if decent financing were available, raises the cost of housing, shifts the inventory to a class of owners who take poorer care of the properties, and forces lower-income families to seek land-installment contracts.

Hauser, Philip M. and Hekmat Elkhanialy. *The Hauser Report on Lending Practices of Savings and Loan Associations in Chicago, 1977*. Report prepared for Federal Savings and Loan Council of Illinois, Chicago, Illinois, September, 1978. Analyzing the lending practices of twenty-two federal savings and loan associations in Chicago during 1977, this study reveals that the city's higher income areas receive substantially more mortgage funds than do its lower income areas. While the latter areas were those found to be most heavily populated by blacks, when various factors such as median income, home sales price and structural age were taken into account, "the explanatory value of race grew so small as to be appropriately considered as negligible."

Heidkamp, Ann and Stephanie Sandy. *Red-Lining in Milwaukee: Who Is Destroying the Westside?* Milwaukee, Wisconsin: Council on Urban Life, n.d. This report focuses on redlining practices in one neighborhood on the Westside. It analyzes the different disinvestment stages and techniques and also reviews the impact of such lending practices.

Helper, Rose. *Racial Policies and Practices of Real Estate Brokers*. Minneapolis: University of Minnesota Press, 1969. This study extensively documents the mortgage financing problems (as well as other discriminatory practices) faced by blacks. It notes the prevalence of land contracts in minority neighborhoods.

Housing Training and Information Center. Informational Pamphlets. 4207 W. Division Street, Chicago, Illinois 60651. This community-based

organization disseminates information on redlining. Literature in-
cludes: "The Grass-Roots Battle Against Redlining," "Redlining
Disclosure," "Glossary," "Redlining and FHA," "The Phases of
Neighborhood Deterioration."

Illinois Governor's Commission on Mortgage Practices. *Homeownership in
Illinois: The Elusive Dream,* 1975. The Commission, established by the
Governor, reports on redlining in the State and presents legislative
proposals to remedy the problem. Chicago neighborhoods affected by
redlining are identified but the report states that data is insufficient to
determine extent of redlining. Regulatory agencies tend to have the effect of encouraging redlining through regulations and administrative
practices, including failure to define a lender's primary service area
and the movement of the lender's main office out of the central city.
The study also discusses other ways to curtail urban disinvestment including changes in the Illinois foreclosure law, modification of certain
clauses in mortgage forms, and revisions in the FHA process.

Illinois Legislative Investigating Commission. *"Redlining" Alleged
Discrimination in Home Improvement Loans.* March, 1974. The commission investigated specific complaints of redlining of home improvement loans in Chicago. It found no pattern of redlining, although it
reported two separate instances. The study does not examine discriminatory practices involving mortgage loans in specific areas.

Illinois Legislative Investigating Commission. *Redlining-Discrimination in
Residential Mortgage Loans.* 1975. Authorized by the State
Legislature, the Commission spent 18 months investigating the lending
practices of 66 of the 200 lending institutions in the Chicago area. The
Commission worked independent of the Governor's Commission. The
report includes conclusions and recommendations.

Jaffee, Dwight M. *Credit for Financing Housing Investment: Risk Factors
and Capital.* Report submitted to HUD as part of the National Housing Policy Study Papers, NTIS document PB-229 980, June, 1973. The
paper discusses the economics of redlining and finds that "both theory
and evidence indicate that the major cause of redlining is the fact that
the objective risk of lending in certain areas is either unmeasurable or
so high that usury ceilings make it impossible for lending institutions
to be compensated for it."

Johnston, Verle. "Financing the Inner City," *Federal Reserve Bank of San
Francisco* (October 1969), 199-210. This article discusses the problems
of urban financing. It then discusses a broad range of reform strategies
including establishing special insurance programs and service corporations, allowing the use of more flexible mortgages, encouraging
minority owned banks, etc.

Joint Savings Bank—Savings and Loan Committee on Urban Problems.
*Urban Financing Guide.* New York, 1968. This report summarizes

scores of innovative urban financing programs effected by many banking institutions. It discusses the lenders' role—what they hoped to
achieve as well as the practical problems they encountered.

Kain, John. *Background Paper on Housing Market Discrimination and Its
Implications for Government Housing Policy.* Report prepared for the
National Housing Policy Task Force. Washington, D.C.: National
Technical Advisory Service, June, 1973. This paper overviews discriminatory practices in the housing market and how this affects
minority groups. It notes the obstacles minorities face in attempting to
obtain mortgages and proposes, among other recommendations, the
establishment of a minority mortgage loan program.

King, Thomas A. *Redlining: A Critical Review of the Literature with Suggested Research.* Research Working Paper #82, February, 1979,
prepared for the Federal Home Loan Bank Board, Office of Economic
Research. Research Working Paper No. 82, February, 1979. This
report surveys and evaluates the redlining literature.

Koebel, Theodore. *Housing in Louisville: The Problems of Disinvestment,*
Louisville: University of Louisville, Urban Studies Center, July, 1978.
This study considers home mortgage lending practices of Louisville
financial institutions. It evaluates such data as the volume of first and
second mortgages, by neighborhood and economic characteristics
such as age of housing and average resident income.

Larkin, Edward W. "Redlining: Remedies for Victims of Urban
Disinvestment," *Fordham Urban Law Journal,* Vol. 5 (Fall 1976), 83-
102. Comment examines "the legal alternatives open to the victim of
redlining. These include pertinent sections of the Civil Rights Acts of
1866, 1964, 1968, and a recently enacted statute requiring disclosure of
lending policies. This note also reviews the possibility of corrective
measures by federal agencies."

"Lenders Allocate Loan Funds to Finance Low-Income Housing," *Journal
of Housing* (January 1970 ), 30. This article discusses numerous pool
programs to increase the mortgage flow to urban areas. It examines
such efforts as the Better Boston Urban Renewal Group, and urban
lending programs in New York State and New Haven, Connecticut.

Leyland, George P. *Determining Priorities of Need for Guaranteed Mortgage
Funds.* New York, N.Y.: New York State Legislative Institute, un-
dated. Using home mortgage data provided by 82 banks in New York
State, this study reports an association between neighborhood racial
characteristics with neighborhood loan availability.

Library of Congress, Congressional Research Service. *The Central City
Problem and Urban Renewal Policy.* A study prepared for the Subcom-
mittee on Housing and Urban Affairs of the Committee on Banking,
Housing, and Urban Affairs, U.S. Senate, 93rd Cong. 1st Session,
Washington, D.C.: U.S. Government Printing Office, 1973. Sections

of this study examine the problems of urban mortgage lending. The
analysis also explores the magnitude and variety of financing for
inner city mortgages.

Marshall, William T. "Mortgage Red-lining," *Savings and Loan News,* Vol.
95 (June 1974), 30. Three articles examine what individual savings and
loan associations and other business interests are doing to answer the
critics of redlining. Cases in Chicago, Milwaukee, Minneapolis-St.
Paul and Baltimore.

Mazin, George Jay. *The Impact of Credit Availability on Housing Abandonment: The Case of the Mid Bronx.* Unpublished masters thesis, Cornell
University, June,1974. This thesis argues that disinvestment in one
neighborhood in the Bronx was a factor accelerating its decline and
leading to abandonment. In contrast, the author shows that a
neighboring area where institutional financing remained available was
spared such deterioration. The thesis then discusses various strategies
for encouraging adequate urban mortgage financing.

Michigan, Department of Commerce, *The Governor's Task Force on Redlining,* December,1976. This is a Final Report of the State of Michigan's
Task Force on Redlining. A case study of mortgage lending practices
in Flint indicated that a relatively small proportion of loans were made
to neighborhoods with an old housing stock and a high proportion of
black residents, but that overt discrimination on the basis of either the
race of the applicant or the location of the property was relatively insignificant. The Task Force made a number of subsequent recommendations that included mandatory disclosure by lenders of all mortgage
credit, a rejection of mandatory credit allocation as an acceptable
strategy to combat redlining, legislative enactments against discrimination on the basics of property location and personal characteristics not associated with risk, and a three-point approach for the
development of a loan pool system for use throughout the state.

Michigan, Governor's Task Force on Redlining. *Final Report.* Lansing:
December, 1976. This 76-page report is the final version of the interim
report which was issued in August, 1976. "The major factual finding
of the Task Force is that no standards exist governing mortgage
lending decisions as they relate to the availability of credit, and, consequently, of housing opportunity, in a geographic area . . . proposes establishment of a new and more equitable relationship between loan
applicant and lender, development of standards for appraisal and underwriting practice and accountability in lending through voluntary or
mandatory disclosure . . . recommends that the state take steps to assure the availability of mortgage credit to credit worthy individuals for
structurally sound properties located in high risk areas . . . proposes
broad long-term strategies to deal with the problem of urban disinvestment."

Movement for Economic Justice. *Organizer Notebooks.* Vol. 2, *Redlining.* 1609 Connecticut Avenue, N.W., Washington, D.C. 20009. This organization prepares and distributes information on redlining. This volume contains copies of newspaper clippings, planning documents, reports and local ordinances for Minneapolis, Milwaukee, Chicago, Indianapolis and Jamaica Plain, Massachusetts, in addition to general articles. Material informs the organizer how to undertake an anti-redlining campaign.

Naparstek, Arthur J. and Gale Cincotta. *Urban Disinvestment: New Implications for Community Organization, Research and Policy.* Chicago: National Training and Information Center, 1976. This 45-page brochure is a joint publication of the National Center for Urban Ethnic Affairs and the National Training and Information Center. It presents a history of the Chicago and national anti-redlining movement, discusses the problems of neighborhood decay, and argues the importance of disclosure legislation. Reprinted in House Banking Committee Hearings on National Neighborhood Policy Act.

National Center for Urban Ethnic Affairs. *Neighborhood Reinvestment. An Annotated Bibliography.* Compiled by Karen Kollias, Oct., 1976.

National Committee Against Discrimination in Housing, Inc. *Patterns and Problems of Discrimination in Lending in Oakland, California.* Mimeograph. February 1972. Report of a study by the NCDH/HUD Urban Renewal Demonstration Project (Calif. D-8) examines practices of three savings and loan associations in Oakland, California. Recorded data for all their mortgage transactions from April, 1970 to March, 1971, totaling 323 loans, shows that most loans went to whites. The two black savings and loan associations previously serving the inner city had folded.

National Housing and Economic Development Law Project. *Redlining and Disinvestment: Causes, Consequences, and Proposed Remedies.* Berkeley, California: Earl Warren Legal Institute, University of California, 1976. This 174-page background paper was prepared under contract for the U.S. Department of Housing and Urban Development's hearings on redlining held July 14-16, 1976 in Philadelphia. It discusses the role of federal financial agencies, appraisal and underwriting practices, state and federal disclosure laws or rules, remedial anti-redlining efforts, and legal and non-legal strategies to eliminate redlining. An appendix contains the California anti-redlining regulations and appraisal and underwriting guidelines.

National Urban League. *Issues in Equal Access to Housing.* Washington, D.C., August, 1973. Chapter three examines urban financing problems. It delineates four neighborhoods by their level of conventional financing—full investment, disinvestment, uninvestment, and reinvestment—and demonstrates that those areas experiencing an outflow of funds also usually experience housing deterioration. The report presents a strategy to stem disinvestment and housing decay.

Northwest Community Housing Association, Inc. *Mortgage Disinvestment in Northwest Philadelphia.* (June 1973). 28 pp. Study reveals a sharp decline in the degree of mortgage lending in northwest Philadelphia by institutional lenders. A racially changing area in the northwest is compared with an all-white northeast area of similar building types and employment and income characteristics of residents.

Northwest Community Housing Association. *Redlining in Philadelphia: The Attempted Murder of Five Neighborhoods.* Philadelphia: Northwest Community Housing Association, 1976. This 27-page report examines the five Philadelphia communities of West Oak Lane, Germantown, Logan, Franklinville/East Park and East Mt. Airy, using the Real Estate Directory for the City of Philadelphia as the primary data source. The study concludes: "The problem faced by the five neighborhoods in the study is *not* the absolute absence of conventional mortgage funds. Rather, it is the *preponderance* of federally insured-mortgages, and particularly, of unregulated companies whose mortgage lending portfolios are dominated by those mortgages."

Nourse, Hugh O., and Donald Phares. "The Impact of FHA Insurance on Urban Housing Markets in Transition—the St. Louis Case," *Urban Law Journal,* Vol. 9 (1975), 111-128. This paper is one of a number of reports on neighborhood change in St. Louis. "The shift in FHA policy in 1966 to an explicit disregard of neighborhood conditions and trends in establishing credit worthiness caused FHA-insured mortgages to be increasingly employed in areas shifting from white to black occupancy. No indication exists that price variations differed in these neighborhoods as a result of the added financial assistance. Nevertheless, the burden of subsequent drops in value may have fallen on middle-income black families first integrating a neighborhood rather than on prior white residents, as was previously the case."

Orren, Karen. *Corporate Power and Social Change.* Baltimore, Maryland: The Johns Hopkins University Press, 1974. This study examines the role, attitude, and impact of American life insurance companies on the urban environment. It documents racial discrimination and other biases in the life insurance industry mortgage investments. The study also explores the recent industry response to the urban financing dilemma, the $2 million Urban Investment Program.

Raftner, Gail G. (Ed.). *Crisis in Urban Lending: Myth or Reality?* Chicago: Institute of Financial Education, 1975. This 260-page collection of articles and essays examines urban disinvestment from a variety of views. It contains reports of trade-journal articles which discuss the problems facing lenders and appraisers who deal with inner city property. Included is the U.S. League of Savings Associations' Special Management Bulletin, "Guidelines for Management Response to Activist Groups," and "Lenders Can't Ignore Economic Facts of Life."

Rapkin, Chester. *The Real Estate Market in an Urban Renewal Area.* New York: New York City Planning Commission, 1959. This report analyzes the real estate market in the West Side of Manhattan, an area undergoing urban renewal in the 1950s. Chapter 6 examines how properties in the area were financed. The report repeatedly notes the growing difficulty and cost of obtaining financing, the prevalence of non-institutional mortgage lending and the negative impact of such disinvestment.

Reidy, Daniel F. "Urban Housing Finance and the Redlining Controversy," *Cleveland State Law Review,* Vol. 25 (1976), 110-137. This article discusses the perspective of financial institutions in the redlining controversy and discusses legislation (including the Cleveland ordinance) and litigation. It concludes that the "redlining controversy will probably intensify during the next year or two . . . Offices of lending institutions can use their resources and influence to combat the pressures generated by the anti-redlining movement, but the scenario would probably be a series of retreating skirmishes with spectre of credit allocation hovering in the background . . . The best strategy for lending institutions may well be to voluntarily intensify affirmative action to pump home loans back into savable urban neighborhoods."

Renne, Paul A. "Eliminating Redlining by Judicial Action: Are Erasers Available?," *Vanderbilt Law Review,* Vol. 29 (May 1976), 987-1015. Article discusses "the concept and effects of redlining, the relevant statutes and administrative regulations [with attention to California] and the use of class action litigation as a means of eliminating the practice." It concludes: The statutory tools exist to eliminate the destructive practice of redlining. The fact-gathering mechanisms are being created that will provide the necessary predicate to successful class action litigation based on these statutory prohibitions. All that is needed are skillful and determined litigants prepared to assume the responsibilities of preparing and litigating such attacks."

Searing, Daniel. "Discrimination in Home Finance," *Notre Dame Lawyer* (June 1973), 1113-144. This article discusses the mortgage financing problems faced by minority groups. It discusses proposals to strengthen the financial institution regulatory agencies' ability and willingness to combat such discrimination and examines what actions have been taken.

Schafer, Robert. *Mortgage Lending Decisions: Criteria and Constraints.* Cambridge, Mass.: Joint Center for Urban Studies, 1978. Using mortgage data from the five largest SMSAs in New York State, the author found that while some redlining had been extant, most lending practices are based upon objective criteria such income, loan-income ratio and net wealth of the applicant, value of the property, and requested loan-to-value ratio. The report concludes with recommendations pertaining to fostering competition among mortgage lenders, developing risk programs and enacting anti-discrimination laws. Other recommendations include the adjustment of the market interest rate, each lender should publish their lending criteria, neighborhood residents should be allowed by the State to make joint decisions on exterior maintenance problems, and the scope of anti-discriminatory laws applying to the race of mortgage applicants should be expanded.

Solomon, Arthur et al. *Financial Institutions and Neighborhood Decline: A Review of the Literature*. Report submitted to the Federal Home Loan Bank Board. (November 1974). This 120-page study explores different theories on neighborhood decline. It includes an annotated bibliography and discussion of credit rationing and underwriting practices.

Stegman, Michael. *Housing Investment in the Inner City*. Cambridge, Massachusetts: M.I.T. Press, 1972. This study examines the dynamics of housing decline in Baltimore, Maryland. It explores some of the non-conventional mortgage financing devices found in the inner city such as the Land Installment Contract (LIC) and analyzes the reasons for the prevalence of such financing forms and their impact on housing maintenance and value.

Sternlieb, George. *The Tenement Landlord*. New Brunswick, New Jersey: Rutgers University Press, 1966. This study focuses on the social, economic and housing problems confronting Newark, New Jersey. It analyzes the dynamics of housing deterioration in the city. As part of this analysis, it reviews how the older housing stock was financed and discusses mortgage difficulties and the impact of such problems. Included are the results of interviews with both property owners and financial institutions.

—————. *The Urban Housing Dilemma: The Dynamics of New York City's Rent Controlled Housing*. New York City: Housing and Development Administration, 1972. This study examines rent control in New York City, focusing on the mortgage financing procedures for much of the city's older housing stock. Included are results of extensive interviews conducted with both property owners and banking institutions.

—————. and Robert Burchell. *Residential Abandonment: The Tenement Landlord Revisited*. New Brunswick, New Jersey: Center for Urban Policy Research, 1973. This book is the follow-up study to the senior author's earlier work, *The Tenement Landlord*. It extends the time horizon of the earlier analysis and examines the accelerated social, economic and housing decline of Newark, New Jersey. Interviews with both property owners and banking institutions reveal a lessening of credit availability with a concomitant negative impact on housing maintenance and equality.

University of Chicago, Center for Continuing Education. *From Redlining to Reinvestment: Using State Regulatory Authority and Capital Expenditure to Leverage Private Capital Expenditure and Credit.* Report submitted to Conference of the Governor of the State of Illinois, September 1-2, 1976. This study is a collection of articles, statements, testimonies, and reports on redlining and reinvestment issues submitted to a conference sponsored by the then-Governor of Illinois, Daniel Walker.

Von Furstenberg, George and Jeffrey R. Green "Estimation of Delinquency Risk for Home Mortgage Portfolios," *American Real Estate and Urban Economics Journal.* Vol. 2 (Spring 1974), 5-37. This article discusses some lender and property variables linked with mortgage delinquency and foreclosure.

Von Furstenberg, George M., and Jeffrey R. Green. "The Effect of Income and Race on the Quality of Home Mortgages: A Case for Pittsburgh," in Von Furstenburg, George M. and Ann Horowitz (Ed.). *Patterns in of Racial Discrimination:* Volume 1, *Housing.* Lexington, Mass., Lexington Books, 1974.

Voyles, Robert P. "Redlining and the Home Mortgage Disclosure Act of 1975: A Decisive Step Toward Private Urban Redevelopment," *Emory Law Journal,* Vol. 25 (Summer 1976), 667-703. Comment discusses redlining as the catalyst for the disinvestment cycle, traditional methods of attack against housing discrimination, and the Home Mortgage Disclosure Act, which is seen as a commendable effort to confront a complex problem.

Williams, Alex, Williams Beranek, Robert Byrne, James Kenkel and David Pentico. *A Study of the Factors Associated With, or Contributing to Risk in Urban Mortgage Lending.* Study conducted for the Federal Savings and Loan Insurance Corporation. FHLBB contract 73-41. 1973. This study analyzes factors associated with urban mortgage foreclosure and delinquency. Through regression analysis, it concludes that mortgage foreclosure delinquency and slow payment are associated with numerous factors, including occupation of mortgagor, age of structure, and type of financing.

OTHER REFERENCES

Benston, George J. "The Persistent Myth of Redlining: the Malevolent Mortgage Lender Who Discriminates Against Whole Neighborhoods Exists Mostly in the Minds of Some Fire-Breathing Activists," *Fortune* 97 (March 13, 1978), 66-69.

Brazas, Florence Milton. "Red-lining...the Systematic Restriction of Home Mortgage and Improvement Funds by Financial Institutions,"

*Building Official and Code Administrator,* (July-August 1974), 50-53.

Brimmer & Company, Inc. *Risk vs. Discrimination in the Expansion of Urban Mortgage Lending.* Report prepared for the United States League of Savings Associations. Chicago, 1977.

Center for New Corporate Priorities. *Where the Money Is, Mortgage Lending.* Los Angeles: Center for New Corporate Priorities, 1974.

Cincinnati Coalition of Neighborhoods. *Housing Analysis in Oakley, Bond Hill and Evanston, January 1960-April 1974—Financial Investment Patterns.* Cincinnati, Ohio: Coalition of Neighborhoods, 1974.

Cincotta, Gail and Randy Vereen. *Regulatory Agencies and Redlining Disinvestment Process: A Report.* Mimeograph. Chicago, 1977.

"Cities and States Adopt New Anti-Redlining Measures," *Housing and Development Reporter,* Vol. 3, Number 6 (Aug. 11, 1975), 264-266.

City of Seattle, Reinvestment Task Force. *Report of the Mayor's Reinvestment Task Force—Community Members.* Draft (April 1976) and Final (June 1976). Darel Grothaus, Staff Director. Office of Policy Planning, Artic Building, Third and Cherry, Seattle, WA 98102.

DeVise, Pierre. *The Anti-Redliners: How Community Activists Have Forged a Devil Theory of Urban Decay,* Working Paper II. 24 Chicago Regional Hospital Study, September, 1976.

Hodes, Laurent V. "Beyond the Redlining Battle," *National Savings & Loan League Journal* (June 1978), 30-38.

Holbert, Kenneth. "Redlining: A New Dimension in Fair Housing Policy," HUD *Challenge,* Vol. 7 (April 1976), 20-22.

"Home Mortgage Disclosure Act of 1975: Will it Protect Urban Consumers from Redlining?", *New England Law Review* 12 (Spring 1977), 957-990.

"Home Loan Disclosure Plays the Numbers Game," *National Journal Reports* (Dec. 11, 1976), 1780.

"How to Live with Loan Disclosures", *Savings and Loan News* (August 1976), 50-56.

Hunter, Oakley, "Boosting Housing for the Inner City," *Nation's Cities,* Vol. 9 (1971), 11-12, 23.

Hutchinson, Peter M. et al. "A Survey and Comparison of Redlining Influences in Urban Mortgage Lending Markets," *American Real Estate and Urban Economics Association Journal* (Winter 1977), 463-472.

Kollias, Karen. *Disclosure and Neighborhood Reinvestment: A Citizen's Guide.* Washington: National Center for Urban Ethnic Affairs, 1976.

Kollias, Karen. *Neighborhood Reinvestment—An Annotated Bibliography.* Washington: National Center for Urban Ethnic Affairs, 1976.

Lindsay, Robert et al. *Mortgage Financing and Housing Markets in New York State: A Preliminary Report.* Albany, New York: New York State Banking Department, 1977.

McConnell, Dennis D. "Investing in Neighborhood Revitalization: (how Atlanta, Ga. has dealt with redlining, the practice by lending institutions of denying or limiting mortgage credit in certain neighborhoods)," *Atlanta Economic Review* 28 (March/April 1978), 22-24.

Pfunder, Margaret S. "The Legality of Redlining Under the Civil Rights Laws," *American University Law Review* 25 (Winter 1976), 463-495.

"The Philadelphia solution to redlining: analyzing neighborhoods block by block; $19 million lent, only 6% delinquent," *Business Week* (May 9, 1977), 54.

Phoenix Fund. *Savings and Loan Activity in the City of St. Louis—A Phoenix Fund Update for 1974.* St. Louis, Missouri and Phoenix Fund, 1975.

Pike, Mary L. and Ann Meglis. *Readings on Redlining.* Prepared for a March, 1976 meeting of the Potomac Chapter of the National Association of Housing and Redevelopment Officials (NAHRO).

Public Technology, Inc. *Disinvestment in Urban Neighborhoods.* Washington, D.C.: U.S. Dept. of Housing & Urban Development, 1977.

Radics, Stephen P., Jr. "Redlining: Facts Behind the Press Reports," *National Savings and Loan League Journal* (Sept./Oct. 1977), 18-20.

"Redlining and the Home Mortgage Disclosure Act of 1975: A Decisive Step toward Private Urban Redevelopment," *Emory Law Journal* 25 (Summer 1976), 667-703.

"Redlining Solution Requires Unified Approach: Part I, The Complex Process of Neighborhood Decline," *Mortgage Banker* (April 1977), 46-52.

"Redlining: Why Make a Federal Case Out of It," *Golden Gate Law Review* 6 (Spring 1976), 813-50.

Rose, Daniel. "The Redlining Controversy: One Viewpoint," *Real Estate Review* (Winter 1978), 94-97.

"Savings Banks Reject Redline Charge," *Savings Bank Journal* (January 1977), 9+.

Schlafly, Joseph. "A Proposal for Eliminating Redlining: The Missouri Financal Institutions Disclosure Act of 1976," *Saint Louis University Law Journal* 20 (1976), 722-753.

"The Search for Solutions to Save the Communities," *Savings & Loan News* (June 1974).

Urban League of Rhode Island, Inc. *Disinvestment in Central City Areas.* Providence, September, 1973.

Urban-Suburban Investment Study Group. *The Role of Mortgage Lending Practices in Older, Urban Neighborhoods—Institutional Lenders, Regulating Agnecies and Their Community Impacts.* Evanston, Ill: Center for Urban Affairs at Northwestern University, 1975.

Van Alstyne, P.J. "Redlining—The Cure Worse than the Illness, *Journal of Contemporary Law* 3 (Spring 1977), 264-277.

Westside Action Coalition. Housing Committee. *Redlining on Milwaukee's Westside.* 1974.

"The Whites Fled, But the Bank Stayed," *Business and Society Review,* (Summer 1976), 58-61.

Wisniewski, Robert E. "Housing Mortgage Redlining: An Introduction to the Parameters of Federal, State and Municipal Regulation," *The Municipal Attorney* (February 1977), 47-50.

Woodstock Project. *Reinvestment Strategies in the Context of Neighborhood Maintenance and Development.* Northwestern University, Evanston, Illinois. Unpublished. Chicago: Woodstock Project, 1976.

# Index